An Irreverent Guide to Washington State

D1028040

AN
IRREVERENT
GUIDE
TO
WASHINGTON
STATE

by
Jim Faber

Doubleday & Company, Inc.
Garden City, New York
1974

ISBN: 0-385-06692-9
Library of Congress Catalog Card Number 73–22798
Copyright © 1974 by JIM FABER
Printed in the United States of America
First Edition
BOOK DESIGN BY BENTE HAMANN

This book is for my daughter Nicola,
who wanted to call it *Our Washington*.

CONTENTS

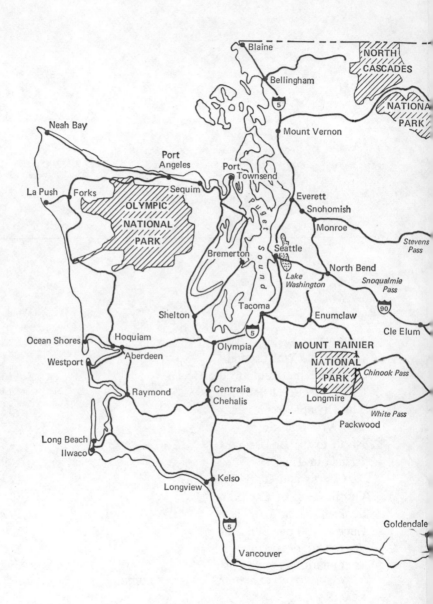

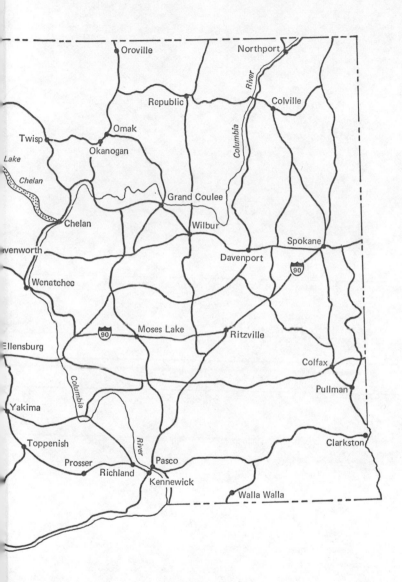

FOREWORD

As I write this from my office looking across the street at the Bread of Life Mission in Seattle's Skid Road (a view I found has spurred my lagging efforts) I see people on the move. Overhead, a 747 swings low for its approach to Sea-Tac airport. A block away on the waterfront, a big blue ferryliner readies its departure for Alaska. Nearby, campers and station wagons line up for the Bremerton and Winslow ferries. Old Seattle streets are filled with ambling sightseers. It's the first week in December and a gray day—as all but four in December are here, on the average—and one glum with reports of alarums and excursions at home and abroad. But people are on the move.

An Irreverent Guide, following Dr. Johnson's advice that no book is worthwhile unless it helps the reader "better enjoy life, or better endure it," is written to open a few new vistas of an enchanting state.

Although I consider myself a charter member of a no-growth group called Lesser Seattle, I have never subscribed to proposals discouraging exploration of this far corner. Those unwilling to share their natural bounties usually become mean-minded. Insularity, not familiarity, breeds contempt.

It is my hope that *An Irreverent Guide* will help nurture an appreciation of Washington's fragile resources of seashore, mountains, and deserts and perhaps will aid those working to keep the bulldozer from paving over the past in our cities.

Although I have augmented my lifetime wanderings through Washington with ten thousand miles of exploration by highway, plane, and train during the past two years, I recognize there are areas I have missed. I trust the irritation of those slighted will be offset by those relieved at the oversight.

As America enters a period, however brief, when unrestricted automobile travel may not be feasible, this guide offers innumerable tours within the immediate hinterland of most any Washington community. Washington too is fortunate in that its railroad routes not only connect major communities, but provide equipment that ranges from good to excellent. The main Amtrak route from Vancouver on the south to the Canadian border is one of the world's most scenic train trips, skirting farmland and seashore. Cross-state, such historically great trains as the *Empire Builder* and its sister, the *North Coast Hiawatha,* link Seattle with recreational base camps such as Everett, the Tri-Cities area, Yakima, Wenatchee, Ellensburg, Ephrata, and the 1974 World's Fair city, Spokane. Air West provides plane service to Spokane as well as Walla Walla, Wenatchee, Yakima, and Hoquiam on the coast. Supplemental lines can take you to the most remote resort area.

To my longtime friend, Murray Morgan, the Pacific Northwest's ranking Baedeker, historian, and bemused observer, my thanks for correcting my history papers, and hopefully permitting me a passing grade. The errors are mine. Thanks too to Murray for his generous permission to quote extensively from two of his finest books, *Skid Road* and *The Last Wilderness.* Other local works that have proved particularly helpful have been those of Ruth Kirk, David Richardson, and the late Nard Jones.

I'm grateful to Don Richardson of the state's tourism office for his assistance in reviewing the chapters. Thanks too to the Washington State Highway Department for making available the map, provided as an assist to visitors. For more detailed coverage, I suggest writing the Washington State Department of Commerce and Economic Development, Tourist Promotion Division, Olympia, Wa., 98501, for the State Highway Department's excellent highway map, which includes detailed strip maps of all freeway routes.

Finally, I'm appreciative of the patience of my fellow traveler, Ann Faber. Thanks to her for her missionary work on behalf of my lapsed syntax, and to Carol Barnard for her library and newspaper file research. My thanks too to my colleague, Seattle columnist Emmett

Watson, who, when the going got tough, never failed to come up with some words of supportive counsel, usually, "Let's have lunch."

I am also indebted to the Seattle–First National Bank, Home Oil Co., the Madrona Pharmacy, and others too numerous to mention.

Have a good trip.

JIM FABER
Seattle
December 1973

SEATTLE,
THE WALKAROUND CITY

You find the good and true of a city by walking around.

Ernest Hemingway said that. If he didn't, then it was Stewart Udall or Justice Douglas. Or George Plimpton.

Anyway, walking is the best way to savor Seattle. Hills and all, it's a hero sandwich for strollers. Order it to go.

Do you have an appetite for the market: fruits, vegetables, fish, meats, poultry, spices, cheese, and flowers, hawked with the raucous shouts of Les Halles West? Would you prefer the smells, sights, and sounds of the waterfront, a combination of fish and chips, oysters, clams, and shrimp served indoors and outdoors on docks once crowded with Gold Rush ships and now housing ferryboats, import shops, and trained seals? Is your dish antiques, paintings, pottery, delis, and vintage architecture? Would you rather feed a flock of ducks and watch the passing boats? Ruminate in the gloom of a virgin forest? Or stroll around the international food stalls, fountains, greenswards, and exhibits of the old Seattle World's Fair grounds?

Those are just a few of Seattle's walkabouts, none of them more than thirty minutes from a downtown hotel. Let's sample a few. Along the way, we'll walk gently over a few graves and read some head-stones marking Seattle's gaudy past.

A few thoughts while you're lacing your shoes:

Back before America's dirtiest four-letter word became "city," Seattle yearned for bigness. It lied about its size for decades and pompously styled itself as "the largest city in the world for its age."

To back up this dubious claim, its pitchmen pointed out that one of the city's original settlers, David Denny, a babe at the time of Seattle's encouchment in November 1851, was able in his twilight years to fly over his former playpen and see below a metropolis of nearly a half million.

Those first families christened their landfall, New York, Al-ki, meaning in Chinook jargon, "New York, by-and-by." Today with a metropolitan area population of more than a million (half that within its corporate limits), Seattle hasn't quite realized that early boast. But you won't find many who regard this as a shattered dream. For after a century and a quarter of growth, Seattle has decided it might like to be the San Francisco of the forties, perhaps. But not much larger, thank you.

True you can still find a few self-ordained executors of Seattle's pioneer bequest hunkered down in the Rainier Club or some other Establishment watering hole, savoring dreams of megalopolis by and by. But they constitute a silent and senior minority. The majority, particularly the young and those emigrated from larger cities, see a threat to livability in continued heavy growth.

"You're lovely," Seattle murmurs to its reflection. "But if you get much bigger, I'll leave you."

Some of this concern stems from the fact that Seattle already has the highest population density of any Western metropolis, its half million residents living in a city covering but eighty-two square miles. (A few comparisons: San Diego, 187 square miles, Phoenix, 299, Oklahoma City, 299, and Dallas, 254.)

But apart from a fear of growth, Seattle, like most American cities, is concerned over threats to its environment, a fear honed by its unique quality of livability.

By most any test, Seattle would get passing grades on elements that constitute the good life: better-than-average schools, colleges, and two universities; clean government; high wages for those working (for those not, the highest FHA foreclosure rate in the U.S. outside of Detroit), and attractive neighborhoods.

For all but the lowest wage earner, Seattle has a residential selection that includes a whole range of hillsides overlooking Puget Sound and three in-city lakes. One of these, Lake Washington, was a cesspool before voters a decade ago approved a $140 million bond issue to clean it up. Summertime along its thirty-two-mile shoreline, a dozen parks are filled with swimmers. Sail and power boaters dot the clear waters. Sports fishermen take up to twenty thousand migrating salmon each year from its renewed waters. (Twenty years ago only a dozen migrating sockeye were counted. Credit for the renewed run goes to Dr. Lauren Donaldson, the University of Washington's wizard on artificially induced salmon migrations.)

Fleeing the city (many do—the city's population showed a slight decline during the past decade while suburbs doubled in size) the Seattleite can move to a bucolic island only a thirty-minute ferryboat commute from downtown or seek another isle even closer via a floating bridge. An hour away are forest and farm tracts that make Walden Pond look like Levittown. (And some developments that have the opposite effect.) Within Seattle's metropolitan surroundings, families head for a wide choice of uncrowded salt and fresh water parks, a score of golf courses, a wilderness camp, an explorer's cove, or a ski slope.

Summertime, the city's big-attendance event is Seafair, which is what a saturnalia would be if programmed by Kiwanis International. The August fiesta ends in a street parade lavish with bands, drill teams, and floats filled with leggy girls perched on thrones and cogs and cornucopias and bowers of flowers spelling out words like Progress, Vacationland, and Vote. On Lake Washington, some very powerful motorboats compete for the Gold Cup unlimited hydroplane championship or its counterpart, the Seafair Cup.

Along with this T-shirt lifestyle, Seattle maintains a lively, if not wide-ranging interest in the arts. Attendance at symphony, opera, ballet, galleries, and theater provides culture with a larger boxoffice than all the city's sporting events combined. That statistic as yet includes no pro football or baseball, but does encompass ice hockey, horse racing, University of Washington football, and the city's hustling pro basketball team, the Sonics. Such an attendance imbalance once led Jim Bouton, then pitching for the one-season-and-out Seattle Pilots, to remark:

"A city that spends more on culture than it does on sports can't be all bad." The observation has become palatable even to the jocks now that Seattle's $40 million domed stadium will by 1975 give them their innings.

After that, Seattle will be ready to satisfy just about every appetite save those unforgivably carnal.

Having proven its *machismo* during a lusty past, the Queen City is ambivalent, if not lethargic, about vice today.

"I always think of Seattle as a place where the leading call girl has a pulldown bed," publicist Tex McCrary once said of the city. This is true. The elegant bordello disappeared from Seattle in the early forties, along with the Chinese lottery house and slot machines.

Today the vice squad tolerates gay bars, blue movies, and a little discreet pot smoking, but raids burlesque and night club skin shows at the drop of a pastie.

(Seattle permitted topless dancing but twice: during the World's Fair, which brought a sort of Doris Day giddiness to the city, and a decade later when Superior Court Judge Robert Winsor ruled that city ordinances prohibiting topless dancing were violations of the First Amendment. Again, joy was unconfined. *Village Voice* columnist Nat Hentoff nominated Judge Winsor for the U. S. Supreme Court. But the judge's decision was overruled, the dancers went under cover and bartenders went back to yawning.)

"Don't expect much in the way of nightlife," was the advice offered by a *Business Week* columnist sent to Seattle to take its pulse in 1973. "A better use of your time would be to retire early and rise early to take in the sights."

This is not entirely true. A few in-town spots offer name entertainment and scores provide live music and acts. Bars around the Seattle-Tacoma International Airport and in such suburbs as Bellevue and Burien attract most of the swingles. But the action is limited, as Western International Hotels found after dumping a half million dollars into a big name supper club that folded after one year.

A wide-open city until World War II, Seattle has since fallen into respectability. This has been given many explanations, the most popular being a contention that the technocrats imported by Boeing created a large measure of slide-rule squareness. Others blame the Norwegians and Swedes, who were once Seattle's largest immigrant group and who brought with them a strong dose of Lutheran morality. But today less than a fourth of the city's foreign born are Scandinavian. Most of them are too busy waxing their skis to pay much attention to sin.

A more believable explanation was offered by one of the city's leading call girl madams of the sixties who finally threw in the towel and left town. "There's no action in a town where everyone does his eating and lovemaking at home," remarked this lay philosopher on her departure.

If Seattle's livability accounts for its virtue, it seemingly has had no effect on its godliness. Seattle rests at the bottom of the list nationally in per capita church membership, estimated at less than thirty percent of its population.

One explanation for this apostasy, provided by a leading Seattle divine, differs but slightly from that of the madam:

"Attractions of boating, camping, skiing, fishing, and other activities simply outdraw the churches; and for those inclined to an informal pantheistic religion, making constructive use of the great outdoors is as good a way as any of finding their religion."

Although the city does have some streets so mean that even the muggers work in pairs, its crime rate in recent years has dropped steadily. Among its peers, Seattle ranks low in villany; boosters maintain that what crime exists is committed by local talent, rather than the franchised variety. The Boswell of the Mafia, Gay Talese, lists Seattle as one of the few U.S. cities lacking any evident membership in that organization. (Yes, we have no Bonannos.)

Some see all these new priorities of livability-first as examples of a greening of Seattle, a final rejection of New York, Al-ki. One of these is the University of Washington's director of clinical psychology, Dr. Nathaniel Wagner. When asked to diagnose Seattle's past hangups, he observed:

"Most of our identity problems have arisen from attempts to make ourselves over in the image of an urban, first-class city. I think we've always tried to emulate San Francisco, but now we're wondering if perhaps Portland isn't a better model."

That's a little like advising a confirmed Martini drinker to switch to low-cal Shirley Temples. Seattle's *beau idéal* has always been San Francisco.* It regards Portland as a nice town on a river. But the analysis illustrates the city's *angst* over growth. If Seattle does have an identity problem, I'd suggest it is no more acute than the pangs of a pimply kid wondering what he's going to be when he grows up. After all, Dr. Wagner, Seattle's population didn't reach a thousand until 1870. Our voice has just stopped changing.

"Seattle is a success, but the city has yet to acquire the assurance of success," Murray Morgan wrote in *Skid Road*. "It may take another generation for Seattleites to be able to enjoy all phases of their

---

* One of Seattle's defiant boasts is that "we now have just as many good restaurants as San Francisco." Not true. We don't have as many tourists or expense accounts. But we do have enough to satisfy just about any diner save Craig Claiborne. Suggestions: Continental: Rosellini's 410, Mirabeau, Brasserie Pittsbourg; Steaks: El Gaucho, Canlis; Italian: Gasperetti's Roma; Mexican: Guadalajara; Seafood: Captain's Table, Windjammer; Oriental (see page 27). For a revolving view, the Space Needle, for one at sea-level, Hidden Harbor; eclectic gourmet: Trader Vic's; late dining: 13 Coins; plain but adventuresome: Mr. D's (Greek) or Ivar's Salmon House. Best hamburgers: The Turbulent Turtle, Andy Nagy's Diner, Burgermaster. NOTE: These are personal recommendations that make no attempt to cover the Seattle scene in depth. Nor do they embrace some excellent suburban restaurants (notable omissions: La Provençal in Kirkland, and Henri de Navarre in Edmonds, both notable for French cuisine, and the Yangtze in Bellevue for Szechuan cooking).

history in the way San Franciscans do, though beat generation poets now read their works in Skid Road bars, and the land below the slot is once again a minor mecca for tourists. For many Seattleites, though, the era of the dirt street and the plank walk is not yet far enough distant to be romantic: too many people can remember mud on the living room rug, too many suffered ridicule and lost wages because Easterners of influence and capital considered Seattle a waypoint to nowhere, a village of wigwams."

The ridicule has abated since a decade ago when Alistair Cooke described Seattle as a rain-soaked fishing village midpoint between San Francisco and Alaska. But the city still gets jangled by Easterners who insist we're all coming to a bad end. Like the assessment made by *Harper's* writer George Leighton. After looking us over Leighton concluded:

"So there she is beside Puget Sound; Seattle, settled by migrants, resting upon a region in which migrants still predominate. Her chief industry is in trouble . . . a large proportion of her population relies on Government aid. Stricken the region is now, its pioneer economy a wreck."

That summary appeared in the August 1938 issue of *Harper's*. They have been rewriting the same obituary ever since.

WALKABOUT NUMBER ONE:
THE PIKE PLACE MARKET

Nowhere in America do so many farmers, tradesmen, artisans, and customers share a locale that is as earthily colorful and genuine as the time-wrapped labyrinth known to all Seattleites as simply The Market.

Clinging to a hillside overlooking the city's harbor, it is strewn along two sides of Pike Place, a narrow, thronged, bricked street just west of First Avenue between Pike and Stewart streets. Started in 1907 by farmers who parked their wagons and hawked produce, it grew crazily over the years into a two-level hive of shops and stalls. A collection of architectural compromises, warped and wearied by neglect and the assaults of those who want to save it by tearing it down, it has few rivals for Seattle's carefully bestowed affections.

Its upper corridor, opening onto Pike Street at First Avenue, is a long sheltered esplanade, interspersed by decorative Victorian colonnades, and lined on both sides with shops and stalls. One side offers displays of meat, poultry, eggs, fish, and other seafoods, delicatessens, and quick lunch dining.

The other side, abutting Pike Place, is a mad array of fruits and vegetables, scrubbed and gleaming under hanging green-shaded lamps, piled as if awaiting country fair judging, and sold from stalls so narrow their proprietors shout their wares almost shoulder to shoulder.

Farther north, the stalls feature the handiwork of the Granola generation. Bearded and beaded, in buckskin and shawls, the young merchants display the products of young hands and eyes, rather than those of the soil. Here are candles, carvings, pottery, belts, paintings, and other creations that are quietly offered, not hawked. Just beyond, in spring and summer, are flower and garden plant stalls.

The lower level, and the ramps serving it, is a warren of shops selling everything from used clothing to home brewing equipment, flowers, hashish pipes, antiques, posters, candles, leather goods, sculpture, paintings, old records, spices, coffee, teas, pastas, and foreign foods. Hole-in-the-wall counter restaurants provide million-dollar views of the harbor below.

This bounty, with its eclectic appeal to young and old, affluent and poor, hip and straight, has made the Market Seattle's mixing bowl. Renters of stalls at $1.50 a day or proprietors of more elaborate shops, they infuse the market's drafty grottos with accents as varied as their surnames: Primero, Genzale, Ordinio, Domingo, Padua, McDonald, DiLaurenti, Levy, Lowell, Desimones, Mossafer, Tadique, Korazija, Erickson, Di Pietro, Yokoyama. Before World War II, most of those names would have been of Japanese origin, farmers who for generations worked the rich valley lands to the south. Herded into concentration camps after war's outbreak, and in many cases panicked into selling all they owned, most of them never forgot or forgave. Nor did they return to till what they had always proudly considered their native lands.

The Market's patrons themselves are a living demographic chart: the affluent seeking gourmet spices, the poor searching for bargains, all sharing a moment and a turf; loosened up by the cajolery, blandishments, and the wares of the sellers.

To savor the Market's full flavor, time your walk between eight and ten in the morning, when the sellers begin readying their wares; noisily cutting, plucking, washing, trimming—fashioning pyramids and mosaics of vegetables, nests of eggs, trays of fish and poultry, arrays of beads and leather belts, and other offerings as another day begins. Take your morning coffee or plan breakfast at the Athenian or Lowell's, two low-cost restaurants favored by the marketeers. Both provide broad views of the harbor and, on a clear day, its backdrop of islands and mountains.

The Market is open daily except Sunday from 9 to 6. Breakfast there is a great way to start the day. Not as cosmopolitan as Les Halles, perhaps, but that is past tense. The Pike Place Market narrowly escaped a similar demise, a threat poised by an urban renewal plan that would have surrounded it with a grid of high-rise apartments and high-ticket shops. Led by Victor Steinbrueck, a maverick University of Washington professor of architecture (and designer of the Space Needle), a group, united under the banner of Friends of the Market, turned back this move. Just to make sure the rout of the bulldozer was complete, voters embraced the entire area in a protective zoning ordinance.

Today, as plans move ahead to shore up its sagging timbers and morale, the Market is a happy, sometimes squabbling bazaar run by eighteen differing nationalities, a place to shop for a bagful of munchies, an antique, a bouquet, an Indian hand-knit sweater, or a roach clip. And it's a place to lunch on Swedish hotcakes, steamed clams, liverwurst on a bagel, or a bowlful of freshly simmered vegetable soup. Or dig people and a view in a noisy tavern that offers thirty foreign and domestic brands of beer, and muse over an enclave that is, as another Seattle architect, Fred Bassetti, describes it, "an honest place in a phony time."

WALKABOUT NUMBER TWO:
THE WATERFRONT

Despite the intrusion of a noisy, ugly viaduct, Seattle is one of the few American ports that offers a strollers' wayfare, Alaska Way.

If you want to avoid the hillside descent to the waterfront on foot, take any southbound bus on First Avenue and debark at Marion Street or Yesler Way. The ride is on the house. In 1973, Seattle became the nation's first city to provide free bus service anywhere within its downtown area. Maps at each stop delineate the borders of this service. Seattle's municipal buses and trackless trolleys are gaily decorated in pleasing colors, interiors are clean and seats unripped. But their most popular features are their drivers, as demonstrated by one Easterner who, when asked to identify what he considered Seattle's most pleasing quality, answered:

"It's the place where the bus driver says good night."

If you're a true stroller, you'll head for the waterfront from the Market—on foot—down a set of worn stairs and a hillside path. Or walk to First and Marion Street and take the pedestrian overpass leading to the Washington State Ferry Terminal.

Here each year more than four million passengers arrive and depart to and from the Navy Yard city of Bremerton (fifty minutes), Bainbridge Island (thirty minutes), or via highways to Hood Canal, the Olympic Peninsula, and Washington's ocean beaches.

Let's use the terminal as our walkabout starting point.

Take the escalator to the terminal's top level and step out on one of its viewing platforms. You are looking at Elliott Bay, a harbor born of an Alaska Gold Rush, eclipsed in succeeding decades by San Francisco and Los Angeles, only to spurt ahead during the sixties to become the Pacific Coast's first port for Far East imports bound for Midwest and East Coast markets.

The lower level of the terminal houses a seafood restaurant, Dungeness Dan's.

From the ferry terminal walk a few paces south for a look at Ye Olde Curiosity Shop, founded in 1899 by an inveterate collector, Joseph (Daddy) Standley. Under his ranging eye and acquisitive hand was created a dizzying collection of artifacts and memorabilia, curios and junk, ranging from mummies and shrunken heads to Indian totems, canoes, baskets, ivory carvings, shells, narwhal tusks, Gold Rush pans, old guns, net floats, fleas in dresses, and Ripley's name inscribed on a human hair.

All this plunder is still there, in wall-to-wall and rafter-high profusion and confusion. But unfortunately since Standley's death in 1944, the offerings are gradually being outnumbered by a gift shop array of musical decanters, smartass posters, incense burners, mirrors framed in ship's wheels, and other examples of Future Schlock.

In the lee of the Curiosity Shop is a fish and chips stand with dockside tables. It's one of many along this waterfront stretch, a place to munch, muse, and watch the passing parade of ferries, ships, tugs, and seagulls. Just beyond is The Fish House, where you can ship an iced salmon home or shop for other seafood, including walkaround crab and shrimp cocktails.

You're now at the foot of Yesler Way, not far from where Henry Yesler, one of Seattle's founders, erected the city's first industry, a sawmill.

Here on the seawall you will find one of those bronzed baby shoes of a city, a historical marker, this one celebrating the Battle of Seattle, as it is billed locally, and which reads like a rerun of an F-troop sequence.

The Battle of Seattle was a twenty-four-hour skirmish. It occurred during the winter of 1856, after a confederation of Eastern Washington Indians who had been shafted by a peace treaty decided on violence rather than working within the system. So upwards of a thousand strong they attacked Seattle, with an area population of about one hundred seventy. After the first Indian volley, the village volunteers withdrew to the blockhouse, or as a witness, a local doctor, unkindly described it, "they ran so fast the very bones in their legs bent under them."

Fortunately, the U.S. sloop-of-war *Decatur* was in the harbor. The day was saved in the last reel by the *Decatur*'s gunfire and that of the Marines. The militiamen came out of their blockhouse refuge, later becoming leading speakers at civic clubs and Fourth of July celebrations. The Indian losses were put by one of the *Decatur*'s officers at twenty-eight dead. One of the Indian leaders, Leschi, later was captured and hanged after an unsuccessful attempt by H. R. Crosby, an attorney and ancestor of Bing Crosby, to free him. Later, Seattle named a park after Leschi.

Next, at the end of Pier 51, is the Polynesian, a restaurant with the waterfront's best view for diners. Just beyond is the Alaska Marine Highway Terminal where each week big blue-and-white ferryliners depart with cars and passengers bound for the forty-ninth state.

A few steps farther south is a seventy-year-old cast-iron pergola and a slip that once housed the Seattle Harbor Patrol. Today the facility at the foot of Washington Street is destined to accommodate a collection of historic Sound vessels. Included for inspection is a seventy-five-year-old three-masted schooner, the *Wawona*, a one-time carrier of lumber, copra, and halibut, and if space permits, an early-day steam tugboat, the *Henry Foss*. The venerable tug saw duty during the Gold Rush, shared the limelight with Wallace Beery and Marie Dressler in the 1933 motion picture *Tugboat Annie*, and was the last vessel out of beleaguered Wake Island during World War II. The MGM film was inspired, with a great amount of embroidery, by Thea Foss, who with her husband, Andrew, parlayed a couple of rowboats at Tacoma into one of the world's biggest towboat fleets.

There is little to explore farther south save for the working waterfront which with its cranes and terminals now ranks as third in the nation for containerized cargo volume.

More fitting we should head north, for beyond the Ferry Terminal lie the hoary remnants of the old docks that hosted the Klondike Gold Rush, the Famed Trail of '98 that turned Seattle from milltown into world port.

It all began on July 17, 1897, with the arrival of the Alaska steamer *Portland,* carrying prospectors laden with $700,000 in gold dust and nuggets. The treasure was burnished by a newspaper reporter's description:

"At three o'clock this morning the steamer *Portland* from St. Michael to Seattle passed up the Sound with more than a ton of solid gold aboard."

The place where the *Portland* docked today is covered by the new waterfront park at the foot of Union Street. But the docks just ahead along this old waterfront strand had an equally gamy role.

At the peak of the Gold Rush this strip was derby-deep in throngs of gold seekers and those who plucked them. As many as twenty thousand adventurers a month departed on schooners, steamers, reclaimed ferries, tugs, barges, and just about anything that would stay afloat long enough to collect the fares and bribe the steamboat inspectors.

Producer of heroes and heroic legends, the Klondike Gold Rush was, as author Pierre Berton described it, "in some ways the weirdest and most useless mass movement in history," but it made Seattle a city.

In 1899, the year after the Rush began, more than twelve hundred new homes mushroomed in Seattle's tiny city limits. When the Klondike and the succeeding rush to the beaches of Nome subsided in 1900, Seattle had a population of eighty thousand—doubled in but a decade.

More importantly, Seattle business interests had locked up a captive market. By 1905 they controlled ninety-five percent of Alaska shipping, and, allied with Eastern interest, set out to colonize its timber, fishing, and mining resources.

Today, Seattle talks soothingly of our "sister state," and tries to act like an avuncular advisor to Alaska. But Seattle's commercial ties, if not as chafing as in the past, are still strong and viewed by many Alaskans as bonds. (There are many in Alaska who refuse to forget the fact that the Seattle Chamber of Commerce was alone on the Pacific Coast in refusing to support Alaska's bid for statehood.)

The Gold Rush waterfront, its stubby piers no longer suitable for today's shipping, is undergoing yet another change. A few docks still house small canneries, and an occasional fishing boat chugs in to unload salmon or halibut. You'll find a sail loft or two and a couple of fishermen's supply houses selling searchlights, anchors, nets, crab pots, float buoys, compasses, or a set of yellow slickers. But most of the mile-long strip has become a bazaar, now being developed into a salty waterfront park.

Part of a $150 million park development program approved by voters, the fifteen-acre park will extend along Alaska Way from Spring to Pine Street, embracing most of the existing Gold Rush docks with esplanades and connecting floating modules. Development includes plantings, berths for historic ships as well as pleasure craft, facilities for concerts and vendors' kiosks, and a $3 million viewing aquarium.

One of those who wrested the old waterfront from decay and turned it into a visitor attraction is Ivar Haglund, who operates the

Acres of Clams restaurant at the foot of Madison Street, next on our walking tour. Ivar drilled his first test well on the waterfront in 1937, opening a dime aquarium. An early-day radio balladeer, he unabashedly plugged his aquarium and a subsequent fish and chips stand in song and inspired publicity, such as matching Tony Galento against an octopus in a wrestling match. Today on a good summer day some five thousand customers will eat in Ivar's gaudy seafood restaurant or in its outdoor dining areas.

Adjoining Ivar's is the waterfront firehouse and moorage for one of Seattle's fireboats. If you're a fire buff, young or old, take time to inspect an 1898 American LaFrance pumper, once steam-powered, now still operative with a seventy-horsepower gas engine, installed in 1916. The engines and Seattle's big fireboat can be inspected between noon and 4 P.M., Sunday included.

Pier 54 is home too for the doughty 65-foot *Cathylynn,* a harbor tour boat that makes hour-long inspections of Seattle's terminals, including its new grain terminal abutting waters so deep—72 feet— they can accommodate ships up to 250,000 tons. Fare: $1.50.

Immediately north of Ivar's is the southern boundary of the projected waterfront park which is encompassing, but not eliminating, most of the old docks you see just ahead.

Heading north past the Washington Fish Company pier, housing Ivar's as well as packing facilities for freshly caught salmon and halibut, the next old waterfront dock is Pier 56, home of Trident Imports, the Cove restaurant, with a shaded pierside area for outdoor dining, and an aquarium offering viewings of a variety of fish as well as trained seal and dolphin acts.

Usually the aquarium also features a killer whale act, but these are tryout bits. Once these amazing black-and-white mammals have their numbers polished, they're shipped off (via air freighters) to the marinelands in San Diego, Honolulu, and others on the piscatorial big-time circuit.

(After millions of viewings at marinelands and on television, we have transformed the killer whale into a sort of deepsea Bambi. We affectionately watch their teeth being brushed and delight at the trainer sticking his head in that grinning mouth. Out of captivity, the killer whales have another neat trick. When they locate a gray whale —a larger but completely docile mammal—they cow it into immobility, then force open its jaws and chew its tongue off.)

The aquarium is open daily, 9 to 7. Admission: adults, $1.25, children 50 cents.

Just abeam of Pier 56 are the floats of Seattle Harbor Tours, departure points for hour-long inspections ($1.75 for adults, and 85 cents for children) of Seattle's working waterfront, leaving at 12:15, 1:45, 3:15, and 4:30 P.M. Tour boats also leave from here (twice daily—once on Sunday) for Blake Island, just twenty minutes away. There you can eat salmon Indian style, baked over an open hardwood fire, be entertained by interpretive Indian dances, and inspect a collection of contemporary Indian carvings.

A more encompassing water tour departs at 10:30 A.M. and 1:30 P.M. from the Olympic Hotel, connecting with the Grayline tour boat *Sightseer*. The morning tour departs from Leschi Park, moves down Lake Washington and Lake Union and into the Hiram Chittenden through the Locks and finally docks just abeam of the Ferry Terminal. The route is reversed in the afternoon. Fare for the two and one-half hour trip is $4.25.

Pier 57 houses the Pirate's Plunder—another import supermarket with its own outdoor dining area, the Sourdough, this one featuring alder-smoked salmon and halibut, in addition to steamed clams and plump, mealy french fries.

Pier 59, distinguished by its curving false front, is a sturdy old relic reminiscent of New England. It houses the Seattle Marine and Fishing Supply Company, a mart for chunky fishing boats that tie up at its float. An upstairs loft is the working area for some of the nation's last makers of fishnets for the gillnetters, seiners, and trawlers that range the North Pacific for salmon, halibut, and other seafood.

If by now you've got your sea legs and want to continue, it's about a mile to the northern end of Alaska Way. There's not much to distract your attention from the bay save for a few small canneries and the Canadian Pacific pier. There one of America's last grand old steamers, the *Princess Marguerite,* sails on daily cruises to Victoria, British Columbia. Just north is the Port of Seattle headquarters. Next is the Edgewater Inn, with sea-view dining and rooms from which bemused guests occasionally land a salmon, and finally at the very end, Pier 70, a thronged complex of import houses, ships, a tavern, and two restaurants, Captain Bob's and the Smuggler, the latter with a smashing harbor view.

Along with all the treats for eye, stomach, and nose, Seattle's waterfront is one of the few that maintains appropriate salty sounds— thanks to a few cranky citizens. Most harbors today are virtually noiseless, for vessels no longer need to signal their arrival and terminals are so constructed as to eliminate backing whistles. A few years ago some narrow-necktie type in the State Ferry Authority decided that our ferries no longed needed to signal as they approached the terminals for docking. So the long-familiar long-and-two-short docking blasts were ordered stopped.

The silence along the waterfront was so deafening that citizens angrily demanded the return of the toots. Bureaucracy bowed. Today the ferryboat whistles continue day and night to warm the waterfront with pleasant flatulence. All save those of the state's two newest super-ferries. They sound for all the world like a Texas Cadillac demanding attention at a service station.

WALKABOUT NUMBER THREE:
OLD SEATTLE

The wave of nostalgia which has swept America, threatening to inundate us all in tides of Tiffany shades, pioneer villages, and restored slums, has washed into Old Seattle, cleansing its deserted Victorian office buildings, transforming flophouses into office communes and its missions and taverns into trendy shops, restaurants, and galleries.

Old Seattle is easy to find. Just keep walking downhill and you'll arrive, which is the reason why the city center originated there. Back when Henry Yesler's mill was sawing its first lumber for California markets, trees were skidded down a roadway of greased logs to the waterfront mill. Lumbering prospered. The area for a time became an enclave of saloons, brothels, restaurants, and rooming houses catering to the loggers, giving it a name that has become a colloquialism borrowed by cities everywhere: Skid Road, sometimes corrupted into Skid Row.

Today as Skid Road undergoes an expensive face lift to restore its age and wrinkles, it prefers to be referred to as Old Seattle, thenk yew. Its hub is Pioneer Square at the confluence of First Avenue, Yesler Way, and James Street. As we said, it's just about downhill all the way, as any Skidroader can tell you.

You can reach it via most any southbound bus or trackless trolley on First, Second, or Third avenues. There's no charge. Better you should walk. There are a few bonuses en route.

From midcity around the Olympic Hotel walk up to Seventh Avenue to see a mistake City Hall is trying to cover up. This is where a 4.5-acre park that will put a lid over two blocks of the freeway gulch that runs through downtown Seattle. When the park is completed in 1975, you'll be able to escape into a man-made canyon, thirty-five feet deep, surrounded by plantings and a series of waterfalls which will blot out the sight and sound of traffic below. Another feature is to be a glass wall covered by a thin veil of descending water through which you will see the rushing traffic below.

The park and adjoining below-street parking will cost around $6 million. Back before the freeway was completed, a leading Seattle architect and planner, Paul Thiry, advanced a plan to deck the entire eight-block length of the big ditch with a parkway lid. The estimated cost was less than today's cosmetic greensward, but the plan was dismissed as being extravagant and impractical.

Seattle today, conscious of the fact its downtown has become boring, if not downright ugly, is playing a game of catch-up ball, allocating a total of more than $20 million for development of parks and esplanades in the downtown, waterfront, and Old Seattle areas.

From the Freeway Park, start heading south on Sixth Avenue, passing the splashy handiwork of one of Seattle's most talented sculptors, George Tsutakawa, whose fountains bring enjoyment and solace to a half dozen United States cities. Another enjoyable example of Tsutakawa's sense of shape and hydraulics can be found a few blocks away at Fifth and Spring in an entrance to the Seattle Public Library. Here again the fountain's design was inspired by the ancient Japanese art of piling stones into visually pleasing shapes. At the Library, water flowing through rounded hollows creates a flow and murmur so solacing that local poets have been known to dedicate an ode to it, leaving it on the fountain's rim, weighted by a pebble and a sigh.

Fountains and sculpture have been badly neglected in Seattle until the past decade. But they are gradually finding favor with status-conscious architects as is evidenced in the entryways of the Library's tall neighbors. (Also in the IBM Building plaza, where a fountain by sculptor James FitzGerald is featured.) The new Bank of California tower is flanked by a pleasant mall. Across Fourth Avenue, Henry Moore's massive bronze "Vertebrae—1968" graces the plaza of the Seattle-First National Bank Building.

Also warming the plaza are two small Tsutakawa fountains, a cast tile sidewalk mosaic in Indian motif by Guy Anderson, and four granite benches carved in deep bas relief with a wildlife theme by James Washington.

The Bank's executive floors house what is recognized as one of America's finest collection of corporate-owned art. If you'd like to view the collection, check at the information desk in the main lobby. Unless you're barefooted or a member of Representative Wright Patman's House Committee on Banking, you'll be provided a guided tour.

From the First Bank Building, walk south on Third Avenue, passing—or pausing at—Shorey's Book Store, opened in 1890 and today a bookworm's deli containing 750,000 books as well as maps and prints.

Just ahead as you move southward is the city's nondescript civic center, distinguished only by an almost-forgotten series of murals in the lobby of the new County Administration Building at Fourth Avenue and James Street. They are from the brush of Kenneth Callahan, whose paintings grace some of the world's top galleries and museums. Callahan, a member of Seattle's famed trinity of painters, which includes Mark Tobey and Morris Graves, is best known for his abstract works. These murals are of a different vintage, lusty paintings of forty years ago. Their black and white shadings and the very titles capture the vitality and defiance of men of the sea, circa 1930s— "Life Boat Drill," "Hiring Hall," "Engine Room," and others, all worth a contemplative stop.

As you walk south, you will see a venerable boundary marker for Old Seattle, the white dunce cap of the Smith Tower, which until the fifty-story Seafirst Building was completed in 1969, was Seattle's tallest. When completed in 1914 by typewriter tycoon L. C. Smith, it was billed as "the world's largest building outside of New York City." (Today, it's fifty-sixth.) Just in case someone didn't bother to look up at it and count, four bronze plaques are emplaced on the building's front, announcing: "Smith Tower, Forty-two Stories." The claim to glory is somewhat stretched. The building acquired its touted stature only by counting the tiny attic rooms housed in its peaked spire. It's worth a visit.

The pale-tinted marble lining the high, narrow lobby creates a golden glow reflected from bronze elevator doors. Above them, on either side, a dozen carved Indian heads look down, as painted, feathered, and fierce in visage as any cigar store Comanche. The lobby, the tiled floors above, and the mail chutes still labeled "Telegrams" are as unchanged as the operator-manned elevators. In 1971, when the building's Florida-based owners began paneling over the elevators' interior bronzework, a public clamor forced a halt. But the owner left one elevator encased in this plywood grandeur to show the local Philistines their error. You can eat your heart out on your way aloft to the Smith Tower Observatory (admission: 65 cents).

The observatory features a decor of carved Oriental teak, now faded into a Grauman Chinese dinginess, and a view, between the bars of a suicide barrier, of city and harbor. At your feet is Old Seattle, a few square blocks of low buildings, their cornices shorn by the Big Quake of 1949. They sandwich in a big slice of Seattle history.

Down there grew up a rickety milltown of forty thousand, built of wood from cupola to board sidewalk. In 1889 it went up in a puff of smoke as Seattle was leveled to the ground by fire. Annealed by the flames, a new-found city pride emerged. Tideflats were filled, streets straightened and leveled. The city's few architects and those as far away as New York enjoyed the surprise and challenge of designing $10 million worth of brick Romanesque and gothic Revival buildings to replace the now-banned wooden downtown. Within a year, new office buildings, hotels, and other commercial structures including theaters and an opera house introduced Victorian splendors and excesses seldom dreamed of in the sawdust city.

A decade later, about the time Seattle was sobering up in the morning-after of an economic panic, gold was discovered in the Yukon. Prosperity returned to the district, fattened it with more banks, mercantile houses, suppliers, dives, and other operations designed to separate the gold from the gold seeker. Of the more than one hundred thousand adventurers who headed north out of Seattle, only a few thousand ever reached the Klondike. Of these, but a few hundred struck it rich. Seattle ended up with the pay dirt by outfitting most of those one hundred thousand, collecting their fares and monopolizing most of the freight movements.

As Seattle grew, the city center began moving north. The exodus left behind a cast-off district of flophouses, pawnshops, Chinese gambling joints, missions, whorehouses, and taverns. Sin held out until World War II military brass closed the last brothel and slammed shut the slotted doors of the Chinese lottery and chuck-a-luck parlors. The tenderloin was replaced by mission stew.

In 1961, when Skid Road hit the bottom, uptown realtors moved ahead to pave over what was left with parking lots and urban renewal developments. But as in the successful campaign to preserve the Pike Place Market, they were defeated, blocked by a mixed bag of antiquaries, including clubwomen (and some club persons, too), architects, artists, and a few aware politicians, led by Seattle Mayor Wes Uhlman. Overriding opposition, they helped pass a historic preservation ordinance that has become a model for cities anxious to prevent the blacktopping of their past.

Restoration began in the mid-sixties under the aegis of a talented maverick architect, Ralph Anderson, and a cohort, Richard White, whose art gallery became the district's first business success. Public funds accelerated the rush to nostalgia, creating a tree-shaded pedestrian mall, tree plantings, and old street lighting. Let's go down and take a look.

From Smith Tower, head for Pioneer Square. On your left across Second Avenue is the drug store where in 1890, John Considine, proprietor of bawdy theaters, gunned down Seattle Police Chief William Meredith in a classic shootout. Considine beat the murder charge, giving credence, if any were needed, to a saying, "There is no law south of the Deadline." Adjoining the drug store is a rundown Victorian structure that once served as a depot. Through those Occidental Avenue arches moved a stream of interurbans bound for destinations served today by diesel buses (slower, noisier, and more expensive than the electric cars they sent to the junkyard).

Ahead is Pioneer Square, the hub of Old Seattle and long the favorite drying-out spa of the city's Tokay wine society. Pioneer Square, which is a triangle, has been restored into an amiability it enjoyed, however briefly, in the past. Tourists, uptown locals, and wineheads share benches surrounding a cobble-stoned park encasing a sixty-foot Indian totem, an old horse trough supporting a bust of a brooding Chief Seattle ("the white man's God cannot love his red children or he would protect them") and a glass-and-cast-iron pergola that would have delighted Bemelmans.

The assignment of restoring the pergola, once a waiting station for cable cars, was undertaken voluntarily by a nostalgic Chicago businessman, James Casey. Casey is head of United Parcel Co., a nationwide operation he founded as a 1904 Skid Road messenger boy. A few years ago while visiting Seattle, he viewed the rusted ruin and, in a burst of sentimentality, United Parcel came up with $150,000 to restore the pergola's turn-of-the-century elegance.

The totem pole has a history less ennobling. It was carved by Indians as a WPA project after the original was set afire and destroyed. The original cedar totem, carved in 1897, was stolen from an Alaskan village by a Seattle Chamber of Commerce delegation touring Alaska to create goodwill.

From Pioneer Square, head south and begin wending your way through Old Seattle, where the paint, plastic, and plywood of today is being peeled back to reveal the timbers, brick, and dead dreams of another century. You are now in Seattle's hip pocket.

When Lou Graham, Old Seattle's best loved madam, wanted to stimulate business, she'd load up a carriage with her newest doxies and the word went out, "new girls in town," as they moved through the streets at a tart's trot. Lou's old red brick bordello at Third and Washington today is a mission rest for women, the Friendly Inn. Today in antiseptic Old Seattle, traffic and appetites are generated by the words "new restaurant in town." More than a dozen new dining establishments now dot the area, and while many are long on price and decor and short on service and culinary craft, there are exceptions.

A four-star rating already has been accorded the Brasserie Pittsbourg, located down a flight of worn marble stairs just off Pioneer Square. A noisy, aromatic, ever-crowded delight of French cooking that ranges between pleasingly peasant and gourmet, the Brasserie is the lifetime dream of François Kissel, an ex-Parisian who had the crazy idea that a down-at-the-heel basement cafe called the Pittsburg Lunch could someday make the national haute cuisine list, which it has. The Brasserie now draws so many of the city's in-crowd (including politicians eager to relate to whatever is new) that the term "Pittsbourg liberal" has become a recognizable description. With work scheduled to start in mid-1974 on converting the venerable Pioneer Building into an office and shopping complex, the Brasserie may be moving its recipes and copper pans to another nearby locale. It's worth looking for.

Across Yesler Way from the Pittsbourg is the Merchant's Lunch, popular even before the Klondike made it a favorite of gold seekers and rogues. Like many of Old Seattle's renewed enterprises, the Merchant's Lunch is the handiwork of a sentimentalist. It was opened and restored, including its two-level interior of brick, dark wood, brass, and a thirty-foot mahogany back bar, by Howard Rolie. An ex-newsboy from Skid Road, Rolie deserted his career as the successful operator of a San Francisco air freight firm to "do something I always wanted to do, run a restaurant back here where I used to peddle papers."

The Merchant's Lunch features an eclectic menu that ranges from Norwegian fish cakes to Frittata and a long list of sandwiches, cold cuts, cheese, and salads. For dessert, the bane of weight-watchers, a German seven-layer cake. Downstairs, tucked under Yesler Way, is a bar seating but a dozen in subdued light shining in from old-fashioned sidewalk grills overhead.

Nearby, two Old Seattle restaurants offer a couple of the city's only opportunities for sidewalk dining. Sidewalk dining in Seattle is not to be confused with that amiable preoccupation in Paris, Brussels, Istanbul, or even Fresno. It simply means you eat out of doors, surrounded by chin-high plantings, ordained by our fossilized State Liquor Board, which after several years of contemplation, finally decreed you could, if shielded from view of passersby, sip a glass of wine or beer with your meal, but nothing stronger, you rakehell, you. On Occidental Avenue, one of these, Das Gasthaus, features a wooden platter overflowing with cheese, fruits, sausage, and a loaf of fresh-baked bread. In addition to the sidewalk annex to its interior dining, Das Gasthaus owes its success to the new-found culinary craft of its young black proprietor, Marvin Timberlake, an ex-Navy pilot whose only previous link with restaurants was working as a bus boy in his home town of Michigan City, Indiana.

Two blocks away at Second and Jackson, another sidewalk cafe, the Salad Gallery, is operated by a trio of crafty youth who picked up the idea of a soup, salad, and sandwich house while teaching school in Japan. Another deli, the Bakery in the Grand Central Building at First and Main, has a similar history. Manning the counters in the popular two-level restaurant finished in natural wood is another pair of teachers. They skipped school to team up with an architect and the owner of a secretarial school—all happy dropouts.

A block away, Washington Street heads a short block west to Seattle's old waterfront where a museum ship, the schooner *Wawona,* is moored. Midblock is the old St. Charles Hotel, where a happy émigré from Holland, Hermine Bergmann, serves up steaming cups of cappucino, espresso, Dutch coffee, and chocolate and plates of Holland honeycake and other pastries at the tiny Cafe Amstelredamme. To the rear is a gaily decorated nursery where for a dollar an hour you can park the moppets while you have a fling at nearby shops.

Old Seattle's international air is further spiced at the Gallery Prague, on First Avenue near Main Street. Here Peter and Katrina Cipri have brought a menu from their native Czechoslovakia that includes bountiful servings of svichova and dumplings, apple strudel and other aromatic entrees. Two blocks to the east on Main Street, a spacious basement restaurant of whitewashed brick and low beams, Mr. Pickwick's Eating House, features Shepherd's Pie, rabbit simmered in ale, and other Old English enticements. If you're in a real Pickwickian mood, you can top off your meal with a glass of mead while you finish your Caerphilly cheese seated on benches flanking the wood-burning fireplace.

A few Old Seattle restaurants and bars remain unchanged. At Larry's Green Front at First and Main, longshoremen knock back bourbon with a beer chaser and mourn for days when cargo was delivered by the slingloads and hooks, not by containers and cranes. But just down the block, the J & M Cafe, Card Room, and Employment Office, where loggers once drank, yarned, dealt, and took their chances with "the slave mart," has cashed in its chips. Today under ersatz Tiffany shades the J & M is a restaurant, catering to young proletarians as hirsute as any booted timber beast, but whose idea of carnality is a noontime game of chess.

Old Seattle's passion for individuality is even more evident in its shops and galleries. Of the latter, more than a dozen have opened and closed since the beginning of Skid Road's renaissance age. Among the survivors in this city of many galleries are two notable Old Seattle galleries, the Foster/Richard White Gallery on Occidental Avenue near First, and Polly Friedlander's at First near Yesler.

While most of the art galleries and the interior decorator shops maintain a studied uptown aloofness, virtually all other wares offered in Old Seattle are crafted from the warm ideas, hands, and eyes of people disinterested in being mere merchandizers. When these personalized offerings remain on the shelves and shops close, no Open Under New Management signs go up. Failures, too, are personal properties.

Few of the district's merchants have had any previous marketing experience. For most it is their first business venture.

Typical is Will Horwood, a Harvard Business School graduate. In his mid-forties, Norwood gave up a career with industry to work at his hobby in the Wood Shop. Here he makes and sells dulcimers and wooden toys and restores furniture amid the quiet pace of Jackson Street.

A few blocks away at First and Main, tenants of the Globe Building, an ex-flophouse now housing architects, landscape planners, and a ground floor bookstore, the Elliott Bay Book Company, make their way to the tiny elevator through a pleasant jungle of plants and flowers. The lobby shop is jointly owned by a secretary, Lynn Anderson, in partnership with a housewife friend, Sue Hawkins.

Across Main Street in another restored hotel, the Grand Central, a doctor's widow, Bettye Greig, has showcased a talent for cooking and travel in the commodious Grand Central Mercantile Company, a multihued array of imported kitchen ware and other items.

Her shop and its neighbors flank a ruddy-toned, spacious corridor reminiscent of European gallerias. This arcade of beams and natural brick is illuminated by old theater chandeliers and warmed by a fireplace around which diners from the Bakery eat and gossip. At its far end, glass and ornamental iron doors open onto a newly created cobblestoned plaza, Occidental Park, dominated by a pergola that resembles a misplaced Texaco station, and beyond it, a pedestrian mall. In late spring, the park leafs out with chamber music groups, jazz combos, and operators of crafts and food stalls.

Among the Grand Central's shopkeepers are David Ishii, a Nisei who said goodby to uptown advertising to open his own bookstore, and a gorgeous Swedish import, Mi Flick, who operates a boutique featuring imported women's and children's clothing.

Across the galleria from Mi Flick's shop, Lillian Clark, a university graduate in communications and sociology, sells what she always thought children's toys and clothing should look like. And on the Grand Central's lower level, three youths, David Stone, Tom Andre, and Gregory Englesby, who learned glass blowing at college, entertain spectators and customers by fashioning vases, bowls, and other creations.

Other do-your-own-thing shopkeepers in the Grand Central feature coins, flowers, lamps, quilts, paintings, sculpture, ceramics, native crafts, cheeses, and a variety of imports.

Some vestiges of the past have defied sandblasting and landscaping. Amid the boutiques remain a few Jesus Saves missions. The windows of the Loggers Loan still feature climbing rigs and saws amid the guitars and wristwatch pledges. At 4 P.M. streets fill with ladies fresh —or wilted—from sewing sleeping bags and outdoor wear in nearby loft buildings.

If Old Seattle has any resemblance to uptown neighborhoods, it is that it too dies at night. The area that once accommodated theaters featuring Maurice Barrymore, Sarah Bernhardt, and W. C. Fields now musters a few devotees of Brecht and Williams who fill the tiny Skid Road Theater at First and Cherry for lunch or evening performances. (A new theater restaurant, Borreca's, at Second Avenue near Yesler Way opened in 1974.) An amiably marinated past is recaptured in places like the Blue Banjo on Pioneer Square, a lively tavern that led the return to Old Seattle with ample servings of beer and song. A few other taverns and restaurants feature trios or solo entertainers, as do the district's gay bars. But nightlife is a faint cry from the days when these streets bested the Barbary Coast in wickedness like they don't make anymore either.

For a family viewing of this sordid past, the Pioneer Square Wax Museum on First Avenue near the square tells how it was in 124 tableaus. And "rapping" up the past is a popular guided "underground" tour created by ex-adman Bill Speidel, a genial oldtown crier whose guides lead visitors through a maze of long-buried Seattle history—much of it apocryphal. Call MU 2-4646 for details.

If Old Seattle has reformed in its comeback, to some it is still a frontier.

"They call this Old Seattle," muses Marvin Timberlake, who has expanded his Das Gasthaus into an underground complex of shops and a new restaurant, "but to me, it's young and romantic. Can you imagine me doing something like this back where I grew up around Chicago? It's all locked up back there."

Old Seattle? Not really, for the old was never that pleasant, much as we try to shove back the mindless hands of today's clock. Fortunately, the art of restoration permits us to scrape the cover off the old brick and leave forgotten the other verdigris of the turn-of-the-century city: the clanking clamor of tired streetcars, the unlighted bricks slippery with rain and horse droppings; the pall of smoke drifting in from waterfront and railyard and streets lined not with trees but towering utility poles.

Scoured by fire in 1889, then rebuilt, Old Seattle has survived earthquakes, panics, and neglect, and probably will survive its latest threat—the crowds and traffic to be generated by the nearby King County Domed Stadium (sometimes sardonically referred to as the Hyper Bowl by those who followed its selling to the voters). About the only element facing extinction is Old Seattle's gypsies—the down-and-outers and pensioners of all ethnic groups who called Skid Road home. Once more they are on the move, being slowly squeezed into other forgotten corners.

Just to the mysterious east of Old Seattle, about a half mile distant, is the International District, once known simply as Chinatown before that term, like Skid Road, became vulgar.

The streets of the district lack the bazaar atmosphere of the Chinatowns of San Francisco or Vancouver. Buildings are elderly and ordinary. Absent are shop windows displaying fans, buddhas, incense burners, and kimonos. Most shops and offices are there simply to serve the social and commercial needs of Seattle's Orientals of an older generation. Here and there are the homes of the Chinese benevolent and family associations, the Hip Sing, Chum Lun, Soo Yuen, and others that decades ago could have been the mysterious tongs we thrilled to in our pulp magazine introductions to Chinatown.

Twice a year, during Chinese New Year and in July when the Japanese hold their Bon Odori Festival, the district crackles with flutes, gongs, fireworks, dragons, and dancers. But for the rest of the year, most visitors are drawn there by the Chinese and Japanese restaurants that are to be found throughout the district.

Unlike all too many American restaurants that survive on the talents of their decorators, those catering to appetites for Chinese and Japanese depend on their cooks. Conceding that there is a possibility of a change in the kitchen lineup, the best bets in the International District are:

Chinese: the Four Seas and the Eight Immortals, both relatively expensive; the Sun Ya, popular with Chinese customers; and the modestly priced Tai Tung, King's Cafe, and Lin Yen.

Japanese: Nikko, where a sushi bar is a favorite after-theater stop, and also features a delicious fish concoction, shiyoaki; Bush Gardens, the most elaborate and popular; Mikado, serving dinner only, and the modestly priced Maneki and Tenkatsu.

Philippine: Tommy's Cafe and the Manila, the latter popular with what police reporters used to refer to as "nightlife people."

Indonesian: the Java.

Most shoppers are to be found at Uwajimaya's, a spacious Japanese supermarket, bazaar, and deli at Sixth Avenue and Weller Street. Step inside and be enveloped in the pleasing aromas of Japanese cooking, spiced by the muted notes of recorded music. Most shoppers are Japanese, studiously surveying the offerings of yam and soy bean cakes, sake, noodles, soups, spices, herbs, and a collection of seafood including dismembered arms of octopi, and scores of other foodstuffs. At a takeout stand, Japanese ladies fashion cooked delicacies. For nondiners, there are bonzai trees, books, magazines, cosmetics, kites, rice paper and writing brushes, pottery, carvings, medicines, and other items proudly carrying the "Made in Japan" label.

From Uwajimaya's, stroll up to Sixth and King for a viewing of the new Hing Pay Park and its Chinese gate designed by architect David Lin. A few blocks away, on Eighth Avenue between Jackson and King streets is the Wing Luke Memorial Museum, a tribute, but hardly big enough, to a young Chinese-American killed in an airplane crash in 1965.

The forty-year-old Chinese-born Luke had been a popular Seattle City Councilman, the first of his race to be elected to public office in the city. (In the 1973 mayoralty election, Councilman Lem Tuai, as conservative as Luke was liberal, lost a close election to incumbent Mayor Wes Uhlman.) Luke played a prominent role in the revitalization of Old Seattle and the preservation of the Public Market and envisioned a museum as a link between past and present in the Chinese-American community.

The museum opened after his death does just that, including in its changing shows: exhibits of departed Chinese gambling equipment as well as displays of contemporary and traditional paintings, porcelains, and other art. A recent show offered the works of Chinese women artists, an amiable coexistence of those who received their formal training in Taiwan as well as those schooled in mainland China. Open Monday through Thursday, 1 to 6, other days, 1 to 8.

WALKABOUT NUMBER FOUR:
THE SEATTLE CENTER

There is little reason to walk to the Seattle Center—a mile from downtown—inasmuch as a monorail will take you there faster and spare you walking through an area known inelegantly as the Denny Regrade, abutting the northern tip of the business district. The Regrade was created in 1928 by sluicing Denny Hill into Elliott Bay, an engineering feat that was to have resulted in an area of spacious malls, esplanades, and other civilized amenities. Today it's a wasteland of used car lots interspersed with some of Seattle's least attractive buildings. (Studies are now being conducted on the feasibility of restoring the hill.)

The monorail terminal is located on the mall at Westlake and Pine. From midtown you can reach it by a stroll down Fifth Avenue, one of the city's leading shopping thoroughfares. The complex of office buildings on Fifth Avenue and Fourth Avenue between Seneca and Union streets comprises the University Center properties, owned by the University of Washington, which in 1861 opened its first classes on the present-day site of the Olympic Hotel.

Here was erected a square, two-story wooden building, coyly adorned with an observatory, a belfry with a clamorous bell brought around the Horn, and four Grecian columns. A picket fence enclosed the tiny campus, as wags said, "to keep the stumps from getting out."

Classes were conducted by a one-man faculty, Asa Mercer, who also served as janitor. Only one of the Class of '61 was ever graduated. Mercer took off to the east coast to import two shiploads of decorous unmarried women to raise the city's cultural level as well as the hopes and morals of the city's bachelor population. Mercer's successor as president, William E. Bernard, a Dartmouth graduate, resigned as University president after but three years. Among his complaints was one that "not one of the misses attending the University the first quarter after our arrival could accurately repeat the multiplication table."

"Society is also greatly disorganized," Bernard went on in his farewell address. "Drunkenness, licentiousness, profanity, and Sabbath desecration are striking characteristics of our (Puget Sound) people and of no portion more than those of Seattle. We have two distilleries, eleven drinking establishments, one bawdy house, and at all the drinking establishments, as at our three hotels, gambling is openly practiced, and Sunday is no exception.

"These are the influences we have had to encounter in our efforts to build up an institution of learning. I need not say it is discouraging and well nigh hopeless."

Undiscouraged, the University moved in 1895 to its present site along Lake Washington's shores. Today its six-hundred-acre campus is covered with thirty-five thousand students and a faculty of twenty-five hundred, not including janitors. The original site, today the city's most valuable real estate under one ownership, is still owned by the University. That includes the Olympic Hotel. Many Seattleites support the University of their choice by regularly tithing at the hotel bars.

The monorail, Swedish-designed with cars made in West Germany, was completed in 1962 to serve the Seattle World's Fair grounds, now the Seattle Center. Since then it has carried almost thirty million passengers. Billed as the forerunner of future rapid transit, it has never been able to attain an average speed higher than thirty-five miles an hour, thus creating, if not the transportation of the future, at least the ride of yesterday.

The most rewarding way to enjoy the Seattle Center is to walk about its seventy-four acres of flowers, plantings, fountains, and buildings, most of them erected for the World's Fair. The next best way is to spend a buck and take the elevator to the observatory of the 605-foot Space Needle, or dine at the Space Needle restaurant. The restaurant's 365-degree view of the city, warts and all, is spectacular, unless you share the feelings of Calvin Trillin, who once observed, "I never eat in a restaurant that's over a hundred feet off the ground and won't stand still."

(For a view that is not as encompassing but has few rivals anywhere, try the Mirabeau restaurant on the forty-sixth floor of the Seattle-First National Bank Building. The cuisine is French, as is the Mirabeau's proprietor, Gilbert Barth, who not only can lead you through its elegant menu and wine list, but will recite the exact location of every game fish in the State of Washington.)

The Space Needle is the brain child of former World's Fair Corporation President Edward E. Carlson, who in 1959 spotted a revolving restaurant in Stuttgart, Germany, and sent a postcard home saying, "This is it for the Fair!" This broke everyone up, it then being but two years before the Fair's opening day. But Carlson, a genial but flinty persuader who started his career as a night clerk in a second-rate hotel to become president of Western Hotels International, and today president of United Air Lines, persisted and prevailed. A corporation was formed that included such big Seattle names as C. Bagley Wright, Norton Clapp, D. E. Skinner, and Howard S. Wright. The $4,000,000 Needle arose in eighteen months. It drew an average of fourteen thousand visitors a day during the Fair and since then has attracted ten million more.

The World's Fair that created the Center out of a wasteland is the most-revered Seattle success story since the University of Washington Rose Bowl teams. After a childhood of penury and rejection, it opened in 1962 and attracted a gate of 9,609,969 during a six months' run. It left behind an $80,000,000 facility which, if not Tivoli Gardens, is one of the country's best-endowed public parks, including a foundation-operated science center virtually unequaled in architecture and contents. The Fair, dubbed the Century 21 Exposition, even finished its run in the black. This was due largely to the fact most of its buildings were erected by public funds, including the Government-built $12,500,000 Pacific Science Center, a tribute to what author Murray Morgan accurately describes as "Seattle's unerring instinct for the Federal buck."

The Seattle Center today is an all-season people's park; a collage of mink and jeans, opera and basketball, carny rides and repertory theater, the leisure-time turf for science buffs and begonia fanciers, conventioneers on the town and guitar players on the grass. It's a place where the fans of Bartók and Bill Russell, Rauschenberg, and Albee join, but seldom mingle. There is a hearty coming together each August in a festival appropriately—for Seattle's climate—called Bumbershoot, which fills the Center grounds with musicians, craft stalls, dancers, and entertainment ranging from chamber jazz to black drama.

Places to pause include:

The Pacific Science Center. A visual treat even if you don't enter its five-building complex, surrounded by graceful arches, fountains, and reflective pools, all the creation of architect Minoru Yamasaki, a former Seattleite. Inside (admission $1.50, children 75 cents) are acres of exhibits that stretch the mind: NASA displays of spacecraft, including a sit-in model of Gemini; a portable Lunar Data Station that receives live data from the moon during lunar explorations, a science theater that may include a Russian documentary on space voyages and a filmatic examination of Ireland's County Kerry; the Boeing Spacearium, where on an encompassing domed screen you may tour the planets, stars, and galaxies, or take a miniaturized trip through the microscopic life in a drop of water; a mathematics area titillating to kindergarten age and grad students alike, and including more than a score of exhibits requiring viewer manipulation. An array of other science exhibits includes a Kwakiutl Indian Ceremonial House whose totems and carvings and exhibits of canoes, harpoons, and implements can take you as far out as Gemini. A gift shop, supporting the Pacific Science Foundation, offers science books for all ages and modest collections of shells, rocks, tapestries, Indian carvings, and toys.

The Food Circus. Its main floor houses an Alka-Seltzer variety of cafeteria food stalls, purveying carry-away containers of Belgium waffles, tacos, fried chicken, tempura, fish and chips, barbecued ribs, and just about anything else your hungry little mind can dream of. A new addition on the level above includes a restaurant with booze, surrounded by masses of plantings.

The lower floor is given over to an international bazaar, the offerings of which run largely to brass trays, cultured pearls, trivets, cuckoo clocks, sarapes, and other offerings suitable mainly for friends and relatives with whom you no longer correspond.

The Fountains. Fourteen fountains spray, bubble, and cascade throughout the Center grounds, including one convoluted skein of pipes and nozzles appropriately dubbed the Mad Plumber. Largest of them all and centerpiece of the lavishly landscaped grounds is the $350,000 International Fountain, designed by two competition-winning architects in Japan, Kazuyuki Matushita and Hideki Shimizu, as a feature for the World's Fair. Here 227 electronically operated nozzles (with piping installed for 150 more) send constantly changing water sculptures shooting more than a hundred feet into the air, accompanied by music from the largest stereo system this side of Woodstock. The outer bowl of the fountain is 185 feet in diameter and no one much cares if you scamper down its sloping sides for a dance through the cascades. But the outstanding Center fountain in any competition would have to be James FitzGerald's bronze sculpture work in the courtyard of the Playhouse—it too is worthy of an ode.

Other Seattle Center attractions include: the Northwest Arts-and-Crafts Center, with an excellent selection of paintings, sculpture, fabrics, pottery, prints, and offerings; the Seattle Art Museum Pavilion, with traveling and Northwest shows of contemporary art; the Opera House, home of the Seattle Opera Company, the Seattle Symphony, and musicals and stage shows; the Seattle Repertory Theater; the Coliseum, featuring ice hockey and professional basketball during their seasons; a museum of old firefighting equipment and airplanes. There is an unimaginative amusement area, the Fun Forest, which offers rides no different from most carnivals but which still squeezes squeals from the young.

The Seattle Center is a very wholesome place.

THE NATURE TRAIL
WALKABOUT

For a stroll that bypasses crowds and commerce, drive about ten minutes from downtown to North Montlake Park adjoining the Seattle Yacht Club on Portage Bay (or take the Montlake bus at Fourth Avenue and Pike Street, getting off at Furman Avenue, just two blocks from the park). Here a pleasant waterside path provides a viewing of moored pleasure craft, then curves briefly along Lake Union to where the narrow ship canal links Lake Union with Lake Washington. The trail then mounts a quay and follows the canal virtually at water level. Lombardy poplars are reflected in the water, reminiscent of a European scene, enhanced by the graceful curve and copper-encrusted spires of the Montlake Bridge and an occasional passing sculler or shell. For a languid exploration by water, canoes may be rented at the nearby University Canoe House, across the canal and just south of the Stadium. After broadening to accommodate a rest enclave overlooking the channel, the trail plunges through willows and catkins to end near the Museum of History and Industry (early Seattle memorabilia, a maritime wing, and lots of stuffed animals and birds). Here a newer and even more rewarding trail begins, a nature walk built for a large part on floats that penetrate, but do not disturb the marshes, a haven for migrating birds. Short side trails lead to lakeside platforms where you can dangle your legs and feed the ducks. Two footbridges are arched to allow passage of boaters and canoeists. The trail ends in less than a mile on a grassy knoll, terminus for other trails leading into the two-hundred-acre University of Washington Arboretum, and less than another mile farther, its Japanese Garden.

THE VIRGIN FOREST
WALKABOUT

A few blocks away from Alki Point, where in 1851 a party of seven men, five women, and twelve children put ashore from the brig *Exact* to become Seattle's first white residents to complain about the weather, is Schmitz Park, virtually unchanged since that birthday event.

The homestead of a pioneer couple who bequeathed it to the city with the proviso it remain undeveloped, the fifty-acre park is a mini-rain forest uncluttered by any of the trappings of a public park, save its network of trails.

You can reach it by car by taking the Alaska Way Freeway to the West Seattle exit, then proceeding via Admiral Way to Southwest Stevens Street, or via the West-Seattle-Alki bus going south on First Avenue. (Sunday service requires a transfer—ask the driver.)

A SHUNPIKING ROUTE
TO THE OCEAN

Washington's salt water coastline, if ironed and straightened out, would reach from Maine to Nags Head, North Carolina.

Its tides, winds, and currents have created the state's major cities and industries. Yet of all American waterways, save those in Alaska, this splendid littoral remains the least changed. Protected by the new-found political clout of its environmentalists, it may even survive as the least defiled.

For the visitor it offers a bright skein of highways and ferry routes —and trails for the ambulatory—that poke into 1,700 miles of coves, beaches, and islands.

Along this salt chuck the wanderer can dig clams and oysters; boat salmon and cod; explore old lighthouses, vintage gun batteries, block-houses, and Victorian mansions; ride an Indian canoe from river to sea; pace the foredeck of the battleship *Missouri;* beachcomb for agates, moonstones, and glass net floats, the latter imported by the North Pacific Current; or mount an Instamatic safari for bear, deer, and elk in a towering forest as big as Rhode Island.

And thanks to the proliferation of motel swimming pools and chemical lotions, along the way you may even swim comfortably and acquire a tan of sorts.

Which is to say if you are seeking one of those sandy Pacific rotisseries peopled by bodies alternately surfing and basting, you'd best start your search somewhere south of California's Laguna Beach. With few exceptions, Washington's salt waters in summertime average fifty-seven degrees. Hours of sunshine are limited even in August.

Such imbalances no doubt are responsible for the remark attributed to Mark Twain that "the nicest winter I ever spent was a summer on Puget Sound." While that quotation is apocryphal, there is a sodden quality beyond invention in the journal entries Captain Meriwether Lewis entered shortly after the Lewis and Clark exploration party reached the Washington coast.

"O! the joy!" he rhapsodized on November 7, 1805, from a viewpoint near Long Beach. (Actually he was viewing Gray's Bay, still sixteen miles from the Pacific.) "Ocean in view!"

"O! how horrible is the day!" he complained to his Journal a few weeks later. On departing five months later, he wrote that he had seen but twelve days of sunshine in five months, a gray statistic that may have wrung from him his final summation of life on the North Pacific:

"Salt water I view as an evil in as much as it is not healthy!"

(Lewis, who had a penchant for capitalizing and misspelling every other word, was a big complainer. En route to his rendezvous with the Pacific, he told of a sleepless night alongside an idyllic wilderness lake dotted with swan, ducks, and geese. In his Journal, he grumbled like anyone's Aunt Martha from Mamaroneck: "They are emensley Numerous and there noise Horid." And his main appraisal of Wyoming's scenic Powder River country was that "the Musquitos was so troubblesom." So much for that cranky Baedeker.)

The rarity of Western Washington's sunny days gives them a vintage quality of intoxicating delight. Clouds roll back, the Pacific winds still, and the tableau of mountains, forest, and water reappears. The citizenry turns on with a glazed-eye ecstasy not ordinarily encountered outside of Scandinavia.

The rest of the time, the locals shrug aside the overcast with gray humor marinated by the rain. "Not too much glare today" will be the deadpan reaction to a day that resembles the rinse stop in a five-minute car wash.

So it goes with Washington's beach addicts. Regardless of the TV weather soothsayers' mutterings of dark days ahead, you'll find them most any weekend heading for the water, hoping their outing can be rewarded by a chunk of driftwood, a bucketful of clams, a fish big enough to be legal, and for the most dedicated, the possibility of a full-bellied gale.

There are few natural highs that match plodding a surf-thrashed beach, leaning into the wind, being cowed by the orchestrated sea fury, and feeling a touch of atavistic terror born of the knowledge that this strand covers a hundred shipwrecks that earned it the title "Graveyard of the Pacific."

Then back to the motel, a warming fireplace and the anticipation of fried razor clams for dinner. Could Puerto Vallarta, Kona Beach, or Torremolinos offer more? You bet they could.

Washington's coast begins at the Columbia's mouth and continues northward for one hundred fifty miles to Cape Flattery, then swings east for another one hundred miles up the Strait of Juan de Fuca before making a wobbly loop down many-fingered Puget Sound and its many islands. Within those pleasant boundaries are eleven state parks, a 350,000-acre national park, Indian reservations, and hundreds of overnight accommodations ranging from fishermen's cabins to motels with color TV, heated pool, Saran-wrapped glasses, instant coffee machines, and bedside lamps with shades as big as silos.

The best way to get to see the Washington coastline is to come up through Oregon on U.S. 101 and, after exploring Astoria, cross the toll bridge spanning the Columbia to Megler.

For those not traveling this route, the grandest way to the ocean or Sound beaches is by ferry.

The State of Washington operates twenty comfortable green-and-white ferries over nine different runs, penetrating just about every reach of Puget Sound that to date has defied eager bridge builders.

Two of the main runs are to Bainbridge Island and to Bremerton, both departing hourly from the Washington State Ferry Terminal at the foot of Madison Street. At the turn of the century several score of steamers served some two hundred Puget Sound communities from this waterfront. Today Bremerton and a few island communities remain as stubborn holdouts against bridge and freeway.

If you're short of time and can't resist the opportunity to beachcomb and dig your toes in Puget's sound, take the ferry to Bainbridge Island. The crossing requires but thirty minutes, provides a spectacular view of Seattle's skyline and harbor, and puts you ashore on a bucolic island scalloped with salty names like Rolling Bay, Hidden Cove, Port Madison, Eagle Harbor and its accouterments, Wing Point and Bill Point. On Bainbridge's timbered shores looking across at Seattle is Fay Bainbridge State Park, with stoves and picnic tables (some sheltered), acres of driftwood, and limited facilities for campers. Lazy voyagers can just stay aboard the ferry and make the round trip of an hour as foot passengers.

There also is a special five-hour ferry excursion for walk-ons, the time limit beginning when the ferry arrives. Fare: $1.50 for adults, 75 cents for children up to twelve.

From Bainbridge Island, the main highway crosses Agate Pass Bridge to the mainland, then passes over a mile-long floating toll bridge that will send you on the way to the ocean via the Strait of Juan de Fuca. But that's not the way we're going today.

The two ferries serving Bremerton (*that's* the way we're going) carry 160 cars and 2,600 passengers, do 20 knots, and at 383 feet in length are billed as the world's second largest double-ended ferries. The world's largest are the *Spokane* and the *Walla Walla,* as long as two football fields, which run to Bainbridge Island and the San Juans.

The ferries depart hourly, which gives you a chance to take an amiable ramble down Seattle's old Gold Rush waterfront that reaches northward for a half mile from the ferry terminal.

Now if you'll wipe the last of that packet of fish and chips off your fingers, we'll board the ferry for Bremerton and the beaches. If the thought of an hour-long ferry ride turns you off, take the freeway to Shelton. We'll meet you there.

The route to Bremerton etches its way across Elliott Bay. After clearing Duwamish Head and Elliott Bay, the ferry passes Alki Point—marked by a lighthouse—the site of Seattle's birthplace in 1851. Rounding the southern tip of Bainbridge Island, the ferry knifes through the entrance to narrow Rich Passage, a limpid, fjord-like channel lined with summer and year-round homes. During World War II, this gateway to Puget Sound Navy Yard was hung with steel netting that dropped to the Sound floor as protection against Japanese submarines. It was opened only to vessels whose skippers could give the password without a sibilant accent.

The old anti-submarine nets are piled up today in a rusting snarl at nearby Clam Bay. In their places are those pens you see from the ferry deck, strung out offshore like a series of floating corrals, which is what they are. They're a joint venture of a diverse group that includes a collection of state and federal fisheries and oceanographic agencies, Union Carbide, and an outfit called Domsea Farms, Incorporated, the vice president of which is Jon Lindberg, son of the famed flier. The corrals are rearing pens in which salmon grow at a rate of ten to twenty times that of natural development. Hundreds of thousands of the corralled salmon are raised each year to pan size—just under two pounds—and sold to restaurants. Another million or so are released into Sound waters to help restore depleted runs.

The Domsea operation is one of the most successful aqua-culture

centers in the United States. Equally spectacular results are anticipated elsewhere along Puget Sound. On the Lummi Indian Reservation near Bellingham, for example, special rearing ponds are growing
steelhead, salmon, and species of super-trout. But the main goal of
the $3,500,000 federal-financed Aquacenter is the raising of millions
of oysters. If that experiment works—which it hasn't to date—next
on the menu will be albacore, lobster, scallops, and crabs—good news
for seafood diners as well as the two thousand members of the
Lummi tribe.

Less than an hour after leaving Seattle, our ferry arrives at Bremerton, home of the Puget Sound Naval Shipyard and the world's
largest turret lathe.

The Bremerton yard has been building and repairing warships
since the Spanish-American War. If you're interested in cranes,
lathes, and a boneyard full of assorted gray-hulled vessels moth-
balled against everything but obsolescence, bus tours of the facilities
depart from the main gate. On the dock there is a Naval Shipyard
Museum that attempts to re-create the glories of maritime history.
The museum runs largely to models of old warships and faded pictures of faded glories, but there is one display that excites the eye—
the figurehead of the U.S.S. *New York.* Carved of pine, it includes a
glowering eagle astride a red, white, and blue shield, flanked on
either side by Liberty and Justice. It's John Philip Sousa carved in
pine. Open Wednesday through Saturday 9:30 A.M. to 4 P.M. Sunday 12:30 P.M. to 4 P.M.

The Kitsap County Historical Museum at 837 Fourth Street has
exhibits of old logging equipment and other pioneer days artifacts.
Open Tuesday through Saturday.

If these are not your bag, pick your way through town on State
Highway 300. The clogged, slow-paced route, apparently designed
by a battleship plumber, eventually brings you to Sinclair Inlet, last
resting place of the battleship *Missouri,* open for visitors Memorial
Day to Labor Day, 10 A.M. to 8 P.M.; the rest of the year, noon to 4
P.M. Monday through Friday, and 10 A.M. to 4 P.M., Saturday, Sunday, and holidays.

Flanked by railroad tracks and a tacky shopping strip and surrounded by a boneyard of World War II hulks, it's a sad setting for
the "Mighty Mo," whose sixteen-inch guns thundered at Iwo Jima
and Okinawa. Later they pointed mutely at the shores of Tokyo Bay
where on September 2, 1945, General Douglas MacArthur accepted
the surrender of Japan to the Allied Powers.

Most of the 888-foot battleship is closed off to visitors, but the
vast foredeck is a popular site for posing the kids under the guns or

over the plaque where MacArthur stood. The few exhibits in the tiny museum section look like they were assembled in the Legion Hall at Lorain, Ohio. Aye, tear her tattered ensign down.

Getting to the ocean from Bremerton is, if not half the fun, at least a visual treat. The first leg over State Highway 3 to Belfair passes through a virtually unbroken corridor lined with fir forest, destined for harvesting in about twenty years. All of the timberland you will see en route to the ocean likewise is second growth forests, much of them sown and grown by mill companies on previously logged lands, a far cry from the practices that once ravished so much of the nation's tree stands.

At Belfair, the highway picks up the easterly leg of Hood Canal which isn't a canal at all. It's a thirty-five-mile natural estuary that runs from the pioneer community of Port Gamble to Shelton at Puget Sound's southern tip, then swings east around the Great Bend to Belfair.

Hood Canal was discovered in 1792 by Captain George Vancouver, who was no shakes for naming things. He first called it Hood's Channel, honoring a British lord best known for waffling on the battlefield when he failed to relieve Cornwallis at Yorktown, thus blowing a war. Vancouver apparently couldn't read his notes when he got home and ended up calling the waterway Hood's Canal. Later it became plain Hood Canal.

Vancouver also couldn't resist changing names others had selected, usually for the worse. He sighted a glistening peak in the Northern Cascades that the Indians had already named Komo Kulshan, or Great White Shining Mountain. A Spanish explorer, Francisco Eliza, fancied a resemblance between the mountain's snows and the robes of Carmelite nuns and poetically named it El Montana de Carmelo. Vancouver scrubbed both designations and in honor of his lieutenant named it Mount Baker. There hasn't been a song written about it to this day.

Hood Canal is a joy any time of year, but particularly in May and June when the rhododendrons, Washington's state flower, bloom in ranks along the sections of the highway.

By now, driving through Belfair, you should be about two hours out of Seattle, assuming you are a legal driver, and instead of snapping, "Why didn't you think of that when you were on the ferry?" have a rest stop at Twanoh State Park. This 175-acre facility offers picnic tables, a wooden campground, oyster and clam digging, boating, fishing, a sandy beach, and temperate waters from which you can emerge more or less the same shade as when you entered. In general, Hood Canal waters are warmer and less likely to turn you blue than any other on Puget Sound, save Birch Bay and Point Roberts at the Sound's northernmost reaches.

Now on to Shelton, one of Washington's more attractive timber towns. Shelton is headquarters for the Simpson Timber Co., whose corporate giantism stems largely from its adherence to sustained yield cutting of its vast forests. Not far from Simpson's headquarters building (built of brick) are the research laboratories of ITT Rayonier, the personnel of which provide Shelton with a sustained growth of Ph.D.'s, one of the nation's thickest, if you'll pardon the expression. If you're a real madcap family pause to tour the world's largest automated sawmill, operated by the Simpson, where ten men and a number of pushbuttons (and some saws, too) can turn out in one hour enough lumber to build a split level three-bedroom home. In addition, Shelton ships out 1,500,000 Christmas trees annually, each one guaranteed to inspire a wife to say, "I think the one we had last year was nicer." At Shelton pick up the ocean highway, U.S. 101. Don your duster and goggles and it's on to the town of Montesano on the banks of the Wynooche.

Montesano has a copper-domed courthouse, scene of the trial in 1919 of nine IWW members following the famed Centralia Armistice Day shootout. The edifice ignores this dark chapter. But there is a plaque commemorating the memory of two deputy sheriffs who among a thousand other members of a posse finally brought down John Turnow, the "Wild Man of the Olympics." Turnow (or Tornow) was a two-hundred-fifty-pound, six-foot five-inch dropout who took to the woods, clothed himself in bark and skins of animals (with whom he conversed at length, it is said), and exercised his territorial imperative by killing visitors, including the two deputies.

The road south is strictly a non-urban affair, passing through forest and foothills and halting only for traffic signals at the lumber community of Raymond, founded by a forgiving sea captain whose schooner was wrecked at the harbor entrance.

Raymond's main industry is timber, including log shipments to Japan. The big Weyerhaeuser mill is open to visitors weekdays between 10 A.M. and 1:30 P.M. If they haven't torn down the old Raymond Hotel as they have constantly threatened, its restaurant serves some of the best fried razor clams this side of San Francisco.

If you stop long enough in the neighboring community of South Bend someone is bound to tell you a story of stupefying complexity of the time South Bend physically wrested the county seat away from Oysterville.

It's worth the risk for a leg-stretching exploration along its main street lined with false-front buildings and middens of oyster shells.

Step into its seventy-year-old corner drug store and poke among the hundreds of antiques and historic junk collected by the Pacific County Historical Society. A favorite among visitors is an Indian peace pipe that can be converted in a twinkling into a tomahawk (Indian speak with forked pipe!).

Finally after curving around Willapa Bay and its oyster beds, U.S. 101 heads for the ocean it has been avoiding all these miles. It arrives there approximately midpoint between the fishing town of Nahcotta, near the Columbia River, and Long Beach, and its narrow peninsula.

"O! the joy! Ocean in view!"

And it is. Twenty-eight miles of unbroken beach, flat as U.S. 101, flanked by the restless Pacific and rolling dunes covered with lupine, eel grass, and delicate plants of sand strawberries.

This was the strand that marked the westernmost penetration of the Lewis and Clark party. William Clark noted this by carving his initials and the date, November 19, 1805, on a wind-pruned pine tree overlooking the dunes at today's Long Beach.

The tree has long since disappeared, which is a pity. Who knows what else Captain Clark carved on that pine?

Could have been "Capt. Lewis luvs Sacajawea." Or even, "Tom Jefferson makes Horid noises."

THE LONG BEACH
PENINSULA

By the turn of the century Long Beach was describing itself as "the Cape Cod of the Pacific," and for a time it even managed to provide amenities to match its hyperbole.

Long Beach today numbers less than a thousand, about the same as when Portland swells arrived at the resort via sidewheel steamers and the cars of the Ilwaco Railroad and Navigation Company, also known as the Irregular Rambling and Never Come. The railroad puffed its last in 1930, disappearing along with the hotels, the boardwalks, and beach parasols that for a time re-created a slice of New England so dear to Portland transplants.

Since those days Long Beach has survived, if not flourished, as a center for sports fishermen, family vacationers, and tourists. The town itself occupies a narrow strand cut off for the most part from sight of the nearby Pacific by a strip of rolling dunes, a wild barrier now threatened by the developer's bulldozer.

The dunes are of recent origin, millions of tons of Columbia River and ocean sands heaped along the shore by more than seventy years of unceasing tidal and wave action. Until two jetties were installed at the mouth of the Columbia at the turn of the century, these constantly shifting sands were traps for navigators, making the river mouth a graveyard of ships. Following construction of the stone jetties, the sands began piling up along the peninsula, creating an enchanting strand of sand hillocks, grasses, wild strawberries, winter ponds, and driftwood redoubts that are the delight of young and old explorers.

Then in 1966 the dune barrier was breached by a decision of the Washington State Supreme Court. The tribunal held that the accreted lands are not public, as previously held, but are the private property of those owning lots and homes flanking the dune lands. The ruling stunned conservationists, but there has been little outcry from the property owners, many of whom found that instead of being proprietors of a forty-by-one-hundred-twenty-foot lot, they now owned one forty by two thousand feet!

Mused one such owner, who had been among those mounting a legal battle to retail the dunes' public status: "We hoped we could keep the dunes the way they always were—that's why we bought here. But when the court told us that we now owned all that land we had been content to just look at, well, I guess I'm no different than the rest. I look out my window, and there's a big Monopoly board out there, running right down to the ocean. And it's mine."

One of the modest beach homes is that of artist Kenneth Callahan and his Danish-born wife, Bett. Since the court decision on the dunes, the couple have purchased a nearby timber tract as a retreat from the anticipated condominium blight. The beach isolation has been a constant inspiration for the painter whose works grace collections in the Whitney, Guggenheim, Sloan, and other U.S. and overseas galleries. Daily beach walks yield objects and impressions that may find their way to canvas or simply are added to the artist's creed:

"Seeing is the thing, seeing with the inner eye and the outer eye the constant flux of life, the processes of forming, growth, disintegration, and death, repeated in all forms."

No developers' banners disturb the beach itself, rolled out like a gleaming aluminum sheet for twenty-eight miles, giving it the pardonably stretched title, "Longest Beach in the World." Along most of those twenty-eight miles you can drive, stroll, surf, fish for sea bass, cod, flounder, and other bottom fish, dip for smelt (runs peak in July and August), fly kites, wade, and if you're naturally anesthetized, swim.

If you're along the beach any time other than July, August, and September, arm yourself with a shovel and pail and stalk one of the sea's true delectables—the razor clam.

The razor clam, with its lacquer-like shell, is at its delectable best when rolled in cracker crumbs and fried to a golden hue. The best locale for razor digging is between the southern tip of this Long Beach

Peninsula and Copalis Beach, Tahola, and Kalaloch. Check regulations on catch limits.

Diggers unearth around fourteen million of these bivalves each year. More than that get away, for the razors are equipped with a powerful foot. When aroused, the clam extends this appendage, fills it with water, and, using it as an anchor, pulls itself down into the sand as fast as nine inches a minute. Look for their necks at the edge of the surf or find a dimple-like hole farther in shore and dig.

Fine eating crabs also may be found occasionally in low-tide water holes. These must measure six inches across the back to be taken legally. The limit is six, and they must be males, which can be distinguished by their narrow abdomen. Females have a wide abdomen with a neck of shell extending up to the eyes. (Sorry, Ms. Steinem.)

The Long Beach Peninsula is another one of those islands in time where neither tide, wind, nor man has managed to effect more than a surface-deep change. As it heads northward, State Highway 503 accommodates an occasional spur road headed for the beach dunes. But aside from the flags of a hopeful developer, it offers little distractions en route to Ocean Park, where it turns obliquely east.

Today a quiet village of a few hundred, Ocean Park by 1889 boasted a railroad depot, a hotel, and a summer resort operated by four ministers. Saving souls was not an unknown activity prior to the arrival of the ministry, for Ocean Park, like most Peninsula communities, listed its share of shipwrecks. The most notable was that of the British sailing ship *Glenmorag*. Blown ashore in a gale in 1896, the *Glenmorag* was a total loss. Two lives were lost, but the rest of the crew were rescued, including the captain and a deck hand, who in gratitude married Ocean Park maids.

From Willapa Bay on the Peninsula's northern tip, to the mouth of the Columbia, one hundred seventy-five shipwrecks have been recorded in addition to the loss of more than five hundred fishing boats. Most of these occurred prior to 1900, when charts and chronometers were erratic, and when the Columbia River bar constantly shifted. Still others were accounted for by fogs and sudden storms. A gale in 1880 swept a score of gillnet fishermen to their deaths in a single May night off the Columbia's mouth.

Modern navigational aids have virtually eliminated shipwrecks. But no year passes without losses among commercial and sports fishermen seeking the Columbia's mouth. During an average year the Coast Guard saves more than a hundred lives along these strands, often launching their forty- and fifty-two-foot surfboats into gales.

The ill winds also result in some tamer salvage efforts as storm watchers take to the beaches to seek glass fishnet floats that have been driven in from across the Pacific. The globes range up to a record fifty-eight inches in diameter. Usually the size of a softball, most have been ripped loose from Japanese fishing nets, some of which are strung out for an unbroken fifty miles in Japan's coastal waters. Guinness hasn't tabulated the record catch of the glass balls, but one Nahcotta beachcomber has unofficial claim to the title, having harvested more than three thousand. Best locales for float beachcombing are along a strip from Long Beach northward to Leadbetter Point, in the Graylands-Westport area, and around Cape Alva, south of Cape Flattery. But carry—and note—a tide chart, or you may end up as another Coast Guard statistic.

Just north of Ocean Park, the highway turns east and crosses the narrow peninsula to Nahcotta, named for an early day Indian chief, and nearby Oysterville, named for an early day amatory food. Both communities front on Willapa Bay, where a unique combination of tidal sand flats, flushed by the sea and waters from the Willapa, Palix, Nemah, and Naselle rivers, creates an ideal water bed on which the oysters lustily propagate.

This bivalve bonanza was discovered early in the nineteenth century. By 1850 the first oystermen were digging and shipping $200,000 worth of oysters a year, mainly to the gourmet tables of San Francisco.

Most of the early-day oystermen were far-out types who adapted to the frontier environment by wrapping it around them and living off its bounty with little thought of tomorrow. One chronicler for this hearty band was James Gilchrist Swan, an 1854 model New England dropout, who for three years lived in what has been described as "a leisurely society of boozy white loafers and friendly Indians."

In his reports of those years (*The Northwest Coast,* University of Washington Press), Swan describes a Fourth of July celebration tossed by the oystermen, a saturnalia that began with blasts of gunpowder, staggered through a well-lubricated meal of oyster pie and ham followed by orations, and ended with the igniting of a huge cedar stump. Recalls Swan:

"It made the best bonfire I ever saw; and after burning all night and part of the next day, finally set fire to the forest, which continued to burn for several months, till the winter rains finally extinguished it. The party broke up at an early hour, and all declared that, with the exception of the absence of a cannon, they never had a pleasanter fourth!"

(Parents who lecture children on the virtues of pioneer days should tear out this page.)

Time, tide, and prosperity tended to smooth out the oystermen, and by 1876 Oysterville was the county seat of Pacific County, offering resort hotels, steamer connections with Portland, and an annual yachting regatta. Nahcotta became the terminal of the narrow gauge railroad that ran all the way to Ilwaco at the mouth of the Columbia.

But the oystermen were about as cavalier in their attitudes to their crops as their predecessors had been toward forests. The native oysters began declining in the eighties, and by 1920 the Willapa Bay beds were cold and empty. South Bend stole the county seat, and the railroad stopped running, even irregularly. For a time it looked as though the shell game were over in Willapa Bay.

Then in 1924 the first experiment in planting the bay beds with oyster seeds grown in Japan proved to be a success. Today the propagation, gathering, and processing of oysters—valued at three million dollars annually—is once more a way of life for the area, with annual harvests of more than a half million gallons.

To observe oyster culture on the half shell, stop at Nahcotta where the Northwest Oyster Farm plant is open for tours. (Daily between June 1 and Labor Day. Weekends only at other periods.) Here a friendly guide will provide you with an encyclopedic discourse on oysters.

Oysters are AC or DC. They maintain the sex they were born with for about two years, then switch. By the time they reach maturity at four years, most have decided they want to be females. (You're welcome, Ms. Steinem.)

If you want to heed Byron's line for Don Juan that oysters are an amatory food (the Nahcotta oyster plant offers a similar inducement equally succinct: Eat Oysters and Love Longer), they may be purchased in three varieties: large, extra small, and mini-delight. For an unforgettable cookout, pick up some oysters already breaded and ready for the pan. A nearby seafood restaurant also features the boastful bivalves.

You can also rent a crab trap for $1.50 a day and if patient and fortunate catch your own shore dinner off the Nahcotta dock. For around $6 a day, a skiff can be rented for a short row across the bay to the old Indian summer campground on Long Island, a good place to picnic, camp, bird-watch, or hunt for Indian artifacts, agates, petrified wood, and fossils.

A mile north, Oysterville slumbers on, shorn of its regatta, courthouse, and resort hotels, offering a restful setting that lovingly embraces century-old houses, a stern church, and a general store overlooking the bay. (Stop at the general store and ask to see the map

of the old town, including its embattled courthouse, which after the
abduction of its title became a college for two years.)

From Oysterville the road leads to and ends at Leadbetter Point,
a fourteen-hundred-acre National Wildlife Refuge and state park,
home and nesting grounds for one hundred sixty species of birds.
Limited picnic and camping facilities are maintained by the state
near the point's entryway. The refuge itself is available only for those
who wish to stroll its pathways—or build a nest.

Returning south down the peninsula, the highway leaves the sea
to course its way through lanes reminiscent of Normandy, passing
rhododendron nurseries (visitors welcome) where more than seven
hundred different species and varieties of Washington's state flower
are grown. Other plots grow azaleas, holly, and cranberries. Like
Cape Cod, the peninsula is one of the nation's big producers of cranberries, with more than four million pounds grown annually. If
cranberries are your bag, turn off Pioneer Road for the coastal
Washington Research and Extension Laboratories. There you can
get the whole story, including how Lewis and Clark in 1805 partook
of the wild berries in a Thanksgiving Day feast prepared by Sacajawea and York, the only black member of the historic party.

Just ahead as we return to the vicinity of Long Beach is a variety
of attractions—among them the lure of the Pacific Coast's richest
salmon fishing grounds, and a necklace of parks, vintage forts, and
lighthouses. Both Long Beach and Ilwaco provide an ideal base for
further exploration.

So does Seaview, between these two points. Here the Shelburne
Hotel has been netting fishermen since 1895 with the lure of bountiful family-style meals and comfortable old-style rooms.

Ilwaco is named for Ilowahka Jim, an Indian and son-in-law of
Comcomally, a one-eyed chief of the Chinook tribe which peopled
the peninsula until disease and civilization thinned their ranks. One
of its first settlers—the second, to be exact—was a black, James De
Saule, a cook aboard the sailing ship *Peacock,* wrecked in 1841 on
the shoals that bear its name.

Time has erased Ilwaco's canneries, lumber mills, and its railroad, abandoned in 1930, replacing them with a thriving industry
based on the pursuit, for profit and sport, of the Pacific salmon.
Catches at Ilwaco are rivaled only by those of Westport, farther up
the Washington coast. Charter boats and gear are available in profusion (also at nearby Chinook) or you can join the thousands who
try for perch, sea bass, cod, and occasionally salmon from the Columbia River's north jetty, where launching ramps are maintained.

The North Jetty, a two-mile long finger of huge rocks and its counterpart across the river were built to sluice the river bar of its burden of silt. It's an ideal vantage point for storm watching or viewing the merging of the Pacific and the outrushing Columbia as it ends its fourteen-hundred-mile journey.

More than four thousand deepsea freighters and tankers pass through this gateway each year, guided across the bar by seventeen river pilots. A pulse-stirring sight is to train your glasses on one of the seventy-eight-foot pilot boats making its way through the swells to an awaiting ship.

Fishing from the old jetty is popular and during peak seasons hundreds line the rocky redoubt casting for perch and cod. Casting from the rocks below nearby Bellview Park, once a port for whaling vessels, is also rewarding. Other favorite perches are at Seal Beach, which offers a moorage ramp and lift, and at Beard's Hollow, named for a sea captain who lost his life, ship, and crew on this rocky indentation. To reach it, drive south along the gravel road from Seaview or west for two miles out of Ilwaco.

From Ilwaco, U.S. 101 bends downriver toward the Astoria Bridge, passing through Chinook, once a major site for fishing traps and before that an Indian encampment. Just beyond Chinook a short side road mounts to a bluff housing Fort Columbia State Park. Built in 1897, the fort once was studded with cannon batteries guarding the Columbia's mouth. Today some of the original officers' quarters have been restored into a museum, an art gallery, and a theater. Grassy picnic grounds overlook the river. The batteries are open for exploration, but their guns went off to the scrap pile long ago.

Another mile farther south is a marker designating the strand where on May 11, 1792, Captain Robert Grey in the *Columbia* scudded his way over this bar, laconically reporting afterward the discovery of "a large river of fresh water up which we steered."

His last entry in his account of discovery is a masterpiece of understatement.

"So ends," he wrote of this great beginning.

Just before Megler, U.S. 101 leaves Washington to continue down the Oregon coast and through the California redwoods, one of America's classic scenic highways. There are those, myself included, who miss the lurching, spume-washed crossing of the Columbia here on the ferry that preceded building of the towering toll bridge that now spans it. One of my favorite travel writers, Richard Bissell in his book *How Many Miles to Galena,* tilts at the highway engineers with this thrust:

"There was a lovely ferry across the Columbia River at Megler,

Wash. but it isn't there now because a nice big goddam miserable bridge took its place. I hope it falls down."

A bit extreme, but imagine Edna St. Vincent Millay ever writing: "We were tired, we were very merry, we had gone back and forth all night on the toll bridge."

So as the Astoria bridge sinks into the sunset, let's leave the Long Beach Peninsula for a look at the world's most popular salmon fishing town—Westport.

Ever since the North West Company and its successor, the Hudson's Bay Company, began salting and shipping salmon to world markets, commercial fishing has been big business in Washington. Up until a few decades ago, canneries and packing houses rimmed waterways from Point Roberts to the Columbia and all along Puget Sound. As late as 1949, Puget Sound canneries alone packed almost seven hundred thousand cases of salmon—forty-eight cans to a case—and Seattle sniffed appreciatively at its rank as the world's largest halibut shipper.

Today the state's commercial fisheries—including shellfish—are still valued at more than forty million dollars annually to its fishermen, placing Washington next to Massachusetts and California in piscatorial payrolls. But save for a few small plants, the canneries and packing houses have disappeared, victims of overuse, pollution, and widespread construction of dams on salmon-spawning streams. Most catches now go directly to local markets and restaurants. Others are frozen and packaged for shipment throughout the world. Replacing the cannery towns are communities whose support comes largely from the sports angler. Of these, the town of Westport is king, attracting two hundred thousand avid fishermen a year, giving it the self-assumed title of Salmon Capital of the World.

Westport is on the coast about eighty miles north of the Columbia, equally accessible from Aberdeen or Raymond, where we paused en route to the Long Beach Peninsula.

From Raymond, State Highway 105 skirts the northern shores of Willapa Bay and passes through the tiny Sholewater Indian Reservation. There, as on many other Washington reservations, the tribe gets revenge for all that firewater we peddled them by manning a roadside stand selling cigarettes, minus the state tax.

A side road leads to the Willapa Bay community of Tokeland, now developing its own sports fishing industry. The old Tokeland Hotel is a fishermen's favorite, with modest prices and immodest helpings at table.

At North Cove, State 105 heads north along lonely beaches broken only by the coastal town of Grayland, and farther on, Twin

Harbors State Park, with picnic and camping facilities. Settled by Finns, Grayland is nurtured equally by sea and soil. Flanking its beach is a real honest-to-gosh tablecloth restaurant, the Dunes, specializing, naturally, in seafood; an art gallery and one of the state's oldest hotels. Back from the road are acres of cranberry bogs, rich in color during June.

But the main harvest and lure of the coastal strand is immediately apparent on entering Westport, five miles to the north. There on a sunny August day when only a handful may be frequenting the beach at Grayland, streets are thronged and parking is at a premium.

Men, women, and children, as single-minded as their quarry, stream from nearby campgrounds or the more than fifty Westport motels, trailer courts, and a fishermen's dormitory. All head for a dozen charter-boat moorages strung along Westhaven Drive. Twenty years ago, only eight fishing boats called this their home port. Today there are more than three hundred, each one touted as "the luckiest boat in the bay," emblazoned with names like *Lucky Swede, Playboy Too, Yukon Queen, Sea Spree, Fury,* and *Santa Claus.* One entrepreneur, in an effort to keep abreast of the times, once featured in his crew a topless bait girl. But most are no-nonsense craft that are pleasure boats only if the salmon are hitting. Fishing gear and bait can be rented, but bring your own lunch. And hope it doesn't end up as seafood.

Some salmon fishing continues throughout the year at Westport, but the main season starts with a blessing-of-the-fleet ceremony in mid-May, and runs through October. Interested spectators at the blessing are sailors stationed at the Westport United States Coast Guard Station, which handles up to seven hundred assistance calls each year, making it the busiest USCG rescue station in the nation next to Cape May, New Jersey. During June and July, a fishing derby, baited with daily cash prizes, draws fishermen bent on beating the local record catch—a seventy-one-pound King salmon. There is good surf fishing and clamming along the beaches, and Westhaven Park near the south jetty provides *machismo* swimming.

Westport charters cost up to twenty-one dollars a day per fisherman, gear and bait included. No charge for the blessing.

THE OLYMPIC PENINSULA

The Olympic Peninsula is as large as Massachusetts and twice as salty, with enough elbow room to accommodate a spectacular diversity in flora, fauna, and people.

The Peninsula's 889,000-acre national park is a chastity belt of virgin forest to be viewed but not violated. Virtually surrounding it are stands of trees bred and trained from birth to satisfy the appetites of man and his mills.

Its waterways include nine hundred lakes, almost a thousand miles of trout streams, and an even lengthier coastline that embraces bays so tranquil they nurture the nation's tiniest oysters and strands so stormy they harvest a new shipwreck each decade.

Peninsula weather is predominantly wet. The town of Forks seldom has a month without rain. Yet thirty air miles over the mountains is Sequim, dry as Los Angeles.

Resorts include Hazel-and-Ed cabins that only a fisherman could love, beach motels done in Early Polynesian, a few vintage lodges and one of the state's cleanest beaches, kept that way by Indians who ban whites from it because they are too dirty.

This is the Olympic Peninsula, girdled by sea and Sound, and walled down its middle by sawtooth mountain peaks so fearsome no road or rail has ever crossed them.

Seldom overcrowded and at points unexplored, it is as author Murray Morgan views it, "unchanged since Lewis and Clark . . . the last wilderness."

One highway—U.S. 101—serves the Olympic Peninsula. The normal traffic pattern is to head north from Seattle via Hood Canal to Port Angeles, continuing down the Strait of Juan de Fuca to the ocean slopes then returning through Aberdeen and Hoquiam.

There is a slight advantage in reversing this flight plan, for on Highway 101's its westernmost leg traffic is usually lightest in the northbound lane. So let us use the Grays Harbor ports of Aberdeen and Hoquiam as our starting point.

At the entrance to Aberdeen just after U.S. 101 crosses the Wishkah River (Indian for "Stinking waters") is a small park. It accommodates a few benches, a statue of a World War I doughboy, a World War II artillery piece and a heroic carving of a robust and jovial logger springing forth from a red cedar stump.

The grouping befits its locale, for this is John Wayne country, a strip of Middle America marinated in the blood, sweat, and rainfall that produced the nation's greatest forests and men to match.

The only major port on Washington's fierce coastline, Grays Harbor was named for Robert Gray, who en route to his historic discovery of the Columbia River, sailed his brig into this "safe harbor well sheltered from the sea." Within a century the protected anchorage was to fill with ships, drawn there by forests unequaled even by the Redwood groves of California's Mendocino coast. (One tract overlooking Grays Harbor was logged continually for thirty years!)

Out of the black, dripping forests came the wealth that created mansions and fortunes for the early-day timber barons, and strife and near-poverty for the men who logged them.

Today the opulence of the timber barons of the past is to be found only in museum pieces like the Lytle Mansion in Hoquiam—twenty rooms of Tiffany lamps, music boxes, a six-hundred-piece crystal chandelier, a rosewood square-grand piano, a third-floor ballroom, and wall-to-wall memories. (The mansion, known locally as the Castle, is located at 515 Chenault Avenue overlooking Grays Harbor. Open to the public 11 A.M. to 5 P.M. daily during summer months. Admission $1.50 for adults, $1 for children under sixteen.)

Gone too are the big sawmills. The scream of their circular and band saws has been replaced by bubbling vats that reduce trees to pulp. With them have disappeared the colorful fleets of lumber carriers: sailing ships, tiny steam schooners, freighters, and their salty Scandinavian crews.

At one time, fourteen lumber ships regularly ran into Grays Harbor with a Captain Johnson on every bridge. The Scandinavian influence finally peaked on a turn-of-the-century day when a lumber schooner docked at Grays Harbor to load for South America. The captain, mate, and cook were named Johnson. The longshore gang consisted of ten men named Johnson. The gang foreman was named Johnson. So was the tallyman who checked the operation for the ship's owner, A. B. Johnson of San Francisco. That was the name of the ship, too.

Grays Harbor today is still the world's largest shipper of timber. But virtually all of it is loaded as logs for Japan aboard big, efficient, and ugly Japanese vessels. None of them is named the *Johnson Maru*.

Downtown in Aberdeen, the bars, the Circle, the Humboldt, the Mug, the Whale, and other honky-tonks have long since been replaced by bowling alleys and cocktail lounges. The neon signs of the VFW, 40 and 8, and Odd Fellows provide the only red lights in town.

A few miles west of Hoquiam, State Highway 109 reaches the sea near Ocean City. Here a leg turns south to the beach resort of Ocean Shores, a scatter of motels, beach homes, shops, an airstrip, a golf course, an Indian museum, and an A-frame church (the Galilean), all monotonously looking like something that emerged full-blown from a developer's plat. Which it did, about twenty years ago, and since then has become the state's most popular ocean resort and convention center.

The fishing is usually highly productive here, including July and August smelt dipping, a well-lubricated sport done with long-handled nets up to thirty-six inches in diameter. Limit is twenty pounds daily. Ocean Shores, with its abundance of feed fish, is among the Washington coast's best salmon fishing grounds too. Mooching from charter boats is popular here, using plugged herring and but four ounces of lead, drifting with the current. But without reservations, you can't depend on finding a charter during the season's peak.

Surf fishing, for red tail perch, sea bass, flounder, and cod, also is popular, using a long rod, a spinning reel, and a fifteen-pound test line weighted with a pyramidal sinker. Clam necks which stay on the hook longer are the preferred bait.

If you want the rare chance to explore a shipwreck, park at the Ocean Shores Marina and walk a half mile to where the good ship *Catala,* a sixteen-hundred-ton coastal steamer that once plied Canadian waters, is permanently beached with a twenty-degree list. The *Catala* served as a hotel ship during the Seattle World's Fair, then completed its decline by becoming a floating marina before being driven hard aground during a New Year's Day storm in 1965.

Ocean Shores State Park offers tree-sheltered camping facilities on the beach, including trailer hookups.

North of Ocean City, a prime clamming area, Highway 109 parallels the coast. You may turn off to drive along the beach at most of its communities from Copalis to Moclips.

At Copalis, there survives a fast-disappearing bit of America—the family resort. Here Iron Springs Resort offers a tiny beach for excellent razor clamming, a swimming pool, and cabins on a bluff overlooking the beach. From the kitchen, the proprietor whips up clam bisque and toothsome pies.

Five miles north of Moclips, on a drive enlivened by spectacular sea views, is a turnout overlooking Point Grenville. Near this jutting promontory the explorers Bruno Hecate, commanding the *Sonora,* and Juan de Bodega, master of the *Santiago,* landed to make Spain's first claim to this coast. The unimpressed Quinaults thought so little of the ceremony they ambushed and killed several of the crewmen.

The Coast Guard maintains a Loran station here as an aid to navigators. (Open Saturday and Sunday afternoon for inspection of exterior facilities.) It's well sited, as evidenced by the still-visible wreck of the freighter *Seagate,* which ran aground here in 1956, and not far off, the rocks where the French bark *Ernest Reyer* was shipwrecked at the turn of the century.

The Quinault Indians still guard their beach against intruders. Near Taholah, the northernmost community along this coastal strip, an Indian guard will politely wave you off this reservation beach. The tribe closed it in 1969 as a protest against paleface litter.

However, for around sixty dollars, a friendly Quinault will take two of you in his outboard-powered dugout canoe on a day-long upriver ride to Lake Quinault. You can fish en route. Summers you may catch rainbow, cutthroat, and Dolly Varden trout. Winters and early spring are good for getting steelhead and pneumonia. If you're interested, send a signal to Richard Charlie, Box 1165, Taholah.

Accommodations along this ocean strand are clean, family-oriented, and, unless you are a fisherman, a big clam hunter, a beach explorer, or quite in love, tend to be somewhat lacking in holiday glamour. The most exciting beach recreation is throwing sticks to Newfoundlands.

Pacific Beach offers a friendly restaurant serving a delicious platter of a seldom-found delicacy—clam balls. But the view of the sea is marred by a cyclone fence protecting a Navy housing project, and the state's unfriendliest sign:

DO NOT ENTER. NO THROUGHWAY. NO TRESPASSING. NO BEACH ACCESS. GOVERNMENT PROPERTY.

Just north of Copalis, at Moclips, the Ocean Crest Resort includes a cliffside restaurant with one of the Washington coast's most spectacular views, and better-than-usual food.

Copalis is the juncture for a side road, which we'll take to get back on U.S. Highway 101. (On the drawing boards is a highway that would link Taholah with Queets to the north, thus closing the remaining gap on this oceanside road that starts at Hoquiam. But the highway would pass through the Quinault Reservation and to date a decade of negotiations between the state and the tribe has failed to effect a right of way agreement.) Immediately after turning inland from Copalis, the highway returns to the conventional Olympic Peninsula format—a blacktop lane lined with files of fir and alder, an occasional meadow, and a glimpse of the Olympics. And but few signs of man.

One of the signs ushers us into Humptulips, named for the river it straddles. (Humptulips means "hard to pole," apparently derived from the contours and currents of the stream.) Across the road from its general store and gas station is a small shingle mill that converts the rapidly disappearing cedars into shakes and shingles. At one time, this area was the center of the thickest stand of Douglas fir on the coast, the famed "Plat 21-9" that led to an immortal boast—and requiem—uttered in one of Humptulip's vanished saloons:

"Give me enough snoose and Swedes and I'll log 21-9 like it was a hayfield, dump the toothpicks into the South fork and ride 'em to tidewater like they was rocking horses."

Just north on U.S. 101, which we rejoined at Humptulips, is a shady roadside park, Promised Land, maintained by one of the area's biggest timber firms, ITT Rayonier. In addition to picnic tables (some under cover), stoves, a lagoon, and restrooms, it includes two antique pieces of logging equipment: a 1910 Shay locomotive and an 1885 model donkey engine brought to Grays Harbor around the Horn in a sailing ship.

The locomotive, last used in 1940, and the old vertical spool donkey engine, which was phased out in 1910, look puny and underpowered for their assignment of wrestling the giant Douglas fir. But they and their successors revolutionized the logging industry, ushering in a day when the machinist, then the engineer, and finally the biologist were to transform logging into the farming of trees—and lumber mills into marvels of automation utilizing every part of the tree except the knothole. This is a sharp contrast to the turn-of-the-century days when more timber was destroyed by fire each year— much of it attributable to logging—than was cut.

Today two concepts of the forest's future—lumber or scenery— mingle about as amicably as would a dowager and a strumpet sharing the same noble. Both recognize the arrangement but are determined not to yield another inch of the bed they share.

"As long as the great trees remain in the park there will be men willing to cut them down, saw them up, and ship them away to all parts of the country," Murray Morgan sighs in the *Last Wilderness*. "And there will be others—I suspect a majority—who would rather come to see them than to have them sent."

Morgan's observation of 1950 has proved correct. At that time, around 15,000 worked in the Peninsula's timber industries with another 10,000 working in service industries, including the harvesting of tourists. Twenty years later, the forest products payrolls had dropped to 12,500 and service industries rose to 14,000.

The trees in contention—the Douglas fir forests—begin to loom larger as we head from the Humptulips area into the Olympic National Forest and thence into Olympic National Park with its six hundred miles of trails and almost a thousand camping sites. The 889,000-acre park was created in 1939 by Congress and enlarged in 1944 by President Franklin D. Roosevelt. The 120,000-acre addition—all of it forested, which enraged many a Peninsula resident—can be attributed at least in part to the shortsightedness of the timber companies. They insisted on logging right up to road's edge, dismissing suggestions that a screening corridor be retained (a strategy now practiced). Part of Roosevelt's decision to add more forest land to the already far-flung park stemmed from an unforgettable view of this desolation. FDR, after lunching at Lake Quinault, where we are now headed, was driven through a stretch of newly logged land. Surveying the treeless landscape, he turned to his Congressman companion and said:

"I hope the son-of-a-bitch who logged that is roasting in hell!"

(Years later, while riding through a similar strip of logged-over land flanking Mount Rainier, Interior Secretary Stewart Udall turned to me and said, "I know now how FDR felt." Neither Roosevelt nor Udall, however, appreciated the regenerative powers of Western Washington forests, for both denuded areas are now covered with growing forests of fir.)

Of the two million or so visitors who each year pass through Olympic National Park, only a small percentage ever see its rain forests, save through a car window.

At Lake Quinault—a two-mile side trip from U.S. 101—the National Park Service and the U. S. Forest Service (about as compatible a doubles act as W. C. Fields and Baby LeRoy) have made it simple to stroll through one of these usually impenetrable nurseries of nature. In fact, one of the lakefront's five Forest Service campgrounds—a bower of sweet-smelling trees overlooking the glacier-fed lake—is but a five-minute walk from a paneled bar offering one of the best-constructed martinis on the Peninsula.

Nearby, not far from the gas-station-and-general-store community of Quinault, is the entrance to Big Tree Grove, served by a self-guiding nature trail of less than a mile and well sprinkled with discreet signs that explain its wonders. And wonders they are! A few minutes from the road, man undergoes an enjoyable put-down. Overhead, dimming the trail into a muted green glow, Douglas firs reach sunward to a height of three hundred feet, as straight as masts. The firs share the rich, foot-deep forest duff with the red cedar, first used by Indians for longhouses and canoes, and the Sitka spruce, from which the first warplanes were fashioned during World War I. Christmas-card Nootka cypress mingles with hemlock and black cottonwood. Surrounding them are the understory forests—maple, alder, and cottonwood, some draped in moss. All spring up from a ground cover of bracken, lichen, moss, fern, and a myriad of other growth, including the seedlings just starting yet another cycle.

More than seventy species of evergreen plants flourish in this arboretum. Among those shouldering their way upward are the hemlock and spruce, heirs-apparent that someday will dominate the rain forests as the Douglas firs die out and crash to the ground to become "nurse logs" for their successors.

Beyond the town of Quinault, the black-topped South Shore road becomes one of gravel, skirting the upper Quinault River for almost twenty miles, then entering into Olympic National Park about ten miles before road's end. This strip provides a drive-through viewing of a rain forest, but its main attraction is Graves Creek campground, operated by the National Park Service. This is a favorite of steelhead fishermen and those taking off for a 10.9-mile hike to Enchanted Valley, a faery gorge of waterfalls, forest plants and creatures including elk and mountain goat, and a trail that if your legs hold out will take you over the Olympics via Anderson Pass, into the Dosewallips Valley and down to tidewater at Hood Canal near Brinnon.

Lake Quinault has other attractions: fishing for Dolly Varden, summer steelhead, searun cutthroat, and rainbow trout on the lake and in the river, and the chance for a day-long ride down to the Pacific fishing on the lake and lower river. Permits or arrangements for boats, including the downriver trip (for either fish or just the fun), may be obtained at the Lake Quinault Lodge, the Rain Forest Resort, or check at the Forest Service Ranger Station at Quinault.

The forty-year-old Lake Quinault Lodge wears its years with distinguished *élan*, its new swimming pool and sauna (concessions to restive "steelhead widows") unobtrusively enfolded by a seasoned framework of cedar shakes, a towering stone fireplace, and a lobby that includes wicker furniture and corner tables set up for checkers, chess, and parcheesi. The lobby, verandah, and dining room look out over a sweeping lawn that drifts down to the lake, passing a rustic bungalow that once housed maids and butlers of guests. In a state singularly lacking in first-class resort accommodations, the lodge is one of the few that lives up to the pamphleteer's designation of "delightful."

Back on U.S. 101 at the Quinault Indian village of Queets, the highway begins an eleven-mile sojourn along the shores of the booming Pacific, one of its brief encounters with the sea. At Queets, you can shop for Indian baskets, masks, and, on occasion, man-sized canoes, hand-hewn from cedar. You also may be able to contract for a custom-carved totem of your own, costing about $100 a foot, a reasonable charge for a fast-disappearing art.

Between just north of Queets and the end of this seaside stretch of U.S. 101, the National Park Service maintains eight well-marked and numbered trails that lead from the highway to the ocean. Ranger headquarters are at Kalaloch, the site for one of the ocean's most popular lodges, a small weatherbeaten structure with a dining room and comfortable cabins looking seaward. Park facilities include camping and picnic facilities, campfire programs, nature walks through the moss-draped forest fringing Kalaloch Creek, and a broad, sandy beach. Razor clamming, always unpredictable, is usually productive here, as well as surf fishing.

Ranger-guided beach walks also are conducted at Beach No. 4 north of Kalaloch, including entertaining introductions to the marine life that thrives in tidal pools along this rugged coast. The beach is another favorite for summertime smelt dippers. No license required to net these tiny, silvery fish, delectable when pan fried. Between Beach No. 5 and 6, less than a half mile off the highway, is the king of the Western red cedars, a giant 130 feet high and more than 66 feet around its ample girth. At Beach No. 6 you can explore the bleached timbers of a sailing vessel wrecked there a century ago. Because all tumbles of driftwood look alike, it's wise to place a marker where you take off from the trail on your beach exploration to avoid a forest grope back to your parked car.

Seven miles beyond Kalaloch, a turnout provides a lover's leap view of Destruction Island. This fortress-like island, four miles off shore, was named in 1787 by an English explorer, Charles Barclay, after some of his crew, who had gone ashore for fresh water from the Hoh, were slain by Indians. This echoed the incident that had occurred

twelve years previously when a similar party of Spanish were killed
back at Point Grenville.

The island today is uninhabited save for thousands of nesting
auklets, its lighthouse automated, a loss to romanticists but probably
of some relief to the lighthousekeepers who hauled ten gallons of
kerosene up the ninety-four-foot tower each night.

Just beyond the Destruction Island viewpoint a road offers an
eighteen-mile side trip into another viewing of the Hoh River rain
forest, this one administered by the National Park Service, which
provides naturalist-guided tours, evening campfire talks, a visitor
center, and camping facilities.

Around the campfire, someone is sure to recount the story of John
Huelsdonk, "The Iron Man of the Hoh," a German immigrant who
carved out a mountainside home for his family in these forests. The
tales that grew up around him are as tall as the trees he lived with,
including accounts of his prowess as a bear and cougar hunter. But
the one best remembered, and most extravagantly embroidered, con-
cerns the time in 1905 when a Forest Service ranger met Huelsdonk
on a precipitous mountain trail. Noting in awe the stove he was carrying strapped to his back, the Ranger asked him if it wasn't God-
awful heavy.

"Oh the weight isn't bad," Huelsdonk is said to have replied. "But
sometimes it's hard to keep my balance on a log when that sack of flour
in the oven shifts."

Ahead is Forks, a lumber-succored community where they still
measure in board feet the effects of a disastrous 1959 forest fire that
swept over sixty square miles: 575 million board feet were consumed.
With a population of around two thousand, Forks is the principal
commercial center of the Peninsula's western slope. Each year it
turns on for a Fourth of July celebration that would pleasure Mark
Twain or Harry Truman.

But with all of its mackinaw proletarianism, heightened by the
bellow of the passing logging rigs, there is a strain of reformation
along the streets of this loggers' citadel. It's a feeling lightened by
the "cocktails" sign antiseptically gleaming from a bar that advises
"no caulks." It's there in the store window that mingles Hawaiian
sport shirts with wool socks and high-top boots. It's even evident in
the massive logger-owned trucks, costing upward of twenty thousand
dollars, with paintwork and chrome as assiduously polished as that
of a rally car.

Like Aberdeen, Forks gives meaning to logging historian Stewart
Holbrook's requiem of the howling timber beast of old, now "tamed
all but out of recognition."

"Civilization had at last caught up with him on this Last Frontier," he wrote, and here Holbrook could have been standing on the Main Street of Forks. "And it had cut him down to size, turned him into a husband, a father, a mere didy-changer, a home owner, voter, and proletarian.

"It was just as well, for if there was no Hump to go over from here, no other mountain to the West, where timber was taller and greener, then he might as well fit himself to live in whatever the Last Frontier was to be."

(I strongly advise not reciting the above aloud in any Forks bar after 5 P.M., particularly on Saturday night. If you do, choose the one that says "no caulks.")

Beyond Forks, U.S. 101 arcs eastward, heading for Port Angeles. But as long as you're in the neighborhood, you really should take a side trip to visit the Indian fishing villages of La Push and/or Neah Bay. The road to the first of these, La Push on the Quillayute Reservation, departs from U.S. 101 just a mile north of Forks, penetrating a restful forest corridor, much of it reforested in 1928.

La Push is a corruption of *la bouche*, French for "the mouth" in this case, that of the Quillayute River, a stream but six miles long which empties into the Pacific at the village's doorstep.

With its ragged scatter of cabins fringing a nondescript business district, La Push has about it an air of the tired poor, possibly explained by the fact the average income of the Quillayutes is $600 a year.

Only a few score tribal members live here year round, but in the summertime, the population of La Push swells to as high as six thousand, most of them sports fishermen in aluminum-covered wagons. When skies clear and marine slips and adjoining waters fill with vari-hued boats heading for the fishing grounds, La Push takes on a pleasing Cannery Row bustle. Beer sales rise headily at Wood's grocery ("farthest West in the contiguous United States"); an extra shift goes to work on the federally funded totem-carving line, and the custom cannery encapsules up to five hundred pounds of sports fishing catches daily.

Early in July, smelt start moving into the Quillayute River to spawn and for the next six weeks Indian families take to their dugout canoes to net the silvery delicacies for Seattle markets.

For ocean fishing, the La Push area is at its peak in July and August when salmon move in to feed, and in September and early October when maturing Quillayute chinook are found off the river mouth. For shore fishing, there are abundant bottom fish along the sandy sea floor and kids can usually haul up a mess of tomcod right from the charter boat moorage floats.

These shores were once the happiest of hunting grounds for the Peninsula's Indian tribes. For them, the bounty included salmon, herring, smelt, candlefish, halibut, cod, whale, seal, crab, clams, mussels, oysters, deer, elk, bear, duck, goose, swan, and various roots, barks, and berries, the latter cooked up into pulpy cake or mixed with whale oil.

So if the Peninsula's nine main tribes, including the Quillayutes at La Push and the Makahs at Neah Bay are poor, and most of them are, it is not inherited poverty. These tribes once were well off, living comfortably in cedar dwellings, eating high and even able to afford the luxury of decorations for home and canoe, and possibly a slave or two to mistreat. (Slaves were not hard to come by—the going rate among the Makahs trading with the Quinaults was two otter skins for one slave.)

Tribal wealth was something to display and give away, rather than accumulate. Awed Port Angeles residents in 1865 reported the appearance for the wedding of a local chieftain's son of some fifty Neah Bay war canoes carrying Indian guests clad in black bearskin robes and carrying furs, baskets, and red and blue blankets as gifts. When a Twana tribesman living on Hood Canal threw a potlatch in 1876 the guest list numbered more than a thousand from twenty-two tribes. They moved into a specially built three-hundred-foot longhouse to party and dine for eight days. Then they staggered home, laden with gifts of canoes, baskets, calico, blankets, and a thousand dollars in cash. There was a catch, of course. The guests were in return obliged to lay on their own giveaway. None of those "didn't we have them last?" excuses, either.

Heading north on U.S. 101, the boundary of Olympic National Park embraces La Push and a narrow strip of the coast to north and south. From the outskirts of town, three trails lead to separate beaches, each with its unique offering of streams, tidal pools, waterfalls, and sand beach. First Beach is but a few hundred yards from the parking area. Second Beach, with views of rocky spires, is about a half hour hike—often soggy—through the forests.

Third Beach, popular with novice backpackers, offers a view of a waterfall spilling into the sea and numerous tidal pools. It's slippery when wet, which it usually is. To avoid being inundated, buy a tide table when contemplating beach hiking or camping.

The Peninsula's most-visited Indian village, Neah Bay, is reached by turning off U.S. 101 at Sappho, once a logging camp for a vanished forest giant, the Bloedel-Donovan Timber Company. Many of Sappho's houses were designed to be hauled into the woods on skids. From here, the road to Neah Bay on the Makah Indian Reservation (State Highway 112) reaches tidewater at the town of Clallam Bay, and for the next twenty-one miles parallels the Strait of Juan de Fuca. Most of the road skirts the beach at virtually water level, providing a spectacular view of the strait, its shipping, and the southern shores of Vancouver Island. (Weekends on this serpentine roadway your view is more likely to be that of an impassable trailer or camper; avoid returning on Sunday, if possible.)

Sekiu, two miles westward of Clallam Bay, is a popular lunch stop for salmon en route to the Fraser River and other spawning grounds. This migratory pattern has slowly shifted Sekiu's identity from that of a mill and log-booming town into one catering to sports fishermen.

Sekiu's waterfront, tucked in a cove that opens into the Strait of Juan de Fuca, is hardly a half mile long. It begins just off State 112 with a collapsing mill and rusting equipment, then gives way to a strip of restaurants, bait shops, a few hardy motels, and two floats for rental fishing boats, all put together with that no-nonsense aura of the fishing resort, including whiffs of herring, which somehow become aromatic. Good bottom fishing is possible from the log boom or breakwater.

If you're a romanticist with explorer's legs, peel off from State 112 and take a dirt road twenty miles to a locale that includes such enticements as a quiet lake nudging the coast, Indian trails and petroglyphs, a wild beach with monuments to the shipwrecked dead, and anthropologists' diggings that uncovered a mystery.

The road leads to Lake Ozette, once the home grounds of an Indian tribe wiped out by smallpox. A small resort offers cabins, gas, a coffee shop, boat rentals, and campgrounds. The National Park Service has provided picnic grounds and a Ranger station. Pick up a map here, showing trail routes that lead to the old Indian village, the petroglyphs, and the sites of the shipwrecks, including that of the bark *Austria,* dashed ashore in 1887, its grave today marked by a rusting anchor and chain.

Nearby are the diggings of Washington State University's anthropologists who in 1972 uncovered a five-hundred-year-old Indian house made of cedar and containing in its rubble metal blades that antedated the earliest known explorations of North America. Around the campfire, looking seaward over the surf-thrashed pillars that give this coast its teeth, you can join the conjecture. Did that metal of five centuries ago come from a wrecked Chinese junk that drifted ashore? Or, to stretch the mind beyond that horizon, could it have been leavings of a legendary expedition that supposedly headed across the Pacific, led by a Buddhist priest, a thousand years before Columbus?

Most of the Lake Ozette attractions of lake, sea, and history can be covered in a day-long hike. But beach hiking along this jagged coast is not for the uninitiated. Before taking off, check with the NPS Ranger —or pick up a copy of Ruth Kirk's *Olympic Seashore,* an unexcelled Baedeker of the entire coast, with detailed maps of trail routes.

Neah Bay, down State 12 almost twenty miles west of Sekiu, got its name from a sea captain who landed there in 1843 to replenish his water supply and met the local chief, Dee-ah. The skipper's recollection, perhaps laced with something stronger than water, came out as Neah, and who is the loser?

Previously it had been known variously as Poverty Bay by the fur traders, Scarborough Harbor by the British, and Bahía Nuñez Gaona by the Spanish. The latter inexplicably envisioned it as a major port despite its location, "five points of the compass open to the sea," as a Yankee skipper complained later.

Two years after Manuel Quimper brought the cross and flag ashore here in the name of Don Carlos IV, the Spanish actually established a colony. The colonists, Washington's first non-aborigine residents, built a rude fort, got into a skirmish with the Makahs, and within four months sailed back to sunny San Blas in Mexico, leaving their dreams of a North Pacific empire to mildew in the rains.

In succeeding decades there were a number of low key incursions and intrigues among the Spanish, British, and Yankees involving the Neah Bay area. They ceased in 1855 when Territorial Governor Isaac Ingalls Stevens ceremoniously signed a treaty with the Makahs and ran up a thirty-star flag. It wasn't until 1926, however, that Makahs were able to celebrate their U.S. citizenship in the first of what today are celebrated in Neah Bay, starting on August 26, as Makah Days.

Neah Bay, like Ilwaco, Westport, and Sekiu is not much of a place for surfboards and bikinis. With the exception of its U. S. Coast Guard Station and facilities of the Bureau of Indian Affairs and the Makah Tribal Council, it is almost completely dedicated to the assignment of transporting or otherwise accommodating groups of men, women, and children who are intent on pulling a fish, preferably a rather large salmon, from the sea, or exploring the turbulent beaches.

A network of upthrusting rocks around Neah Bay provides a year-round lure for the hikers and for fishermen. The jetty provides good catches of black rockfish. For the sure-footed, rockfish as well as greenling and ling cod are taken by casting from shoreline rocks.

These same rocks have yielded their share of shipwrecks, too. More than 150 deepsea vessels have gone down in waters around Cape Flattery, the westernmost tip of the contiguous United States, and reached by trail from Neah Bay. The heaviest toll of life occurred in 1875 when the steamer *Pacific* collided with the sailing vessel *Orpheus,* drowning 275. The *Pacific* also took down with her some seventy-nine thousand dollars in a strong box, never recovered. Bring your shovel.

The latest shipwreck is that of the big two-stack troop transport *Gen. M. C. Meigs,* driven onto the rocks while empty and under tow just south of the Cape in 1971. The broken hull is difficult to view, however, with the Makahs periodically closing the trail to the wreck scene, and the Coast Guard strongly advising against attempting a close scrutiny by water.

The twelve hundred Makahs, of whom about six hundred fifty live on the reservation, are remnants of a warlike British Columbia tribe renowned for their seamanship and canoe making, from small two-man dugouts used in shallow waters to ocean-going war canoes and whalers. Whales were sighted and speared from the dugouts with harpoons tipped with elk bones supported by floats of sealskin that kept the dying whale afloat until it could be beached and converted into meat, blubber, and oil.

Taking of the whales now has been outlawed. Pods of them can be seen all along this stretch of the Peninsula and in the Strait of Juan de Fuca, particularly in the spring when the gray whales return from their Mexican breeding waters. Their migratory pattern takes them up the Strait, feeding on the bottoms from shellfish, clams, and other goodies, then rising to the surface to blow out the sand and water. Gray whales average fifty-five feet in length and sleep with their heads and tails under the surface, dreaming about what they're going to do when they get back to Mexico.

Heading back from Neah Bay, two highways lead to Port Angeles; our now-familiar U.S. 101 and State Highway 112. The latter browses along the Strait of Juan de Fuca through a continual forest corridor. Side roads lead to Lake Crescent and to Crescent and Agate beaches, both popular with rockhounds, campers, and fishermen. Features include a fine beach, good motel units, boat-launching ramps, and other facilities for camping, fishing, and just plain beachcombing. Just east of Crescent Beach is the Salt Creek Recreational Area, which includes the old tunnels and gun emplacements of Port Hayden, a onetime coast defense bastion.

We'll take U.S. 101 at Sappho so we can make a fourteen-mile side trip to Sol Duc Hot Springs, which offers a dip in a warm-water mineral pool and a view of Sol Duc Falls, just down the trail from the campgrounds. Facilities include a motel, lodge, mineral baths, and a bar. Turn off fifteen miles east of Sappho for Sol Duc.

Another favorite Peninsula spa is Lake Crescent, rivaled only by Lake Quinault for its appeal to today's mobile Thoreaus who seek deep forest solitude with a fast link to the nearest freeway. Almost twelve miles of Lake Crescent's shores border on Highway 101, but a forest curtain allows it to capture a feeling of remoteness. The lake is a welcome respite from the logging trucks that frighten the hell out of most anyone as they pass at a beyond-the-limit clip along this winding highway. And at most any hour, under any weather, the combination of mountain and forest reflected in the deep-hued lake takes on a postcard unreality.

Three lodges provide overnight accommodations along its shores. The Log Cabin Resort and trailer park is a cluster of newer motel units amid the trees and along a lakeshore lawn. A few miles away, the old Lake Crescent Lodge has rooms featuring a view but little else, a dining room and bar (never on Sunday) and motel units. At the lake's west end, Fairholm Resort offers dining and bar facilities and one of the lake's most spectacular panoramas. Storm King Visitor Center, operated by the National Park Service, is located near Lake Crescent Lodge and will gladly turn you loose, maps in hand, on the region's network of trails.

The lake itself has a depth of six hundred feet or more and is famed for its Beardslee trout—a sort of landlocked steelhead. They're found only here, fight like a salmon on speed, and weigh in at up to thirty pounds. Smaller Kamloops trout also are taken. No license required.

Just beyond Lake Crescent, Lake Sutherland is a haunt for lunker cutthroat trout and hybrid rainbows. Two resorts cater to fishermen and also to swimmers attracted by the lake's warm waters. Beyond Lake Sutherland, take time to peel off from 101 long enough for at least a look at the Elwha River Valley. A few minutes on this road and you're into real Marlboro country; a country lane lined with old cedar fence posts on one side and on the other the brawling Elwha. Straight ahead is the snow-capped barrier of the Olympics and a campground.

Port Angeles, just sixteen miles from Lake Crescent on U.S. 101, was named Porto de Nuestra Señora de los Angeles by Spanish explorer Captain Francisco Eliza in 1791, thus erasing its Indian name of Yennis, which simply means "good place."

Now a major log exporting seaport, Port Angeles lives up to both early-day billings. Summertime, pleasant streets are hung with flower baskets. Visitor accommodations are among the Peninsula's best. Prevailing winds usually dispel the old-gymnasium-rafter aroma of the ITT Rayonier Kraft pulp mill, which strengthens the economy, if not the attractiveness, of Our Lady of the Angels. Open to visitors, Monday, Tuesday, and Friday, except holidays, 10:30 and 2. No children under twelve, no cameras.

At the city's edge, virtually crowding into its limits, are the foothills and crags of the Olympics. To the north and west, the San Juan Islands are scattered over the Sound. Behind them, the Cascade Range and Baker's snowy peak. At the city's doorstep stretches the Strait of Juan de Fuca, dotted with salmon and halibut fishing boats, both commercial and sporting, as well as the occasional ferry to Victoria. Good place, indeed.

From here, the ferry *Coho* of the Black Ball Line makes the ninety-minute run to the British Columbia capital city of Victoria four times daily, May 27 through September 20, daily thereafter. The *Princess Marguerite,* a noble Canadian Pacific steamer, makes one crossing a day June 16 through September 4. Both carry cars. You also can arrange a one-day excursion. Or you may leave your car overnight near the dock.

Before it became wedded to tourism, Port Angeles underwent a couple of false starts. President Abraham Lincoln proclaimed it the nation's second national city, but not much came from this honor save for a picky squabble over the thirty-two hundred acres so set aside. An attempt to establish an early day commune called the Puget Sound Cooperative Colony likewise foundered. After that the economy followed a familiar road: sawmills and shingle mills humming, then rusting away to be replaced by the pulp mill, and finally, the beds, tables, and shops for tourists.

Most popular of the Olympic Peninsula's visitor attractions is Hurricane Ridge, eighteen miles above the city over a road lyrically named Heart O' the Hills. En route, where the highway begins its ascent, is National Park Headquarters, the Pioneer Memorial Museum, and an interpretive center. Beyond is a campground and a view lookout where you sense the emotions that led explorer John Meares in 1788 to bestow on Mount Olympus its name, vowing it "a fit abode for the gods." The designation later inspired the name given the entire mountain range. A day lodge at the summit provides meals, an exhibit area, guided nature walks, and lectures. Open May 30 through Labor Day, also during skiing season.

Almost as spectacular and less crowded at peak season is the view from six-thousand-foot Deer Park, reached by an unpaved road that turns off U.S. 101 six miles east of Port Angeles.

For water-level sports, salmon move through the Strait from late April through early October. In September, an entry fee of $10, a little skill and luck can qualify you for the Port Angeles Salmon Derby where twenty thousand dollars in prizes is awarded for the biggest salmon caught. Biggest to date in the thirty-five-year-old derby: forty-two pounds. Halibut and rockfish also are caught. Launching ramps and rental boats are available at various points. Ediz Hook, a natural sandspit shielding the city's harbor, offers a picnic grounds and boat launching ramp. For the kids, Lincoln Park features a trout pond for those under twelve as well as an authentic Clallam Indian longhouse.

Farther east, the two-hundred-acre Dungeness Recreation Area on the bluffs overlooking the Strait provides camping sites, heated showers, restrooms, a dumping station, and picnic tables. From the woodland bluff, trails lead to the Dungeness Spit, a peninsula five miles long and covered with driftwood clumps of wild roses, and a scattering of agates. A National Wildlife Refuge, the spit is closed during waterfowl migratory season. At its southern tip there is a small campground for backpackers and boaters.

At the town of Dungeness, stop and enjoy a meal of one of America's true seafood delicacies, the Dungeness crab, and view a state historic site, the old three-story Dungeness school, topped by an old bell tower and restored by the Women of Dungeness as a community center. From here, the winding seaside road heads south and joins U.S. 101 at Sequim (pronounced Skwim). As it does for other communities in this "banana belt," the Olympics wall off Pacific storms, making Sequim one of the driest areas in western Washington, with but sixteen inches of rainfall annually. This necessitates irrigation for crops, including mint. (Washington produces around sixty percent of dyspeptic America's supply of this chewable commodity.) Sequim's agricultural bounties have for seventy-five years been celebrated in the Irrigation Festival, held the first week in May.

At Sequim's east end is Pioneer Memorial Park, with picnic grounds, a pioneer cabin, and an Indian dugout and totem poles, but no restrooms, which says something about the durability of pioneers (or the function of totem poles). Farther east on U.S. 101, Sequim Bay State Park is another well-equipped forest and beach park.

Between Sequim and Port Townsend are a number of attractions worthy of a detour. They include one of the state's oldest and best-tended resorts, Chevy Chase. It features golf, tennis, a pool, cottage units, and a dining room in a house built in the seventies and shaded by a grove of seedling cherry trees. The nearby beach is more suitable for exploring than swimming. Legend has it the sands conceal a treasure—the stolen payroll buried there by a defaulting railroad paymaster, who departed this world still mute over the locale of his loot.

Back in 1890 when Port Townsend was very young, it dubbed itself the Key City, the "inevitable New York." Why not? Was it not already a great port, equaled only by New York in the number of vessels entering harbor? Weren't three transcontinental railroads about to select Port Townsend as their coveted western terminus? Wasn't the smelter planned at nearby Irondale going to expand into a great rolling mill with ready customers in the big Navy yard that was going to be built next year? And wasn't the Port Townsend and Southern already laying steel that would tap an unsurpassed timber belt to the south?

Believers were everywhere. Three companies were running street cars over sixteen miles of track that bent through the stumplands of tomorrow's Gotham. Lots sold for ten thousand dollars each—almost five million dollars' worth in 1890. Dudes from Seattle built office buildings, hotels, and fathered six banks. Others betting on the future opened a brewery, a cigar factory, saloons, and brothels. Just south at the suburb of Whiskey Flats the cry went up:

"We're as big as New York, only the town ain't built yet!"

Then the bubble burst. The Port Townsend and Southern went into bankruptcy. The other railroads which a newspaper had said "were certain to make this bay a common terminus" decided otherwise. The streetcars sought other fare cities. The smelter closed, the Navy yard was built in Bremerton, the drydock was towed away. Even the whores went looking for more promising street corners. The two thousand dazed denizens who were left behind rattled around in a city built for twenty thousand. Then they started picking up the pieces.

Today, Port Townsend is undergoing a face-lifting to make it look older, recapturing and merchandizing those days of the gay nineties. Downtown, old office buildings are havens for antique shops, boutiques, and craft centers. The old City Hall, including the basement jail where Jack London once slept it off, has been restored, and includes a historical museum. (Open June through August. Consult the Tourist Information Center, 385-2722, for hours.)

A block west, an 1874 structure houses the Port Townsend Leader, which has been prescribing uppers for the city for more than ninety years. The building, along with four residences and a church, is listed in that blue book of antiquity, the National Register.

Not far from the Leader Building is a small plot in which a Tree of Heaven grows. The century-old tree was the gift of the Emperor of China. He thought it was going to San Francisco. But then Port Townsend thought it was going to be New York.

It is in Port Townsend's hilltop residential area that the community's determination to move backward is best evident. There, overlooking the harbor explored by Captain Vancouver in 1792, the tower of the Jefferson County Courthouse looks down on shady

streets changed but little in the eighty years its clocks have been
tolling time.

Down the street is St. Paul's Episcopal Church, built in 1865. Its
bell guided sailing vessels into the safe harbor below. Another old
bell, used to summon volunteer firemen, hangs from a newly constructed tower. Everywhere, long-neglected Victorian residences have
been restored by those who would rather live in the past—with an all-
electric kitchen. Most famed is the home of Herbert Foot Beecher,
onetime customs inspector, son of Henry Ward Beecher and nephew
of Harriet Beecher Stowe.

Another hilltop attraction is the seventy-eight-room Manresa Castle, built as a residence by a German immigrant with an eye for Bavarian pomp. It later became a Jesuit retreat, then a resort hotel.

Among the few homes open to the public is the Rothschild House
at Jefferson and Taylor Street. Built in 1864 it has been restored, fur-
nished in period, and is operated by the state as a museum. Open
Memorial Day through Labor Day, 10 to 5, Tuesday through Sunday.
The rest of the year, 12:30 to 4:30, Wednesday through Sunday.

(A few years ago, the Rothschild House was the setting for a civic
reception honoring pop artist Robert Rauschenberg, who was partici-
pating in Port Townsend's annual summer art festival. This, mused
one critic, was "about as predictable as meeting Ma Kettle in
Monaco.")

Less than a mile from the Rothschild House is Chetzemoka Park,
honoring one of the city's first leaders, an Indian chief who became
better known as the Duke of York. Although the name carried with it
the patronizing air of settler to Indian, the inscription on the chief's
grave (not in the park) reads simply, "Chetzemoka, June 21, 1888.
The Duke of York, the White Man's Friend. We Honor His Name."

The park looks down on Port Townsend Bay. There each day
strings of those fickle railroad freight cars arrive—by barge from
Seattle.

If you want to hang around Port Townsend, there is good salmon
fishing just about year round at nearby Oak Bay, Liplip Point, Partridge Bank, Marrowstone Point, and other feeding grounds. Ramps,
a boat haven, and other facilities are along the waterfront, which also
accommodates the visitor center of Point Hudson. The Crown Zellerbach paper mill, Port Townsend's leading industry, is open to visitors
daily at 9, 11, 1, and 3. No children under eight. Three miles south
of town is old Fort Townsend State Park.

Heading south from Port Townsend, you have the happy option of
ferrying (summertime only) to Whidbey Island, then crossing to the

other mainland via either the Deception Pass bridge or via another ferry from the island's southern tip.

Most favored, particularly in the spring when the road is lined with blossoming dogwood and rhododendron, is to follow the coastline to Olympia over U.S. 101.

Heading south along Hood Canal, U.S. 101 for the next sixty miles is a happy highway. To the west rise the white teeth of the Olympics and their evergreen buffer of foothills. Eastward, across the fjord, are the misty outlines of the Cascade Range. The Olympic foothills, laced with streams tumbling from melting glaciers, are dotted with seven U. S. Forest Service campgrounds, and another, at Lake Cushman, operated by the state. A scatter of motels and three state campgrounds are located at waterside.

By now you must have been assailed by tales of a giant clam, the goeduck, some of which reach ten pounds or more, and which are sought for the satisfaction their capture brings, rather than their taste, which is pallid, unless whipped up into fritters or chowder. They can be taken only on extremely low tides, most of which occur in wintertime. If you're determined to pit your wits against this mean-minded bivalve, some likely locations are at the mouth of the Dose-wallips River, at Quilcene Bay in Jefferson County, and on Hood Canal near Hoodport.

An alternate route south takes off just below Port Townsend near Discovery Bay, where State 104 heads across Hood Canal over a floating toll bridge. From here you can head south to Bremerton or cross the Agate Pass bridge to Bainbridge Island, with its ferry link to Seattle.

A pleasant bonus on this route is the old town of Port Gamble, established in 1853 by two Maine timbermen, Andrew Jackson Pope and Frederick Talbot. Keystone to a timber empire that grew to rival that of Weyerhaeuser, the old Port Gamble has been restored into one of those freeze-frame pictures out of the past; Victorian houses, some dating back to the seventies, an old general store now housing a museum in its lower level, and a park overlooking the mill dock and channel. Nearby is a pioneer graveyard. Some of its tomb-stones bear eloquent witness to the rigors of the time:

"John T. Connick, Dec. 6, 1881, 42 years, 3 mo. 14 days—Native of New Brunswick . . . Life's work well done, Life's race well run, Now comes rest."

"Gustave Englebrecht, coxswain, U.S.N., U.S.S. Massachusetts, killed in a battle with Northern Indians at Port Gamble, Nov. 21, 1856." Englebrecht became the first U. S. Navy man to die in Pacific military action.

The tombstones perhaps provide us with a more honest picture of the times than do the pleasant tree-shaded streets of Port Gamble, which, like most of today's restorations, are shaped as much by decorators as they are by historians. The restored manses of the company executives remain. But cropped from this picture of the past is the rest of the company town, described by a visitor of the thirties as being composed of barracks and cottages that were "drab brown, the color of baked beans, with yards treeless and flowerless."

Across the Hood Canal Floating Bridge from Port Gamble are the remnants of another key lumber port of pioneer days, Port Ludlow, now emerging as a complex of condominiums, a resort hotel, the Admiralty, and one of the Peninsula's best restaurants, the Harbormaster.

Three miles beyond Port Gamble on State 3 is Kitsap Memorial State Park with camping and trailer sites, and beaches for swimming, fishing, and clamming. Just down the road (State 305) is Poulsbo, founded in 1882 by Norwegian fishermen. If you look squinty-eyed at its fjord-like setting, its moorages of fishing boats and a hillside town dominated by a white-spired Lutheran church, you may agree that Poulsbo lives up to its billing as "Little Norway." The Scandinavian blood has run a bit thin since the codfish packing plant closed down, but seventy percent of Poulsbo's residents still claim that heritage. They celebrate Norway's Independence Day on May 17 each year with a Viking Feast complete with *National Geographic* folk dancing.

Between Poulsbo and the ferry landing at Winslow is Suquamish, headquarters of the tiny Suquamish Indian Reservation and burial ground for Chief Seattle. "A firm friend of the whites," reads his headstone in the cemetery beside St. Peter's Catholic Church. The Suquamish are now contesting the treaty Seattle's friends drew up, resulting in the payment of ninety cents an acre for the eighty-seven thousand acres the Suquamish gave up.

Prophetically, Chief Seattle remarked of the terms, "Today it is fair, but tomorrow it may be overcast with clouds."

Three years later he was to say, "I have been very poor and hungry and am sick now. In a little while I will die. I should like to be paid for my lands before I die. Many of my people died during the cold winter without getting their pay. When I die my people will be very poor. They will have no chief, no one to talk for them. You must not forget them when I die." Sic transit.

Nearby is what is probably the last totem ever to be carved by an Indian leader. Fashioned from a thousand-year-old tree, it was carved by the late Chief Joseph Hillaire to honor Chief Seattle and another

Puget Sound chieftain, Kitsap. En route back to the highway look for the tablet marking the spot where Seattle and Kitsap lived in the Old Man (Oleman) House. The historic dwelling was destroyed a century ago by the U. S. Army.

Someday when Seattle tires of restoring its old buildings, some group may find the means of gracing this strand with a replica of this communal house of the Suquamish tribe. The dwelling, possibly the largest habitation built by Indians in America, was erected along the beach at Agate Passage near present-day Suquamish. Built of fir and cedar planking, it was, studies indicate, about nine hundred feet long and sixty feet wide, housing forty separate family apartments, each with its own fireplace. Hanging mats separated living areas, but apartment doors were of wood, hung on wooden hinges. Corner posts fronting Seattle's commodious apartment and that of his subchief Kitsap were decorated with carved figures. Others served as observation points in case of attack.

The restoration of Oleman House could be a down payment on our forgotten debt to Seattle, firm friend of the whites.

THE WEST SIDE
STORY

Those viewing western Washington for the first time have been known to take to their pens with vigorous inspiration.

One of the very first to be moved was Archibald Menzies, botanist and member of the first exploratory party to penetrate the fjords of Puget Sound. Aboard Captain George Vancouver's flagship Menzies rhapsodized over the landscape and the "salubrious and vivifying air impregnated with the balsamic fragrance of the surrounding pinery . . ."

A century later the advance man for another explorer, Jay Cooke, president of the as yet unbuilt Northern Pacific Railroad, took a whiff of that air, counted the pinery and the salmon he saw being "pitch-forked out of the streams." Then he sent this ode to his boss:

"Jay, we have got the biggest thing on earth. Our enterprise is an inexhaustible gold mine!"

In the eyes of succeeding beholders, western Washington has been viewed as either a scenic postcard or a bonanza. Which is among the reasons it became Washington's heartland, the seat of its government and industry, commerce and population, and in the eyes of the state's East Siders, of mischief and wickedness.

We've explored the ocean reaches of this West Side and visited its islands. Now let's tour its inner reaches, a belt running north from

Vancouver to the Washington–British Columbia border. It's a slice no more than fifty miles wide. But it's packed with scenery that nourishes eye and soul as well as some additives that make both weep.

It's bounded on the west for more than half its longitude by Puget Sound, with 1,157 nautical miles of shoreline. For three centuries these mountain-guarded waters have been a funnel for adventurers and traffickers in fish, gold, timber, and commerce. In their wake enough settlers followed to make this enclave the heaviest concentration of people in the Pacific Northwest corner of North America. Almost sixty percent of the total population of Alaska, British Columbia, Washington, Idaho, Oregon, and Montana live within a 150-mile radius of Seattle.

Let's start at Vancouver on the Columbia and then head north for a look.

The Interstate 5 freeway that crosses the broad Columbia at Portland and sweeps into Vancouver has made that community but another hurry-through city. Which is a pity, for streets are lined with history in this oldest of Washington communities.

There is a bit of hyperbole in a marker that proclaims, "The Civilization of Washington Started at Vancouver." Some of the decimated Indian tribes along the Columbia might even view the tablet as an epitaph. But the boast is pardonable. For in the early 1800s, Vancouver was emerging as a major trading post and port at a time when the nation's center of population (thirteen million) was in West Virginia.

Sir George Simpson, governor of the Hudson's Bay Company, baptized the frontier fort in 1825 by breaking a bottle of rum on the flagstaff. He led a cheer for King George the Fourth, dispensed a few drams to "the Gentlemen, Chiefs and Indians assembled," and went back to the counting house.

A few years later, it would take a staff of thirty clerks just to keep books at Fort Vancouver. By then it had become a major depot for a fur trading empire that stretched from the Rockies to the Pacific, from the Canadian Arctic to the Sandwich Islands with outposts in Utah and on San Francisco Bay.

Turn off Interstate 5 at the Mill Plain Boulevard Interchange to the Fort Vancouver National Historic Site. It's a worthwhile foray into a chapter of America's past that climaxed in the 54-40 or Fight confrontation.

Here on the brow of a hill overlooking the Columbia plain, a National Park Service museum houses artifacts, exhibits, and dioramas limning the days when Fort Vancouver was a great fur port. Open weekdays, 8 A.M. to 4:30 P.M.; weekends, 9 A.M. to 5 P.M. Admission free.

On the Columbia plain just below the museum promontory, the Park Service has reconstructed a portion of the original stockade. Someday when priorities are reordered in the Department of Interior the NPS may realize its dream of reconstructing the old Hudson Bay post in its entirety. Until then, you'll have to re-create its outlines from the exhibits. Then step outside, look down at the lush Columbia vale below, and take your own trip back to the 1830s:

Envision, less than a mile distant, a cedar stockade fringed by a village that straggles down to river docks. Inside the stockade are retail stores, warehouses, workshops, a chapel-school, a cannon-studded blockhouse, and a scattering of rough residences that house a population of several hundred. One, a two-story house, is painted white and softened by plantings. It is that of the post's towering factor, Dr. George McLoughlin.

The main business of Fort Vancouver was business, thirteen hours a day, twelve on Sunday, with but three holidays annually. From his crude seat of empire, McLoughlin collected and moved men, animals, crops, and materials and dispatched them across mountains, rivers, deserts, and seas. His instructions sounded like the cards in some early day game of Monopoly. That, even then, was the name of the game.

Within his domain, bigger than Western Europe, were ships, canoes, and bateaux to be built, repaired, provisioned, and dispatched; thousands of cattle and sheep, shipped from Mexican California, to be bred, fattened, and slaughtered; sawmills, grist mills, smithies, and carpentry shops to be manned; grain, butter, and cheese to be shipped to Russian Alaska; shingles to be sold in San Francisco, and above all, furs—eighteen thousand beaver pelts in 1830—to be sent to London.

In keeping with colonial policy of stiffening spines and awing the natives, dinners at Fort Vancouver were reminders that this corner of a foreign field was also Forever England. Or so it seemed at the time.

To the accompaniment of a kilted piper, the Hudson's Bay Company officers and guests dined from tables laid with proper napery, glassware, silver, and china. The menu included the best regional offerings of beef, swine, game, fowl and seafood, vegetables and fruits, served by liveried Kanaka houseboys. McLoughlin, now attired in frock coat and breeches, led the toasts. They included, we may presume, those that provided a reserved recognition of Indian chiefs present, not unlike those proffered by a latter-day political boss to his ethnic ward heelers.

What a place this outpost of empire must have been! Noblemen, church prelates, and scientists like botanist David Douglas mingling with mountain men out of the Rockies, sea captains from Canton; Kanakas, French Canadians, Iroquois, Crees, Flatheads, and Ojibways, or a shuddering missionary from the Sandwich Islands, all under the watchful, bookkeeping eye of Dr. McLoughlin, the White Eagle, King of Oregon, a master colonial administrator, who, refusing to bend, died broken and broke not far from this Columbia strand.

Just across tree-lined East Evergreen Boulevard from the Fort Vancouver Historic Site lies another swatch of history—a row of verandah-girdled quarters for U. S. Army officers of the mid-1800s. Now museum pieces, they were quarters for a succession of young blades then in training to become historic figures. Ulysses S. Grant, Philip Henry Sheridan, George B. McClellan, George E. Pickett, and Philip Kearny were among those sweating out their tours of duty here at Vancouver Barracks, which after the boundary settlement in 1840 emerged as another outpost for a newly emerging world power.

An occasional troop was dispatched into the Indian wars of the midcentury, but most post assignments were more likely to be resolved with the surveying transit than with rifle and cannon. Grant, a commissary lieutenant, spent much of his time plowing and harvesting a crop of potatoes. He explained he raised them because a man couldn't eat properly in Vancouver Barracks on an officer's pay. But to martinets like McClellan, the sight of an officer, if not a gentleman, plodding unkemptly behind a team of broken-down wagon horses, swearing and puffing cheap cigars, was unforgivable, seeding an animosity that came into full flower during Civil War action.

Grant's quarters, built of logs sheathed in planking, is now a museum housing Indian artifacts and antique glassware and furnishings used by him. Open daily except Thursday, 1 to 4 P.M. Admission: 50 cents for adults, 25 cents for children.

Another house in the compound row, built in 1886, is the one in which General George C. Marshall was billeted between 1936 and 1938. In 1937, the father of the Marshall Plan, created to contain Soviet expansion, was on hand to greet two Russian airmen who had completed the first polar flight from Moscow to the United States. They landed not far from where Dr. McLoughlin watched the recession of another empire that was to have been Forever England. Sic transit.

Other worthwhile historic sites in the Vancouver area include the Covington House at Leverich Park, built in 1864 for the Hudson's Bay Company (open 10 to 4 Tuesday and Thursday during June, July, and August); the Clark County Historical Museum, 1511 Main

Street, housing Indian artifacts; a pioneer doctor's office and a country store (open 1 to 5 daily, except Monday); and the Old Slocum House in Esther Short Park, built in 1867 and now a National Historic Site housing an intimate theater (no, Madge, that does not mean X-rated movies). For additional information call on the Vancouver Chamber of Commerce, 817 Washington Street, or telephone 694-2588.

From Vancouver, Interstate 5 bores north on our route to the Canadian border. If you're a shunpiker, and have time to enjoy the bucolic, depart from the freeway just north of Vancouver onto State Highway 503. A meandering road will introduce you to such tiny communities as Battleground, Bush Prairie, and Amboy. The road skirts the Lewis River, provides pastoral viewing of Mount Adams and Mount St. Helens, and offers fishing holes along the Lewis River and at Lake Merwin, Yale Lake, and Swift Creek Reservoir. A well-equipped park for picnicking and swimming can be found farther on at Merwin Dam.

They tell me there is a nine-mile hike along the Lewis above the Swift Reservoir that will provide you with a gulping view of waterfalls and gorges of the river and a chance to eyeball an elk. Check with the U. S. Forest Service ranger at the Lewis River Ranger Station who will arrange an introduction.

Back on Interstate 5, Longview is the next stop if you're interested in touring a very large sawmill operated by the Weyerhaeuser Timber Company. Open for visitors Monday through Friday, 9:30 and 1:30, June 15 to Labor Day; 1:30 only rest of year. No children under five. Also to be viewed is the site of one of America's first planned contemporary cities. Longview is located on the north shore of the Columbia where the Cowlitz River enters and sometimes stays too long. Like it did in the 1860s, when floods erased the nearby hamlet of Monticello and its short-lived eminence as territorial capital. Longview was founded in 1920 by lumber baron R. A. Long who built the world's largest sawmill. As another monument he also created a planned city that included a chain of parks, public buildings, sunken gardens, and boulevards.

Growth has made Longview into something not quite what Long envisioned. But midtown, at Sacajawea Lake Park, Long's baronial ideas are reflected in the lake and its surrounding seventy acres on which flourish fifty-eight varieties of trees and thousands of shrubs, perennials, and bulbs.

This model city was dedicated in 1924 in a seven-day Pageant of Progress. On the seventh day no one rested but turned out to hear the Reverend Billy Sunday deliver an inspirational sermon. The speech left unconverted the editor of the local IWW paper who tucked his review under the headline: BELL HIRES JESUS MAN TO QUIET SLAVES.

Spanning the Columbia at Longview is a bridge linking it with Rainier, Oregon.

Nearby Kelso offers visitors a look at frontier life at the Cowlitz County Museum. Open Tuesday through Saturday 10:30 to 4:30, Sunday 2 to 5, closed on holidays.

Less than a dozen miles north of Kelso, an hour's drive over State 504 will take you to the foot of Mount St. Helens. The peak, youngest of the Cascade pinnacles, rises 9,677 feet in symmetry not unlike Fujiyama. A volcano, it last erupted in 1842, throwing ashes as far as The Dalles, sixty miles away. The peak was discovered in 1792 by Captain Vancouver, who named it in honor of Britain's ambassador to Madrid. The first ascent was made in 1853 by Thomas J. Dryer, founder of the Portland *Oregonian*. There is no record of the publisher attempting to change the name of the peak to Dryer as a counterpoise to Rainier.

Since then, thousands have made the trek up slopes that tower over Spirit Lake (elev. 3,199 feet). Steep timbered walls rise some two thousand feet above the lake, which is stocked annually with rainbow trout.

Accommodations may be found at several lakeside resorts or at Spirit Lake Campground which offers piped water and boat ramps. Several smaller campgrounds are accessible only by boat or trail. During the summer the Forest Service provides evening visitor information programs, and several self-guided tours are available. Other attractions include the St. Helens lava caves (one of them the longest in the world), hiking trails, and late summer trout fishing and huckleberry picking in the St. Helens back country.

Returning from Mount St. Helens, you can shorten your northward journey and see the pleasant vales of the Cowlitz River by taking State 505 through Toledo, thence rejoining Interstate 5. Toledo, nestled against the willow-bordered Cowlitz, got its name from a sidewheel river steamer that would bring passengers and freight here to make connections with stages and wagons.

Looming ever larger ahead, assuming the sun is out, is the one bit of scenery over which just about every Washingtonian becomes unabashedly sentimental, Mount Rainier. Lost in the clouds for more days than it is visible, Rainier's emergence stirs the sourest curmudgeon. "The Mountain is out" becomes a greeting, the affirmation of a bright day ahead.

Mount Rainier has many claimants as its gateway. Seattle, Tacoma,

Yakima, and other cities rightfully share the title. On our present route, turn off Interstate 5 at Mary's Corner and onto U.S. 12 for a scenic circling of the peak and a closeup enjoyment of its glaciers, wildlife, waterfalls, and forests. If you're in doubt about weather conditions around the peak, telephone the National Park Service at Longmire (569-2233 or 569-2211).

(A recent ecology textbook by a University of Washington professor maintains you can predict the weather by watching the Mountain. If you see Rainier, it's going to rain, if you can't see Rainier, it's raining.)

State 12 passes through the Cowlitz Valley hamlets of Ethel and Salkum, sites of the world's largest salmon and trout hatcheries, both open for inspection, and just beyond, two Tacoma City Light dams.

The dams, Mayfield and Mossyrock, were built by the City of Tacoma after it overcame the opposition of those who saw but two more salmon tombstones. To keep alive the big Cowlitz River salmon runs, twenty million dollars of rearing facilities augment the blocked upstream spawning beds. Near Salkum you can view one of these programmed nurseries. When up to twenty-five hundred fish hourly move upriver, the action is as fast-paced as the airport control tower at O'Hare.

Within this elaborate hatchery, salmon and trout bound upriver are sorted by push-button controls and diverted into various holding ponds. Ripe salmon are killed and eggs placed in trays for fertilization. Reared fingerlings are later released to head down the Cowlitz into the Columbia, and finally out to sea. In three or four years they return to repeat the cycle.

Trout are similarly propagated. Fish not required for pond raising, once the annual quota of 480,000 pounds of released fish is reached, are moved by big trucks with aerated tanks to Davisson Lake behind Mossyrock Dam, then released into their natural spawning route. Fingerlings heading downstream from this hatch are diverted into a big pipe that bypasses the dam, sparing them destruction in the turbines.

Tours of Mossyrock Dam begin at a "Hydrovista" facility near Mayfield. It includes a viewpoint, a museum, and nearby picnic grounds. Two parks, Mayfield Lake State Park and Lewis County Park, both on Mayfield Lake, provide additional locales for swimming, boating, and trout fishing. Davisson Lake behind Mossyrock Dam also offers recreational facilities.

At the old logging town of Morton, head for the Rainier National Park entrance at Longmire (summertime only—other months continue on U.S. 12 to circle the mountain) and on to Paradise Valley, probably the most exciting—and overused—of Rainier's attractions.

En route, there's time to digest a bit of history, dating back to the time when Indians venerated this peak as "the Mountain that was god."

To the Indians, Rainier's alpine valleys were places for medicine men to meditate and become endowed with great healing powers, much as medicine men do today at Palm Springs, Acapulco, and Miami. For the less godly, it was a sanctuary, inviolate even to the angered kin of a murdered tribesman (tribesperson?).

Mount Rainier was named by Captain George Vancouver for a British Naval officer, who never saw it. He did see combat duty during the Revolutionary War, headed a squadron in the waters of the East Indies, and died leaving a portion ($1,250,000) of his sizable fortune toward reduction of Great Britain's national debt.

The 14,410-foot peak—sixth highest in the United States—was for more than forty years the center of Pecksniffian debate over whether it should remain known as Rainier or whether it should be named Tacoma—or Tahoma—on the claim that this was its original Indian name.

The debate reached its peak in 1924, when the Tacoma adherents succeeded in getting the U. S. Senate to pass a bill in their favor. But the Rainier forces bottled the bill up in a House committee where, thankfully, it died.

During the debate, the Tacoma-based opponents of Rainier harangued Congress with wild charges. Rainier, they claimed, "raided our shores, captured our citizens, and burned our cities." (He never sailed within sight of our shores and was in action but once, against an American privateer at sea.) Not only that, claimed the friends of Tahoma, the admiral's tarnished name was adopted at Washington, D.C., by the National Geographic Board in 1890, after "a midnight orgy." During this revel, they said, a carload of Rainier beer was used as a lubricant and bribe, "thereby prostituting this noble mountain to be an advertising agency for a brand of intoxicating liquor." This despite the fact that the brewery that adopted the name didn't come into being until three years after.

As for the validity of the name Tacoma, there is strong evidence that this designation was conjured up by a publicist for the Northern Pacific Land Company, which was then hustling lots in Tacoma. And he quite probably took his cue from Theodore Winthrop, who either invented or first used the name Tacoma in his early day classic, *Canoe and Saddle*.

Other Indian monitors maintain Winthrop probably heard an Indian describe the peak as "tkohph," which meant "white," and once scoured of its gutturals it emerged as "Tacoma." But you can still get caned in the Tacoma Club for suggesting this.

While Mount Rainier's admirers include those who like to ski, hike, climb, fish, and maintain census counts of birds, forest creatures, and alpine flowers, the Mountain probably can best be described as the state's most popular drive-in. Of its annual count of more than a million visits annually, most are day trips by locals answering that mystical call, "if we don't get out of the house with the kids, I'm going to climb the wall."

So off they go to the Mountain, a million strong each year, dismounting long enough to picnic, buy postcards and souvenirs from the Ginza West gift shops, sniff fresh air appreciatively, and return home tired and laden with enough exposed film to drive Eastman stock up another point. For the car-less, Gray Lines rubberneck buses circle the mountain daily from May 26 through September 30, pausing for lunch at Paradise, for a tab of $13.50 for adults, half fare for children six through eleven.

There is no air service to Mount Rainier, although nearby Crystal Mountain resort area is served by an air strip for private pilots. Back in 1959, an adventurous pilot landed on Rainier's peak, which to the Mountain's park service guardians was as welcome as a roller skater in St. Peter's. The pilot discovered to his chagrin that his engine wouldn't start for the return takeoff, and for the next forty-eight hours was strafed by waves of competing rescue planes who dropped enough food, medical supplies, and assorted survival gear to stock a surplus store. With the aid of a shove from helpers who had hiked to the summit, the plane finally was catapulted off the peak and made a dead stick landing in the valley below. The pilot was arrested, paid a fine, and disappeared into the bourne of forgotten celebrities.

A less hazardous way to reach Rainier's 14,410-foot summit is to hike, and each year thousands of climbers, ranging in age from subteens to a few over seventy, do so. Guided climbs are available through Rainier Mountaineering Inc., run by Lou Whittaker, brother of the first American to climb Mount Everest. From May 15 to September 15, Lou's school teaches climbing and survival techniques with tuition ranging from $15 for a one-day course to $125 for a five-day seminar. (Rainier Mountaineering Inc. disclaims any affiliation, other than admiration, for a group known as the Rim Club. Membership—now approaching twenty—is restricted to couples who have made love at the summit.)

For those not so inclined, the Mountain has other attractions. Within its thirty-four square miles there are more than eight hundred camping sites (no trailer hookups), two overnight inns, and three hundred miles of trails. One trail, which Washington Governor Dan Evans (a periodic climber of Rainier who confines his membership to the Mountaineers club) claims can give you "a natural high" encircles the peak in an eighty-five-mile loop. It is called the Wonderland Trail and leads past lakes, waterfalls, glaciers and forests. The hike requires two weeks and two stout legs to complete. Shelter huts are provided at ten-mile intervals.

No license is required for fishing Rainier's lakes and streams, but the views are usually more rewarding than catches. Lake fishing begins on July 4, ends on October 31. The stream fishing season is between the third Sunday in May through October. Fishing on the Ohanapecosh River and its tributaries is restricted to fly anglers only.

For most of those who go to the Mountain, contemplation is enough. There is something deep and satisfying in the viewing of Rainier as it looms ever larger until at vantage points like Paradise and Sunrise it completely fills our visual screen.

Rainier National Park headquarters is at Longmire, where pioneer James Longmire opened the Mountain's first visitor accommodations back in the nineties. Here the Venerable National Park Inn offers ten rooms, a dining facility with a limited menu, and a verandah lined with chairs in which little old ladies from Central Casting rock and look up at the glacial peak. Near the inn is a National Park Service museum and information center.

Longmire also has one of the Mountain's most completely satisfying picnic and camping grounds: a fir-sheltered shelf dotted with rounded boulders carried down here by the glaciers that have gone back for another load. The sigh of the trees and the more insistent rumble of the rock-rolling Nisqually River provide the audio for a heroic view of Rainier, framed like a bad postcard by the forest.

The highway from Longmire to Paradise is a head-swiveling upward spiral that passes waterfalls and crosses the Nisqually for a view of Nisqually Glacier's dirty face. At the 3,700-foot level, a parking area provides access to a 1.6-mile trail leading to Comet Falls, and beyond that another turnout offers a view of Christine Falls. The most popular of these cataracts, Narada Falls, has trails leading to pools into which thunders the 241-foot falls, named in 1893 by the Sophical Society of Tacoma for their guru.

Paradise Valley, like Yellowstone and Yosemite, is a tender vale hard-pressed to maintain its alpine fragility under increasing motorist pressures. Located on the very doorstep of the Mountain, it is the center for myriad trails, a visitor center, and the only large overnight facility within the park, Paradise Inn. While somewhat Spartan in its accommodations, Paradise Inn is an honest-to-gosh mountain lodge with a timbered lobby, stone fireplaces, Navajo rugs, stuffed animals, and a dining room full of pretty young waitresses trying to look like Julie Andrews. There is even a cocktail lounge for the devil-may-care traveler. The inn is open from June 16 to September 3. For reservations call (206) 272-2261. If a bear answers, hang up.

In winter months, day facilities, including ski rentals, tows, instructors, and a cafeteria are maintained during ski season weekends. Paradise snowfall averages more than five hundred inches during winter months, and during the 1971–72 winter, piled up to a depth of 1,027 inches, a world record. Tricky weather conditions, generated by prevailing moist southwest winds, have kept Paradise from ever realizing its dream to become the Switzerland of America. (Some Tacomans blame this denial of a birthright on the fact the National Park Service won't build a ten-million-dollar inn and a rank of chair lifts up the side of the mountain.)

Unfortunately, even the National Park Service hasn't been able to tastefully lighten the imprint of man in this vale. The Paradise picnic grounds, once scattered through an all too-fragile alpine valley, are now regimented ranks of concrete tables and benches fixed in black-top, all with a dandy view of the highway. A newly constructed visitor center resembles a Disneyland flying saucer ride, so built that one can obtain a better view of the peak from a Paradise Inn keyhole. (Perhaps the motif is pardonable, for it was over Rainier in 1947 that a pilot reported seeing nine "shiny pulsating objects" soaring by at an estimated twelve hundred miles an hour. With the help of a United Press midwife, the term "flying saucer" was born.)

But if the center's exterior intrudes on the scene, its exhibit halls and interpretive theater are admirably equipped, including a time-lapse film of a glacier looking for all the world like a huge conveyor belt as the slowly moving ice mass is riven and dislodged.

There are twenty-seven of these "ice rivers" moving down Rainier's slopes. At their centers, movements of nearly eighteen inches a day have been recorded. The melted water from glaciers such as Paradise hollows out under-ice tunnels, that, enlarged by air, form spectacular ice caves. Due to differences in the rate of surface snow melt, these are not always open for viewing. Check with the Paradise information center.

From Paradise, turn off just a mile beyond Narada Falls onto Stevens Canyon Road, which passes Reflection Lake and Lake Louise on its way around the mountain. A fine locale for a picnic or just pure unadulterated gaping is the Box Canyon of the Cowlitz, a 155-foot chasm carved by glacier and river erosion. Great Instamatic hunting, too, with periodic views of Rainier, Mount Adams, and the Tatoosh Range.

At the Stevens Canyon entrance (or exit) turn off for a visit to Ohanapecosh, with its visitor center, campfire lectures, and more than two hundred campsites in a deep forest along the Ohanapecosh River. No view of the peak here, but a network of trails wends through groves of hemlock and red cedar, some nearly a thousand years old.

No-license trout fishing (flies only) is popular along the river. A mile from the campground the river poses for a tumble down Silver Falls. Nightly nature powwows are held at an interpretive center which features forestry exhibits.

From Ohanapecosh the East Side Road looks up at Rainier for eighteen miles before leaving the park and heading for Tacoma and Seattle. At midpoint, another highway—State 410—turns east for Yakima over Chinook Pass.

Near the park's north boundary, a sixteen-mile-long side road serves the Sunrise visitor area (open July to September), opening up spectacular views that include Mount Baker to the north, Mount Adams to the south, and Rainier dead ahead. Camping and picnicking are popular at Sunrise. The visitor center includes exhibits depicting the geological history of Rainier, which blew an estimated two thousand feet off its top back ages ago. Rainier, an unrepentant but dormant volcano, was caught smoking only a century ago. Steam, at temperatures reaching 175 degrees, still vents from the peak. Geologists with stethoscopes keep listening for another big burp. One is predicted within the next ten thousand years, but that gives you ample time to clean up your mess and leave.

Leaving Mount Rainier National Park over State Highway 410, the road drops down to the turnoff to Crystal Mountain, the state's most popular winter resort. The spa includes lodges, restaurants, condominiums, and a year-round lift that transports skiers and sightseers to a seven-thousand-foot crest with a snack bar and a dazzling view of Rainier and the Cascade Range.

The view lives up to its billing, but Crystal Mountain in summertime, with its acres of graveled parking lots, scattered huts, and chalets surrounded by peeled hills would make John Muir weep.

Beyond this turnoff, the highway, State 410, begins its gentle descent to the valleys below. This was a favorite route for East Side Indians who came over from the Yakima River, Horse Heaven Hills, and as far away as The Dalles to get a salmon dinner and complain about the rain. In 1853 the first pioneer party to pass this way over the Cascades groaned its way through the cleft, at times lowering

their wagons over cliffs. Of one hundred thirty-six wagons, only two
were lost.

The highway leads down Naches Pass to Enumclaw, a pleasant
lumber and agricultural community where tree-shaded streets and
neat residences belie its Indian name, meaning "place of evil spirits."
Just off the highway is the Farman Pickle Company plant. If you
pucker up just right, you can tour the plant, but call first.

If you're in a hurry to reach Seattle, take State 169 at Enumclaw.
If not, stay in Rainier's shadow a little longer for a visit to Washing-
ton's third city, Tacoma, and reach Seattle via a ride on a couple of
Puget Sound's venerable ferryboats.

State 161 leads to Tacoma via Puyallup, home each September of
Washington's biggest agricultural fete, the Western Washington Fair.
In April fields become carpeted in yellow daffodils. Their arrival is
celebrated by the Puyallup Daffodil Festival, climaxed by a street
parade through Puyallup, Sumner, and Tacoma.

Puyallup's Pioneer Park honors its founder, Ezra Meeker, a veteran
of an Oregon Trail crossing by oxcart in 1852. Meeker, who became
Puyallup's first mayor, prospered as a farmer and built a seventeen-
room mansion which has been restored as a museum. Open Saturday
and Sunday, 1 to 5, and by appointment at other times. Telephone
863-9368.

Leaving Puyallup, take Pioneer Avenue and follow the Puyallup
River to Tacoma over the Old River Road, a meandering pike that
curves through berry and dairy farms and a portion of the Puyallup
Indian Reservation. Despite the shrinking of its spawning grounds
the river continues to attract migrating salmon and is one of the state's
best steelhead streams, a bounty that has fueled a prolonged dispute
between sports fishermen, state agencies, and the Puyallups. The
jurisdictional dispute has produced both low blows and high comedy
and at times the tribe's well-publicized "fish-ins" have enlisted such
disparate allies as Jane Fonda, Dick Gregory, and Eugene McCarthy.
The tribe augments its fishing income with another cash crop, cigarettes, sold minus the state tax, at roadside stands.

A few miles beyond the reservation, the river empties into Commencement Bay, the magnificent harbor that may yet provide Tacoma
with its long-deferred role as a great world port. Here the river delta
is pierced by busy waterways lined with plants producing everything
from pulp, oil, and aluminum to candy, boats, and concrete beams.
Beyond, on streets mounting precipitously from the shore, are the
towers of a city. It's a vista that would warm the hearts of Tacoma's

founders and give affirmation to their sagacity in christening it City
of Destiny.

Alas, the title seems less visionary on entering Tacoma's downtown business district. Though the industrial flats vibrate with activity, much of the city's core area with its proliferation of empty
buildings and stores has the air of a dowager on relief, deserted and a
victim of nonsupport. The nonsupport is a familiar story—merchants
succumbing to the showy enticements of a suburban shopping center.

The desertion is a more painful subject and possibly explains
Tacoma's feistiness whenever the subject of Seattle comes up. Seattle,
in Tacoma's eyes, has been the smooth-talking con artist that robbed
the city on Commencement Bay of its destiny, overcoming by guile
a head start that Tacoma had obtained by its better breeding. For in
the years immediately preceding the turn of the century, Tacoma appeared to have it made. In 1887 the Northern Pacific Railroad, ignoring the blandishments of the con artist, located its terminus on
Commencement Bay. A few years later, the Weyerhaeusers had established in Tacoma their headquarters for a timber empire that
within a decade became the world's biggest producer of lumber. A
thirteen-hundred-seat opera house opened. Stanford White's firm designed a grand hotel of Tudor contours overlooking the harbor.
Henry Villard started construction on another that was to rival Que-
bec City's Château Frontenac. Frederick Law Olmstead, acknowl-
edged as the nation's greatest landscape architect, was assigned to
design the new city. He responded with an inspired plan calling for
sculpturing the hillside with curving terraced drives leading down to
a waterside esplanade. In a single year, 1888, more than a thousand
buildings were erected and the harbor was filled with ships, leading
a London newspaper correspondent, Rudyard Kipling, to write that
this was, indeed, "the boomiest of booms."

In 1893 a panic wiped out twenty-one Tacoma banks. From then
on, events, most of them unrelated, conspired to dim Tacoma's prospects of being Number One as Seattle's brightened. The construction on the château halted. Olmstead's grand plan had been scrapped
in favor of a monotonous grid patterned after Sacramento, California.
The Northern Pacific moved its rail terminus to Seattle. Next to go
were its steamship lines, transferred to Seattle just as the Klondike
Gold Rush renewed Tacoma's hopes. Less than twenty years later
the NP compounded this indignity by moving its entire headquarters
staff off to Tacoma's hated rival thirty-five miles up the Sound.
Shortly after, the Milwaukee Railroad shifted to Seattle, taking with
it a steamship line to the Orient.

Downtown Tacoma survived these reverses until 1968. Then the giant Weyerhaeuser Timber Company, over all civic entreaties, abandoned plans for a multimillion-dollar office building complex that was to have been the core of a renewed core area.

"We'll continue to be your friends and neighbors," the company president said soothingly in making the announcement for moving hundreds of office workers to a wooded site midpoint between the two cities. Small solace to the City of Destiny.

Despite these knockdowns, Tacoma has won a couple of preliminary bouts on its comeback trail. Its industrial base, encouraged by the nation's lowest electrical power rates, continues to broaden. A neglected harbor has bounced back in the past decade, due primarily to log exports and the boom of containerized cargo movements to the Orient. With eighteen hundred acres of tidewater land available for expansion, Tacoma for the first time is emerging as a strong contender against Seattle, which is rapidly running out of space for harbor facility growth.

Despite the launching of a twenty-four-million-dollar urban renewal plan and the announcement by Hilton of plans for a new downtown hotel, attempts to rejuvenate the city's core area have been less successful. The program has succeeded in converting one of Tacoma's main avenues, Broadway, into a pedestrian mall, restful with plantings, covered walkways, fountains, and an escalator link to a big parking garage. But to date the department stores and high ticket shops have not returned from the Tacoma Mall shopping center that generated their exodus to the suburbs.

Hilton's announcement did succeed in filling an embarrassing omission, a downtown hotel and convention center. For despite its potential as a tourist base camp—proximity to Mount Rainier, the Olympic Peninsula, and some of Puget Sound's most rewarding islands and fishing grounds—Tacoma's only downtown hotel was converted into a retirement home in 1973. Until completion of the Hilton, downtown Tacoma has little to attract the visitor, particularly a hungry one. Visitors seeking restaurants usually are directed to Johnny's Dock, which is on the waterfront; to the Cliff House, perched high above the harbor across Commencement Bay; or out of town to the suburban Lakewood Terrace, which many hail as one of Washington's finest restaurants in both service and cuisine. One of the few downtown exceptions is O'Brien's, down a circular stairway in the plaza of the Pacific National Bank Building at Pacific Avenue and Twelfth Street. Looking out on a splashy fountain, it's a good takeoff point for seeing the City of Destiny.

So before heading for Tacoma's chief visitor attraction, Point Defiance Park, stroll a few blocks up A Street, passing what is billed as "the world's tallest totem pole" (105 feet) to a tiny, pleasantly shaded park. The park, ornamented with a Revolutionary War cannon, overlooks Commencement Bay, so deep that early-day sailing ships tied up to trees along its banks. Dominating the scene below are the belching stacks of the St. Regis pulp mill, source of Tacoma's biggest payroll and, alas, its biggest smell. Under state pressure, the Kraft pulp mill has heavily invested in various forms of gargles to reduce its offensive breath. (Back in the early fifties the Tacoma City Council passed a landmark smoke control ordinance but under pressure hurriedly amended it to exclude all white smoke, to the considerable relief of St. Regis and the nearby Tacoma smelter.)

Just a short walk from the park at Pacific Avenue and Twelfth Street, Tacoma's eighty-year-old brick city hall, with its stately clock tower, is being converted into a complex of shops and restaurants.

En route to Point Defiance Park, pause at the Washington State Historical Museum at 315 North Stadium Way, in the shadow of Villard's château, which, after years of standing empty, was converted into a high school. The surrounding residential area with its graceful old homes and shady streets explains why many Tacomans envy not Seattle. The streets and views of harbor and mountains retain the same charm that led an early-day writer to describe them as thoroughfares where it "seems always afternoon."

The museum, in addition to being a valued repository of historical documents, offers a collection of exhibits as varied as a jumble shop or a Georgetown garage sale. In addition to pictorial highlights of state history and cases of Indian and pioneer artifacts, displays include a lock of Narcissa Whitman's hair (see chapter "On the Trail of Explorers"), Chief Seattle's pipe, an aluminum fuel tank from the polar exploration dirigible *Norge,* a pool table on which General George B. McClellan played a cautious game with George Pickett, some of the personal collection of Territorial Governor Isaac Stevens, and much more. Open Tuesday through Saturday, 9 A.M. to 4 P.M.; Sunday, 2 P.M. to 5 P.M.

A few blocks from the museum is Wright Park, at Sixth Avenue and Division Street, a pastoral twenty-seven acres that nurtures one of the West's oldest arboretums, with more than a thousand trees and shrubs as well as a conservatory, picnic tables, and a playground.

From here, a well-marked scenic route leads to Point Defiance Park, bordering and high above the Tacoma Narrows. The heavily timbered park, opened in 1905, covers more than six hundred acres with forest trails, beaches, hundreds of picnic tables, a lake, zoo, aquarium, a children's "storybook land" concession, a vintage railroad, and a reconstruction of Fort Nisqually. Rental boats are available for sports fishermen seeking catches in the salmon-rich Narrows.

For a generation nurtured (or soured) on Disneyland and its imitators, the vintage railroad is something of a disappointment, at least according to the loud reviews emanating from cynical youngsters as the old steam locomotive wheezes along at five miles an hour over a quarter-mile track that loops through the woods. (With but a small investment, the ride could be livened up by programming a mechanical IWW agitator to jump out of the woods singing "Solidarity Forever.") The ride—fare, 50 cents—starts from a facility known as Camp Six, which is a few old empty bunkhouses and a cookhouse, mounted on flatcars. A nearby shed houses what is billed as a museum, consisting of a clutter of old tools and some yellowing photographs, a shabby display for "The Lumber Capital of the World."

Leaving from Point Defiance Park, it's but a quarter of a mile to the dock where the ferry leaves for Vashon Island. The island, like its more well-to-do sister, Bainbridge, to the north, is surprisingly unspoiled. Orchards and berry farms line its country lanes, and there are miles of beach and woodland forest trails to explore. Ask on the ferry for directions to Dolphin Point Walk, a mile-long trail along a headland overlooking the Sound, or to Robinson Point Light Station, where miles of beaches beckon. The light station itself is open for inspection from 1 P.M. to 3 P.M. weekdays, 1 P.M. to 4 P.M. weekends.

From the northern end of the island, the ferry departs for Seattle, docking at the south end of Lincoln Park, about twenty minutes from downtown. Bon voyage.

If you held to the hurryup route and didn't turn off Interstate 5 at Mary's Corner for the Mount Rainier loop, you're now heading north through typical western Washington country.

From Mary's Corner north to the fringes of Washington's capital, Olympia, Interstate 5 rips through rich farm land and wide swaths of second growth timber. These support a scattering of slowly growing communities that increase in number and density until Olympia, where Pugetopolis begins.

If you're an avid viewer of old buildings, pause just north of Mary's Corner at Sheldon Jackson House State Park. There you can walk around one of the first houses (1845) built north of the Columbia. At Chehalis, twelve miles farther north, is the Claquato Church, one of Washington's oldest, with a bell cast in 1857.

Nearby Centralia was founded in 1852 by a former slave, George Washington, who had been adopted by his former master. Washington's memory is honored by a namesake park, but there are no blacks living in Centralia. The only statue in the park is one honoring four American Legionnaires who died on Armistice Day, 1919, when a mob stormed the IWW hall and later lynched a Wobbly who fired two of the fatal shots.

Nearby a park provides a lake open to fishermen under ten, a play area, rose gardens, and picnic grounds and the Borst Blockhouse, built in 1855 during the Indian Wars.

For a glimpse of the forests that carpeted most of the West Side but a century ago, exit from Interstate 5 at Millersylvania State Park, 833 acres of maples, cedars, hemlock, dogwood, and Douglas firs, some of them four hundred years old. The park was willed to the state in 1924 by F. J. X. Miller, surviving son of John Miller and his wife, Anna, Austrian immigrants who settled there in 1881. I'd like to believe the legend that young Miller had been a general and bodyguard of Franz Josef. His bride, the story goes, was the emperor's daughter, a princess who left a Bavarian castle to find true love in the shadows of Mount Rainier.

The park has trailer, camping, and picnic areas, and a stocked lake. There from a rental boat you can trail your fingers in the water while composing some new tales of Viennese love in the woods.

Ten miles north of Millersylvania State Park, another short detour from hurrying Interstate 5 will route you into Tumwater Park. There you can sit in the spray of a Deschutes River waterfall and relive the days when this area became the first American settlement north of the Columbia.

The fifteen-acre park is provided by the Olympia Brewing Company, whose slogan "It's the Water" has made Tumwater famous. The bosky glade embraces two waterfalls, drifts of rhododendrons and azaleas, a riverside restaurant, Indian petroglyphs, picnic grounds, and playgrounds, and during September and early October a viewing of migrating salmon on their way to spawn. Check with the State Department of Fisheries in Olympia for dates of the anticipated runs: Telephone (206) 753-6600 or park headquarters, (206) 943-2550.

Just to the north of the park, a stroll beyond one of the fish ladders will bring you to the Crosby House, built in 1854 by Nathaniel Crosby III, the brother of the great-grandfather of Bing Crosby. The landmark is maintained by the Daughters of the Pioneers. Open only on Thursday afternoons.

Earlier—in 1845—a party of six men had pulled up their mounts and agreed that this, indeed, was the place. They had been on the move with but brief pauses since the spring of 1844 when they left

Independence, Missouri, in a big wagon train that had included eighty wagons and eight hundred men, women, and children.

Below them, the Deschutes wove through forests and grassy plains, then tumbled down this same series of falls into a sheltered deep-water cove opening onto Puget Sound. An ideal spot to stake out claims; just right for farms and mills and a trading center, which they promptly named New Market.

The markets, they rightly surmised, would come in part from just up the Sound where lay the big Hudson's Bay Company stockade post of Nisqually. Beyond it were the vast acreages of the Company of Adventures satellite, the Puget Sound Agricultural Company.

The six stayed. With their families they became among the first Americans the Hudson's Bay Company could not discourage from settling north of the Columbia (another thirty had dropped off farther to the south).

Among the New Market immigrants was George Washington Bush, who with his German wife and six sons settled on a 640-acre donation claim, today known as Bush Prairie. Bush was either a free-born mulatto driven out of Missouri by racial laws as most historians accept, or an East Indian, as is recorded in the Bush family Bible. With either shading in those Wasp-ish days when blacks remaining in Oregon Territory faced arrest and flogging, his ability to survive and flourish is an epic.

The party's leader, a young Kentuckian son of slaveholders, Michael Troutman Simmons, was Bush's benefactor, perhaps because of Bush's ability to help finance the wagon train. Later, as a Territorial legislator, he was instrumental in passage of legislation excluding Bush (but not other blacks or Indians) from the Territory's racial restrictions.

A massive granite block in Tumwater Park marks the spot where Simmons, Bush, and company founded New Market, a name soon replaced by that of local Indians. On your way to Olympia, stop for a tour of the nearby Olympia Brewery (daily 8 to 4:30) where in the taproom you can savor all this heady history.

I can't ever recall bending my route through a state to tour its state capital. But even if you're not a student of history or monumental architecture, you should pause in Olympia, if only to pay homage to the oysters that grow only here.

Tiny but extravagant in taste—and price—the Olympia is one of Washington's few native oysters, most of the rest being Japanese immigrants. They're found in their finest at the Olympia Oyster House, an old restaurant of undistinguished architecture and decor, but rich in good taste from the kitchen.

Not far away is Capitol Lake Park on Water Street, nicely equipped with a playground, a protected beach, and a good view of Washington's grandiose Capitol on the bluff above.

Once Olympia recovered from a childhood dream that it would be a great railroad center and port when it grew up, it set about building a capitol that is one of the nation's finest. That is to say, it's a traditional MGM-style capitol with acres of marble halls, bronzed doorways, flocked wallpaper, and leather seats of government, all topped by a dome that weighs 74,500 tons and is the fourth highest in the world, bested only by those at Washington, D.C., St. Peter's in Rome, and St. Paul's in London.

Newer embellishments include a park-like area on the east campus that houses almost a thousand tree plantings and a series of fountains, pools, waterfalls, and a water garden.

Other accouterments that stir the hearts of visiting taxpayers and demonstrators include a reception room where the glow of two Czechoslovakian crystal chandeliers from Tiffany's lights a ten-thousand-dollar walnut inlay table from W. & J. Sloane.

When this legislative palace was completed in 1928, a writer in *The Washingtonian* was moved to comment:

"Let Samson come. Let this strongman go up the granite steps, brace himself between the guarding columns, and let him push. How futile is the strength of material force." Succeeding generations of petitioners would nod in agreement.

The mystique that better government flows from splendid surroundings had an earlier apostle in 1890. In the successful campaign to retain the State Capitol at Olympia, a local newspaperman wrote:

"Legislators could never enact mischievous or wicked laws in such a place as Olympia, calculated as it is to bring out men's best impulses and promote their better nature."

A year later, the same newspaper viewed the departing legislators and commented:

"The entire state recognized the fact that no more absurd and graceless set of incompetents ever assembled as representatives of the people."

Summer tours through the Legislative Building are conducted from 9:30 to 3:30. Organ recitals are held June 15 through Labor Day: Monday through Friday, 12:30 to 1:30; Sunday, 2 to 4. The Temple of Justice, which looks up (occasionally) at the Legislative Building, is open to visitors 9 to 5 weekdays. The State Library is open daily 9 to 5. The State Capitol Museum at Columbia and Twenty-first Street offers historical exhibits and a small Indian collection. Open Tuesday through Friday, 10 to 5; Saturday, noon to 5; Sunday 1 to 5. Closed on major holidays.

The spacious Capitol grounds are at their best during spring, when Japanese cherry trees are in bloom, and in summer when the sunken rose garden is at its peak. There are scores of fresh-water fishing lakes surrounding Olympia, which is also one of the takeoff points for the highway (U.S. 101) that girdles the Olympic Peninsula.

On our way to the Canadian border, there is a choice of continuing up the Interstate 5 freeway to Tacoma, or reaching that city by a circuitous route via U.S. 101. For the latter, turn off at the Aberdeen exit just south of Olympia. This route will take you through lovely heavily timbered country to Shelton, where a connecting highway (State 5) heads up Hood Canal and, after meandering aimlessly along the scenic waterway, links up with the main highway to Tacoma (State Highway 16).

A few miles down this highway is Gig Harbor, a haven of commercial fishermen, largely of Croatian, Slovene, and Austrian descent, and now emerging as a popular anchorage for artists, craft shops, and visitors.

A favorite dining stop at Gig Harbor is Scandia Gaard, high on a hill with its dining room (smörgåsbord on Thursday and Sunday afternoons) providing a commanding view of the narrow inlet. An old under-the-stairs bedroom alcove in the farmhouse, built eighty-five years ago by a Swedish couple, has been converted into a bar. The old henhouse is now a gift shop and Scandinavian museum. In June, Scandia Gaard is the site of a Midsommarfest, which features a lot of fluttering-apron dances and accordion music.

Another popular restaurant, the Shoreline at the harbor's edge, features seafood. Down the harbor, the old lightship *Relief* has been converted into a maritime museum.

State 16 continues east from Gig Harbor and dramatically enters Tacoma over the Tacoma Narrows Bridge, a 5,939-foot bridge that in 1950 replaced the infamous "Galloping Gertie" span which shook itself to pieces during a windstorm a decade earlier.

(If you continued north on Interstate 5 rather than the side trip through Gig Harbor, an alternate route would be to drive to Tacoma via Steilacoom, Washington's oldest (1854) incorporated town. The highway, reached by taking the Steilacoom exit just north of Olympia, passes through calming farm country and provides an opportunity to explore Steilacoom's streets of Victorian houses and its museum. Ferries leave from Steilacoom for Anderson Island, but the island offers no visitor facilities.)

NORTH
TO THE BORDER

Most travelers heading north up Interstate 5 beyond Tacoma and Seattle, be they local residents or tourists, are bound for either of two Canadian destinations, Vancouver, the swinging gateway to British Columbia, or its capital city of Victoria.

The two cities are as diverse as champagne and stout. Vancouver, Canada's funnel to the Pacific, is a world port seasoned by an infusion of immigrants that give it a flavor not unlike that of San Francisco. Victoria, but a few hours away by ferry, is determinedly, and at times self-consciously, British, from its gracious Parliament building to its ivy-clad Empress Hotel, where high tea has sagged but imperceptibly since Victoria's founding by English colonists.

Our route is a shunpiking trip to the border, an amiable ramble that skirts Interstate 5, which is for those in a hurry. Its northward course moves through quiet towns that nestle in the lap of the Cascades, pauses at a waterfall, a cluster of wilderness dams, then meanders high above Puget Sound, dips a toe in its warmest beach, crosses the border under the Peace Arch at Blaine, and terminates at Point Roberts, a tiny peninsula lying between Canada and the Washington mainland.

A fine hedonistic way to start this trip is to plan breakfast at Snoqualmie Falls Lodge, overlooking a 270-foot cataract. (If you think

Snoqualmie is difficult to pronounce, you might ruminate over the original Indian name, sdob-swahlb-bluh, which means "you call these four-minute eggs?")

From Seattle, head out on U.S. Interstate 90 over the Lake Washington Floating Bridge, joyously exclaiming, "This is the largest pontoon bridge of its kind in the world, costing nine million dollars and built by the WPA with each floating unit securely anchored and weighing four thousand five hundred and fifty-eight tons!"

The highway skirts Lake Sammamish, site of an excellent state park. Minutes out of Seattle the highway enters rolling foothills and begins a climb that will crest at Snoqualmie Pass, which is wall-to-wall with skiers during winter months. During summertime it is about as ugly as its permissive Forest Service landlords will permit.

A few miles west of North Bend, take the Snoqualmie Falls exit, passing through the logging town of Snoqualmie, with a sleepy business district flanked by a pleasant greensward, and turn into the Snoqualmie Falls Lodge parking area.

The old lodge is warmly pleasant, with some tables ranked in alcoves overlooking the Snoqualmie River cataract as it claws its way through serried rock to split into thundering, rainbow-hued cascades and boiling mists.

Over the years a series of proprietors have produced fare to match the scenery; meals inspired by the lumberjacks who first settled the Snoqualmie, worthy of lusty appetites. If you're wondering why I invited you here for breakfast, turn your gaze away from the falls and observe:

For openers: a pitcher of chilled orange juice, grapefruit, platters and bowls of mountain-picked blueberries, strawberries, Yakima peaches, melons, grapes, and baked Washington apples. The apéritifs cleared away, the business of breakfast begins: fried eggs with bacon, sausages and ham; hashed brown potatoes, stacks of hotcakes, and hot freshly baked biscuits. For an encore, the waitress dispenses a serving of hot cooked honey by pouring from a height of three feet. To small fry this is a cataract rivaling that of the falls below. Dinners are equally gustatory.

Not all tables have a view of the falls, and there are days when the demands of a power-generating station reduce the falls to a disappointing trickle. For reservations telephone (206) TU 8-2451.

Adjoining the lodge is a small park, so well kept it looks like it should be in an Abercrombie and Fitch display window, and an observatory, cantilevered over the waterfall's mists. The park is the contribution of Puget Sound Power & Light Company, which first harnessed the Snoqualmie's falling waters in 1898, making it one of the nation's first hydroelectric plants.

Nearby is the Puget Sound and Snoqualmie Valley Railroad yard, a vintage railroad museum with a collection of steam engines, street-cars, and other rolling stock. The museum's operative equipment makes a one-and-a-half-mile run between Kimball Creek and Big Swamp. Open Sundays and holidays 11 to 5. Adults $1, children under sixteen, 50 cents, and $2.50 for family rate.

Other worthwhile local attractions include the Snoqualmie Valley Historical Museum and the Snoqualmie Falls Forest Theater. Here in a hundred-acre forest that looks out on the falls, the outdoor theater is the setting for summertime plays and concerts, and in September a seven-day Renaissance Faire.

The U. S. Forest Service, a sloppy landlord in ski areas and one that all too often measures the forest in board feet, nevertheless maintains some dandy forest sanctuaries for the camper. There are a score of them in the Snoqualmie National Forest and another dozen in adjoining Wenatchee National Forest.

To the three million who annually take to the woods in the 522 Forest Service camps throughout Washington the facilities are a welcome respite from the city. To the backpacker and many conservationists they are woodland slices of Wonder Bread, mass-produced and artificially preserved.

One of the best places I know of to weigh both views is in a forest on the banks of the Stillaguamish River on our shunpiking route to the Canadian border. (If you want to bypass the falls, this destination is slightly over an hour's drive from the Evergreen Floating Bridge toll plaza just outside Seattle.)

Our route heads north from Snoqualmie Falls on State 203 (stop just beyond the foot of the falls for a tour of the Tokul Creek fish hatchery, where you can watch trout being readied for sacrifice) passing through quiet farm country. Just south of the hamlet of Carnation is Carnation Farms, open for inspection between 9:30 and 4 (except Sundays and holidays) if you like inspecting dairy cows.

After passing through dozing Duvall, take the road to Granite Falls, where drifts of alder, maple, and fir border the town's two main streets. The main building in the town of Granite Falls (pop. 750) is a two-story brick edifice built fifty years ago. Its neighbors include a false front structure housing a farm and garden store, a post office still equipped with brass-lined glass letter boxes, an old blacksmith shop now housing an antique shop, a restaurant with a bar appropriately named the Lumberjack, and a firehouse. On Saturdays during the tourist season, the fire rig is moved out into the streets while the interior is given over to a flea market, a favorite for those on the trail of old bottles.

At the eastern edge of the city limits where the young firs form their ranks and begin marching up the foothills, a parking area permits a walk across a bridge spanning the Stillaguamish for a viewing of Granite Falls. The falls, a series of low cascades, have created innumerable quiet pools and sandbars well utilized by trout fishermen.

A dozen miles farther east is Gold Basin Forest Service camp, the first in a trio spaced along the Stillaguamish River. Here, but an hour out of Seattle, you can drive in, park your car in a clearing complete with picnic and camping facilities, and walk down to the river bank. Sit on the bank while the kids wade. You don't have to fish, hike, or yodel. Just sit on the bank, listen to the Stillaguamish foolishly rolling boulders down to the lowlands as it has for ages. Contemplate its broad gray-green waters and look up at the foothills topped off by the snowfields of Mount Pilchuck. Watch a hawk head into the forest corridors and be thankful you got here before the trees are all converted into toilet paper.

That possibility isn't quite as doomsday as it sounds. Time and rainfall have healed over a lot of wounded country in western Washington, as evidenced by the fact that all these forest hills were logged off fifty years ago. And back in a mountain fold a few miles east of here, a sort of seedy Gomorrah flourished at the turn of the century.

That was Monte Cristo, casually named by a romantic prospector who discovered a mountainside of low-yield gold, silver, iron, and lead. All fell into the hands of some talented promoters that included John D. Rockefeller and other Eastern financiers, who temporarily created an El Dorado. Along with a gaggle of eager small-bore plungers, John D. put two thousand men to work building a railroad into these hills. Then they constructed a costly ore refinery, riddled the mountainsides with mine shafts, and created the town of Monte Cristo. Its main streets of Dumas and Mercedes housed seven saloons and a respectable number of whorehouses.

The road to Monte Cristo, which turns off State 92, opens into a valley so rich in scenery that Laurance Rockefeller would have made it into another Jackson Hole and left the ore where it was. At road's end is what remains of Monte Cristo. The old turntable of the Everett and Monte Cristo Railroad is still there. A sagging inn houses a handful of mementos from the early days. But the rest of the town has disappeared, save for piles of planks, shattered and silvered by time.

Wilman's Peak, which serves as a backdrop for Monte Cristo, is pierced here and there by the abandoned shafts of the mines: Lincoln, Peabody, Liberty, Golden Cord, Justice, Mystery, and others.

Some of the mines, perhaps to the surprise of their promoters, actually were good producers—the Pride, Mystery, and Justice alone shipped out almost three million dollars in ore.

But the expense of mining, refining, and shipping ore over the slide-plagued railroad was too great. More important, much of the early assays turned out to be, if not fraudulent, at least wildly overly optimistic. When the Panic of '93 struck, Rockefeller bailed out. The properties in which he had noisily invested his millions two years before were quietly liquidated. He unloaded the railroad—at a loss of two million—and sank the Monte Cristo mines and smelter. Down the same drain went John D.'s investments in the port of Everett, including a hotel, nail factory, and street railway, plunging that city into a panic. When it was all over, Rockefeller had magically made a few million on his Western venture, which he later described as "unfortunate." Whether his sorrow was directed at the stockholders or at the modest size of his profit, history does not say. In 1937 the last rails of the Monte Cristo—Everett line were sold to Japan.

Back on the leisurely trail to Canada, we drive north along the Sauk River to Darrington, a mountain-rimmed town founded largely by South Carolinians, and on to Rockport. Here a side trip requiring less than an hour leads to Newhalem, entrance to the new cross-state highway that spans the North Cascade National Park. But that's not where we're headed this time. For Newhalem has another feature, the starting point of a tour of the Seattle City Light hydroelectric complex that harnesses the Skagit. The tour includes a ride on an incline railway that will lift you up six hundred feet to Diablo Dam, a boat trip down its backwaters for an inspection of the Ross Dam powerhouse, and a logger's lunch served family style with all the seconds you can eat. Cost is $6 for adults, $4 for children; six tours daily between 8:30 A.M. and 4 P.M. Allow about six hours, including meal time. Reservations must be made in advance and can be obtained by telephoning Seattle City Light at (206) 623-7600, Ex. 300, or by writing them at 1015 Third Avenue, Seattle 98104.

While this longer tour requires advance reservations, Seattle City Light also provides a selection of three free mini-tours, one of which includes a ride on the incline lift. Also offered is a four-hour tour that includes a boat ride up Diablo Lake and a viewing of the powerhouse. The tour costs $2. All start from Newhalem.

The main tour begins with a viewing of the crypt of James Delmage Ross and his wife, Alice, who are interred at the base of Ross Mountain. This bit of municipal deism is a tribute to the engineer whose vision led to harnessing the inaccessible Skagit gorges with a trio of dams that since the thirties has supplied Seattle with the nation's cheapest—and cleanest—power.

Just beyond, a woodland trail and a series of planked footbridges crisscross a forested hillside. Here amid the babble of Ladder Creek is the garden of the Rosses; carefully tended plantings and shrubs from throughout the world. At dusk, colored spotlights play on the scene. It's a fairy place of natural beauty, but at night, looking at the shifting pastels that color the woodlands and waterfalls while hidden loudspeakers leak Mantovani from the branches, one can only silently pray for a power failure.

The entire guided tour requires almost six hours and returns you to Newhalem for the logger's lunch served in the employees' cookhouse.

Ross Lake is awaiting a role as the keystone of the new Ross Lake National Recreation Area. Its present limited camping and sports fishing areas are to be expanded into an outdoor recreation facility that will include new nature trails, camping grounds, and a chair lift that will escalate visitors into the North Cascades National Park. Right now, it's one of the state's best lakes for matching wits with rainbow trout who have not grown up spoon-fed in a hatchery.

Access to Ross Lake, other than coming in through British Columbia at the lake's north tip, is somewhat difficult, requiring a short boat and truck ride to reach the Ross Lake Resort, a cluster of modern motel units anchored along the shore near the dam. But the fishing and scenery in this alpine setting are worth the effort. For information, call the resort through the Mount Vernon exchange. The number is 4735, but Myrt, the friendly Mount Vernon operator, has to dial it for you.

Newhalem, which houses City Light employees, is only five hundred nine feet above sea level but has the appearance of an alpine village. Clusters of neat white houses and outbuildings line a meadow sown in lawns in the shadows of mountain peaks. During daytime hours, with men at work at the dams and children off to school (and women gossiping over coffee cups?) it is as tranquil as the Ross crypt. The loudest sound is the tsk-tsk of the lawn sprinklers.

In the Newhalem guest cottage overlooking this scene, a framed notice reads: "In case of attack on Whidbey Air Base, the nearest assumed target, you will have approximately 45 minutes to get in the shelter. Take your time and don't panic, there is room for everyone. But don't delay." Sic transit.

Back on State Highway 20 heading west, we have two options. One is to head north on a quiet-paced road leading to Mount Baker, and thence on to Canada. Or return to Interstate 5 and from there

weave in a few short side trips that visit an Indian reservation, skirt
the Sound for a spectacular viewing of the San Juan Islands, and
pause at some beaches with the warmest sea waters in the state.

For variety's sake, let's take the latter. We'll catch up with Mount
Baker at this chapter's end.

If you're a bird watcher, the Skagit stretch below here from Mar-
blemount to the mouth of the Sauk is, next to Angoon, Alaska, the
nation's best area for viewing the bald eagle. As many as two hundred have been sighted along this strip, heaviest concentrations occur-
ring in winter. Although fierce in mien, the national bird is a real
sissy, living largely off dead fish or run-over rabbits. Brad O'Connor,
the Seattle *Times* outdoor editor, relates a tale of four bald eagles
that spent three days trying to capture a wounded pigeon before giving up.

The route enters the Skagit River delta through the farm community of Sedro Woolley. The logger founders who harvested its stand
of red cedar wanted to call it Bug. But the women folk thought that
sounded silly. So it eventually got its present name: Sedro, Spanish
for cedar, Woolley for an early settler who had platted a rival town-
site.

The Skagit Valley is a kind of microcosm of the best in western
Washington's resources, with exception of the red cedar, which was
logged off down to the last tree. The valley's alluvial soil supports
some of the state's richest dairy farms and grows one third of the
nation's peas as well as other crops. Its delta lands attract large flocks
of ducks, geese, and hunters. Coastal waters support a small fleet of
gillnet boats and pleasure craft fishing for salmon.

A half hour's side trip from the Interstate 5 intersection at Burlington is La Conner, founded in 1867 as a trading post and now determinedly attempting to regain that role.

Along its main street flanking the Swinomish Channel, old false
front buildings house antique shops, arts and crafts boutiques, a seafood restaurant, taverns and clusters of bemused Indians from the
Swinomish reservation. Gillnetters and pleasure craft tie up along its
docks and floats. In winter (January or February) the waterfront is
festooned with fishermen competing in La Conner's smelt derby.
Just up the hill is the Skagit County Historical Museum (open
Wednesday and Sunday, 1 to 4) and views of the La Conner flats
and the channel that separates the town from Fidalgo Island, another
favorite of salmon fishermen.

A bridge crosses the channel to the island and the Swinomish Indian Reservation. Here on January 22, 1855, Governor Isaac Stevens
met with twenty-three hundred Puget Sound Indians and their chiefs

and signed the Point Elliott Treaty. The Swinomish used to have a big three-day celebration commemorating the treaty, but it has waned in recent years, perhaps because more and more tribesmen got around to reading the small print. The treaty promised the Indians $150,000 for two million acres of tribal lands that extended from lower Sound to the Canadian Border. That came out to almost two bucks for each tribesman.

Back on Interstate 5, head north and take the Chuckanut Drive exit just beyond Burlington for a cliff-hugging bypass route to Bellingham. The drive is a winding, two-lane road built for a day when there was little horsepower under the hood and the family dog rode on the running board. But it's rich in tranquilizing views of Puget Sound and the easternmost of the San Juan Islands. There are numerous view turnouts, the road is stoutly edged with comforting stone railings, and two roadside oyster houses provide additional solace.

Where Chuckanut Drive begins its downward course into Bellingham is Larrabee State Park, almost two thousand forested acres of picnic grounds, camping areas, including trailer hookups, and facilities for swimming, clamming, and beachcombing. Adjoining the drive's northern edge is Fairhaven Park with picnic grounds and a twelve-acre rose garden.

The Spanish explorer, Francisco Eliza, first saw the broad bay that is now Bellingham's harbor and named it Seno de Gaston. Vancouver showed up a year later with another one of his after-you changes. Since then it has been a city with as many ups and downs as its surrounding hills and mountains.

Discovery of gold on British Columbia's Fraser River in 1858 sent Bellingham's population soaring in a single year from a few hundred to fifteen thousand and then back to a few hundred again when Canada slammed the door on the gateway. In succeeding years its fortunes rose and fell with those of its timber, coal, and salmon resources. Today its economic base is in pulp and aluminum, augmented by log exports, surrounding croplands, and a large oil refinery at nearby Ferndale.

A swatch of Bellingham's past is taking on new color in the old town of Fairhaven, not far from where Chuckanut Drive enters the city. Here a California multimillionaire is creating a counterpart to Seattle's Pioneer Square and Vancouver, B.C.'s Gastown. The restoration includes the Marketplace, a collection of shops and eating establishments spread through a seventy-year-old Victorian building, where Mark Twain once blew a little smoke in the old Cascade Club. Across the street is Finnegan's Alley, housing a restaurant, art gallery, and shops. Another half dozen buildings are being restored in

Fairhaven. Once this was a town in its own right. Now it's on the way to becoming another waystop on the nostalgia trail, embellished by such nonpioneer trappings as Parisian bronze doors and stained-glass windows, chandeliers from Italy, a Montana saloon bar, and one of those ubiquitous double-decker London buses. All we need is a Swiss Guard bartender in that Montana saloon—serving mai tais.

Another good way to overlook Bellingham's past is to drive up a mile or so to the campus of Western Washington College and Sehome Park that looks out on the bay. In addition to its harbor view, the campus draws visitors attracted by its varied architecture, which ranges from Westminster Victorian to Buckminster modern.

Downtown at 121 Prospect Street is the Whatcom Museum of History and Art, another red-bricked Victorian structure, built as a city hall in 1892. It now houses a major collection of Puget Sound and Alaska Indian art and a gift shop offering local pottery, educational toys, and art works. Other exhibits range from contemporary shows to those of Arctic and African origin. One of the few efforts to nurture the dying crafts of Puget Sound Indians is found here too, with master carvers from the nearby Lummi Indian Reservation passing their knowledge on to young tribesmen. The museum is open Tuesday through Saturday, noon to 5 P.M.; Sunday, 1 to 5 P.M. Closed Thanksgiving, Christmas, and New Year's Day.

The Lummis still race their fifty-foot war canoes each year during the Lummi Stommish in June. The competing teams, sometimes as many as a dozen manning eleven-man canoes, can be viewed from the festival grounds at Marietta, northeast of Bellingham. Adults, $1, children, 50 cents.

If you're a fancier of old choo-choo railroads (and shame if you're not) Bellingham offers a hill-and-dale ride near the southern end of its Lake Whatcom. Cars are of the sixty-year-old red plush variety; there's a private car with an open rear-end platform, and the train is drawn by an old steam engine with a chime whistle that sets the pastures quivering with some mournful notes right out of Tom Wolfe the Elder. Depot is at Park, ten miles south of Bellingham, reached via the Alder exit from Interstate 5. Trains run on weekends and holidays between Memorial Day and Labor Day at 10, 12, 2, and 4. Fares for the hour-long ride: adults, $2, those seventeen and under, $1.50. Advance reservations: write Lake Whatcom Railway, Box 6, Wickersham, Wa. 98285.

For a quieter but equally entrancing backward look, turn off I-5 at Ferndale, about ten miles north of Bellingham, for Hovander Homestead Park, operated by Whatcom County. The hundred-acre working farm includes cows, horses, pigs, ducks, and other livestock and fowl, all amenable to loving touches from kids. Inside the farmhouse much remains the same as when Holan Hovander, a Swedish immigrant architect, homesteaded there in 1903. A big red barn houses old farm equipment and each year fields are planted and harvested as they were at the turn of the century. Picnic and hiking facilities are located along the Nooksack River. At Ferndale, turn south on Hovander Road to Neilson Road and thence by River Lea Road into the farm.

Birch Bay is about fifteen minutes from its Interstate 5 exit, twenty miles north of Bellingham. A roadway and seawall flank the shores of Birch Bay, serving miles of cottages, motels, restaurants, a golf course, a state park, campgrounds, boat ramps, and other beach resort auxiliaries.

Like the red cedar that gave Sedro Woolley its name, the slender birch trees that Vancouver sighted along this sea arm have all but disappeared. Vancouver didn't put ashore to discover the attraction that would make it the state's favorite salt water pleasuring grounds: miles of sandy flats that, warming under the sun, banish the chill of Puget's sound.

Despite its popularity, Birch Bay has an unhurried air. Neat cottages, most of which have resisted cute names, hide in groves of trees. Beyond the sea wall are tumbled ranks of graying driftwood and miles of hard-packed sand flats and tidal pools seasonally filled with sunburned kids.

Birch Bay is at its best for swimming or just viewing at summer eventide when its waters inundate the sun-baked flats and pools. The long runout smooths the incoming warm waters. There's no surf, hardly a ripple, save those stirred by an occasional purse seiner or pleasure boat. And only an expert can tell you if they are in Canadian or U.S. waters.

The Strait of Georgia just beyond Birch Bay is bisected by a zigzag line Kaiser Wilhelm I drew in 1871 when as the arbitrator in the U.S.-Canadian border dispute he divvied up the San Juan Islands. Thus Galiano and Saturna, the islands you see just due west of Birch Bay, and the peaks of Vancouver Island behind them are Canadian. But those lights just coming on a few miles away at the northernmost reach of this waterway are from the summer colony of Point Roberts. And Point Roberts is in the United States, occupying the tip of a Canadian peninsula through which the 49th parallel slices.

The Point's only connection with the rest of the United States is over thirty miles of Canadian roads, barred at two points by customs stations. The Yankee toe in the Canadian boot has been kicking for more than a century at this confinement. For through the border stations must pass the Point's shoppers, school buses, mail trucks, road graders, and even patrol cars. Prisoners must be transported to Bellingham by boat, for sheriff's deputies would lose jurisdiction the minute they drove across the border into Canada. Virtually all maternity cases go to Canadian hospitals and the Point's new arrivals enjoy the distinction of being citizens of both Canada and the United States until they make a choice.

Many Canadians would like to see the enclave brought into Canada through a land swap. If a vote were held in the summer, when the Point is filled with vacationers from nearby Vancouver and New Westminster, such a secession would undoubtedly pass. However, many of the Point's year-round residents, including farmers of Icelandic stock, draw the line against efforts at secession. To them the border is a bundling board, one that permits a proper degree of propinquity with Canada but keeps intact their U.S. citizenship.

Change, fed by U.S. capital and Canadian appetites for vacation homes and Yankee spirits, is everywhere visible in Point Roberts. And where it isn't visible, you can hear it emanating from two cavernous cabarets. It comes in the measured beat of a Lawrence Welk-inspired orchestra playing at the seven-hundred-seat Cannery, a former salmon cannery operated by two Icelanders who correctly surmised there was more profit to be derived from packing in the thirsty. And it's heard even louder from two rock bands holding forth at the Breakers, which, with a seating capacity of more than a thousand, bills itself as the world's largest indoor-outdoor beer garden.

Down the road, fluttering like a banderillero's ribbon in the Point's flanks, are the developer's flags. The most ambitious of these envisions a multimillion-dollar resort complex that would include a golf course, marina, and condominiums spread out over almost two thousand acres, which if realized would occupy more than half of the Point's remaining open space. Many islanders welcome the project, feeling it would end the ticky-tacky sprawl of trailer clusters and cabins that are changing the face of its beaches.

Along the Point's public strands, thousands of Canadian and U.S. vacationers find little to complain about in waters warmed by the same sandy shelf that has made Birch Bay across the channel a favorite for generations. To accommodate the growing crowds, Whatcom County has opened a new beach park overlooking the Strait of Georgia, with ample picnic shelters and a boat-launching ramp that serves one of this inland sea's richest salmon banks.

Point Roberts is about an hour's drive from Blaine, and approximately the same to Vancouver via Tsawwassen, B.C.

Assuming you wish to bypass Point Roberts, the quickest way to Vancouver from Birch Bay is to return from the bay resort to Interstate 5, continue into Blaine, and thence northward over the Canadian freeway. This routing permits a stop at the Peace Arch and its surrounding floral park and picnic grounds. The concrete arch straddling the border was erected by Samuel Hill, an eccentric international gadabout (see chapter "The Lewis and Clark Trail") and dedicated in 1922 by Marshal J. J. C. Joffre of France to commemorate a century of peace between Canada and the United States. It's a favorite site for picture-taking ("Look, ma, one foot in Canada and the other in the U.S."). Less reverent types find it a gas to be photographed under the arch with its innocent inscription, "Children of a Common Mother."

NOTE: If the lure of duty-free booze lures you into one of the two shops selling it at the border, inquire where you are to pick up your orders. In most cases, you're dispatched to a warehouse two miles away adjoining another border station, which you are required to use. This means you not only do not get to view the Peace Arch, but you're sent on your way, not over a four-lane freeway to Vancouver, but via a cranky, ugly, two-lane road with a fifty-mile speed limit. Even Chivas Regal at $5.50 a fifth isn't worth it.

Another route to Vancouver is via Lynden (continue due east from Birch Bay on State Highway 546), a neat community of farmers largely of Dutch extraction. Lynden is the kind of town where they still tie your packages with string from an overhead dispenser and sweep the sidewalks daily. The town's burghers send their sons off regularly for haircuts, support eighteen churches and but two taverns. In March big draft horses, Percherons, Clydesdales, and others from nearby farms, both U.S. and Canadian, compete here in the annual International Plowing Match. (Some also are shown at the Northwestern Washington Fair in August at Lynden.)

From Lynden, continue north to the border station at Sumas and cross into British Columbia. A short link brings you to the fast trans-Canada highway (10) that will wheel you through fat farm country, over the Fraser River at New Westminster and on into Vancouver.

If driving is turning you off, you can eliminate all this nonsense and head directly from Seattle to Vancouver on a real here-comes-the-flyer train. The Amtrak train lurches its way along Puget Sound for much of the run, the rest of its tracks flashing through farmland. It sports a diner and observation cars and only costs $8.75 for the round trip.

We bypassed Mount Baker on this meander to Vancouver, B.C., but it should be added to your Washington destination list. In many ways, Mount Baker provides the state's most satisfying alpine journey, remote enough to offer uncrowded campgrounds, trails and highways, and spectacular vistas.

A fine, shunpiking route to Mount Baker is to head north on State 9 from Sedro Woolley, passing through such hamlets as Prairie, Saxon, Van Zandt, and Deming. Here State 542 heads through the foothill villages of Maple Falls, Glacier, and Shuksan, and then right up into Baker's lap. You can also pick up State 542 at Bellingham.

Now classified as a dormant volcano, Mount Baker covered the countryside with ashes as recently as 1854 and still belches sulfurous fumes. The peak was first scaled by an Englishman, Edmund T. Coleman, in 1868—four years after his party's initial attempt. Plenty of prospectors worked the Mount Baker area, but only two mines paid out: the Lone Jack and the Boundary Red Mountain mines each returned more than a million dollars.

The Mount Baker National Forest comprises one million plus acres of timber, twelve hundred miles of roads, four hundred miles of trails, and numerous camping and picnic areas. Among its many attractions is Baker Lake, a nine-mile-long reservoir offering swimming, fishing, resort and campground facilities, not to mention magnificent vistas of Mount Baker. The lake, reached via State 20 and an unnumbered road from Concrete, also is a favorite for those seeking fall colors.

For closeups of Mount Baker and its oft-photographed companion, Mount Shuksan (elev. 9,127 feet), cut off I-5 at Bellingham to State 542 past Deming and Kendall. One mile past Glacier, Glacier Creek Road offers the best roadside views of Mount Baker and the varicolored face of its big Coleman Glacier. Several miles farther on State 542, Wells Creek Road cuts off to the right and just beyond are the thundering waters of Nooksack Falls. Near State 542's end is the Mount Baker ski area, offering skiing much of the year. Check locally as to whether the lodge and chair lift are operating.

U. S. Forest Service campgrounds are located along this route, some of them fronting the Nooksack River. Most offer piped water and some include community kitchens and wading for children.

ISLANDS IN TIME

Not many in Friday Harbor were surprised a few years ago when a panel of New York and Washington, D.C., environmentalists nominated the San Juan Islands as one of the nation's seven most desirable places in which to live.* Few islanders were pleased with the honor.

"It's like having your daughter selected as a *Playboy* centerfold," complained one. "Who needs that kind of attention? We're already messed up with too many people."

At first glance, such fears seem groundless. Most of the 172 islands in the San Juan chain are lacking in water and thus uninhabited. Total population of all San Juan County is only four thousand, making it one of Washington's most sparsely settled areas. Friday Harbor is the largest community in the islands, with but eight hundred or so. But the boom in vacation and retirement dwellings is beginning to cannonade across the inlets. Land sales on the biggest islands—Orcas and San Juan—have increased heavily in the past decade with buyers coming from almost every state in the United States and as far away as Australia. The chairman of the San Juan County Planning Com-

* The other six: the Sawtooth Range in Idaho; Flagstaff, Arizona; Big Sur, California; Willamette Valley, Oregon; Virginia's Culpepper-Warrenton area; and the Ozark Mountains.

mission is a retired oil engineer from Saudi Arabia. A third of those living on Orcas are retired, and more settle in every year.

So don't delay your visit, for as lovely chunks of unspoiled America, the days of the San Juans may be numbered. Unless they isolate the virus that has afflicted most of this nation's scenic strands, these empty, wave-lapped littorals will be but another stretch of Villas, Estates, Colonies, or whatever tomorrow's developer chooses to call his hives. Let's be on our way.

Last year, the San Juans counted more than two hundred thousand visitors, most of them arriving at the big islands of Orcas or San Juan by ferry from Anacortes or from Sidney, across the channel in British Columbia. Sure, you can fly up if you need to hurry to your relaxation. Or charter a cruiser or sailboat, which is neat if Elizabeth Taylor is working the sheets. But really, the only way to ply is aboard one of those conveyances Walt Whitman described as "inimitable, streaming, never-failing, living poems." The ferryboats.

The State of Washington hauls more people around on ferries (six million a year) than just about anyone this side of Charon. For the most part they do a creditable job. The newest of the twenty-one-vessel fleet—including the *Walla Walla* on the San Juan run—are gross in size, with a capacity of two thousand passengers and two hundred six vehicles. They are warmed by Phoenix beauty parlor colors, so-so restaurants (but no booze), and solariums to protect you from the rain. Now the ferry authority is studying a proposal to add a fleet of hydrofoils to speed up service on Puget Sound, which is akin to suggesting helicopter service to Shangri-La. But Boeing is making hydrofoils and Boeing swings a lot of incense at the statehouse. Pot would be legal in Washington tomorrow if Boeing started making Rizla papers.

While San Juan Island and Orcas Island are destinations for ninety percent of those visiting the archipelago, you can qualify as a San Juan Island visitor by taking a ferry from just north of Bellingham to Lummi Island, across a channel from the home turf of the Lummi Indians. It's also the only place in the world where salmon are still caught by a unique entrapment called reef netting. Originated by the Lummis, reef netting is simply an arrangement of nets that act as artificial reefs, guiding migrating salmon into larger nets suspended in the water between two longboats. When the salmon swim over this net, a lookout cries out a warning and the net is closed and hauled in. Catches average around fifty salmon, but nets have been known to yield more than five hundred during a good run. Best time to view the reef netters at work is during August.

The Lummi Rocks off the island are popular among sports fishermen seeking summer runs of chinook and coho salmon. There is a boat-launching ramp on the island.

The real ferryboat ride to the San Juan Islands departs from the terminal at Anacortes, located on Fidalgo Island about ninety minutes north of Seattle via Interstate 5. Fidalgo is somewhat embarrassed at calling itself an island, as it is separated from the mainland only by a narrow waterway with the uninspiring name of Swinomish Slough. The islands in the San Juan group won't even let Fidalgo into their club as a probationary member.

At one time Anacortes was known as "The Gloucester of the Pacific," with processing plants for Alaska cod and six big salmon canneries, in addition to more than a dozen lumber and shingle mills. Today it's nurtured by an oil refinery and by tourists who would spend a lot more time browsing around town if the head-scratchers in the ferry service didn't keep them all locked up at the terminal skipping rocks and waiting for room on the next boat. They could all be handed numbers and sent off to eat seafood and finger the goods at the shops in the old Keystone Hotel, or inspect mementos of the past at the Anacortes Museum of History and Art and other downtown dens of antiquity.

Anacortes was named for Anna Curtis (originally Cortés), wife of the town's pioneer newspaper publisher. She became the postmistress of Anacortes, but there's no record of her ever having postmarked the family towels.

From Anacortes, the ferry begins its run* to Lopez, Shaw, Orcas, and San Juan Islands and on to Sidney, B.C. You may stop over at any one of the islands. Or, if you have but a day, leave your car at the ferry terminal and cruise through the islands and include a quick tour of Victoria, the Old English capital of British Columbia. Travel time for this one-day excursion, including the bus trip from the ferry terminus at Sidney, B.C., to nearby Victoria and return, is twelve hours. Fares begin at $6.50 for adults and $3.25 for children.

Leaving Anacortes for its initial stop at Lopez Island, the ferry crosses broad Rosario Strait, part of the marine highway used by freighters, tugs, barges, and cruise ships traversing the Inside Passage to Alaska. A good time to post lookouts for showoff schools of porpoise, blackfish, or an occasional pod of whales. Beyond Rosario, the ferry threads its way through narrow Thatcher Pass separating Decatur and Blakely islands, both carpeted with firs and madronas that shade rocky palisades and deserted coves.

* Two hours and forty minutes running time on the superferry *Walla Walla,* three hours on the older *Evergreen State.*

Yes, Junior, those really were smuggler coves. For since their first occupants arrived, the San Juans have served as a conduit for illegal goods from British Columbia, ranging from silk and wool to opium, not illegal at that time, but bearing a heavy duty when imported from British Columbia, where it was openly processed. Later the same routes became funnels for Prohibition-era rum runners.

In their wake the smugglers left legendary figures like Larry Kelly, whose specialty was delivering such Chinese imports as silk, opium, and Chinese. There are those who today say the depth off Orcas Island (the locale varies, depending on who is tending the bar) are scattered with the bleached bones of passengers he dumped over the side to avoid capture. Kelly prospered in import trade for a time, becoming a big property owner on Sinclair Island, where he was elected to the school board (his favorite subject was the Open Door policy). After a number of bad trips that gained him a prison term, Kelly died broke and landless.

A more durable latter-day smuggler was Roy Olmstead, king of the Puget Sound rum runners, a rank he proudly held along with that of captain of the Seattle Police Department. Before he and ninety-four of his ring were indicted in 1924, Olmstead made enough to buy a Seattle radio station, where legend has it his wife coded her kiddie bedtime programs with instructions to her husband's seagoing delivery fleet.

While all this yarning has been going on, we've quietly slipped past Upright Head for our first landing—at Lopez Island. Because Lopez is relatively flat and has the islands' best soil, it's largely agricultural. But there is a secluded resort, the Islander, on its east shore, and you can camp at Odlin County Park or rough it at Spencer Spit State Park at the island's north tip. Like the rest of the San Juans, the island is popular with cyclists. You can pack your wheels aboard the ferries for no extra charge.

From Lopez Landing the ferry enters Harney Channel and after cruising four miles, pauses at the Shaw Island landing on Blind Bay. Shaw has only twelve miles of road, is almost entirely privately owned, and doesn't encourage visitors, even if your name is H. L. Hunt.

You are more than welcome at our next stop, Orcas Island, home for half of San Juan County's year-round residents and heavy with visitor accommodations and attractions. As the ferry is warped into its berth, you begin to understand why this is indeed one of America's most livable places. Cars, station wagons, campers, cyclists, and hikers stream ashore over a ferry slip festooned with geranium planters and head up a madrona-lined road. Hand-carved directional signs capture the rustic tone of the island, pointing to Dolphin Bay,

White Beach, Guthrie Cove, Eastsound, West Sound, Deer Harbor, Olga, and Doe Bay.

Even driving at the posted speed of forty-five miles an hour, it takes but a moment or two to clear Orcas town, which includes a general store, a small old hotel, a liquor store, gift shop, and other amenities. The unwinding roads are free of traffic, billboards, and franchised beaneries. Instead, they are quiet aisles of evergreens and hardwoods arching almost across the roadway. At eventide, shadowy deer meet in meadows. The right of way is shared by quail, grouse, and rabbits whose population growth at times threatens to engulf the islands.

The few remaining farms on Orcas include those of hard-scrabble farmers as well as gentlemen ranchers with well-tended tax shelters housing Charolais and Scottish Highland cattle and Appaloosa and Arabian horses. Not all would make good 4-H counselors. One thigh-slapping tale told about the gentry is that of a wealthy doctor. When he needed to supplement the diet of his blooded cattle not long ago, he ordered a shipment of alfalfa dispatched—by truck from Seattle's stylish Marshall Field department store.

It's not that the islanders are particularly rich, in fact, personal incomes are far below the state average. But Orcas includes a strong strain of those choosy about work. Marlowe Hartung, an ex-ad executive from Seattle who now operates an art center and gift shop in the village of Eastsound, recalls his introduction to this island independence. Balked at efforts to induce a carpenter to begin work on a long-delayed remodeling project, Hartung finally asked in exasperation: "Good night! Don't you want to make a dollar?"

"Mister Hartung," came the even reply, "I got a dollar."

Road's end for most Orcas Island visitors is at one of Washington's few elegant resorts, Rosario, or at nearby Moran State Park, both on the shores of East Sound. Along the way, side roads offer pastoral views of Crow Valley. At the turn of the century, this and other Orcas vales were among the state's best apple producers, with as many as 180,000 boxes being shipped from Eastsound annually. Marketing problems and the emergence of Yakima Valley orchards ended the brief reign. Today Crow Valley still provides a setting of shake-roofed farmsteads and cattle grazing in fields flanked by vine-covered cedar fences. You don't find settings like that much anymore outside of a menthol cigarette commercial.

Rosario can be described as San Simeon done in American Eclectic. Rising from solid rock on a promontory overlooking East Sound, its lines and interiors, grounds and appointments reflect the tastes and caprices of its founder, Robert Moran, and subsequent owners.

Moran was a New York school dropout who headed west, went to sea, and later founded a shipyard in Seattle where in 1904 was built the battleship *Nebraska*. (Moran was $350,000 over on his bid. He reduced it by $250,000 and Seattle raised the rest by public subscription. Today's military contractors spill that much at lunch while adding up the overrun tab they're going to hand Uncle.)

When he retired that same year (he had been told he had a weak heart) Moran designed and built his Xanadu. It included today's main resort lodge, a three-story concrete mansion topped by a six-ton roof of sheet copper and guarded by an ornamental fence of battleship anchor chain. Inside, Moran installed solid teakwood parquet floors, a fireplace fifteen feet long over which hung a Gainsborough painting, Belgian stained-glass windows, a ballroom, pipe organ, bowling alley, billiard room, and indoor swimming pool. He didn't stop there.

Moran built a dam and hydroelectric plant in order to have electric heat (some of the elements still work), dug a lagoon for his canoeist guests, erected a dock and machine shop for the 110-foot sailing yacht he built on ways nearby (the longest trip he made on the yacht was twenty miles down channel), lavished the grounds with flower beds and the figurehead from the clipper ship *America,* and then built three houses for his brothers, and a kinky round house that clings to the cliffside. In 1921 Moran donated six thousand acres of his barony to the state as parkland, the state valiantly resisting all the way. In 1939 his wife died. Alone at eighty-two, Moran moved down the island to a house at Eastsound where he died four years later.

In 1939 Rosario, its waterfront, timberland, mansion, hydroelectric plant, Gainsborough, and all the rest of the estate accouterments created over a forty-year period were sold to a California industrialist. For fifty thousand dollars.

While Rosario falls a mite short of its boast, "one of America's top family resorts," it has few rivals in Washington. The dreadnought solidity Moran built into the main inn has survived decades of good and bad embellishments. The dining room, done in Mediterranean *kitsch,* serves good expensive meals with lesser-priced snacks available at a nearby coffee shop. There's enough lawn to find a quiet place to read or sprawl, beaches to explore, waters to fish. Three swimming pools are available; one fronting the lodge overlooking the channel, a high-decibel pool for kids, and, indoors, a tile-floored pool installed by Moran and augmented by one of those mechanically made maelstroms that are today's substitutes for the fountains of youth. Rates for the lodge and two motel-type additions range from moderate to expensive.

Just down the road a piece from Rosario is the beginning of Moran State Park, the priceless bequest of its namesake and one of the state's most rewarding and popular recreation facilities. The five-thousand-acre park embraces a slice of waterfront, four lakes, a mountain, a staircase of misty falls, and four campgrounds with 125 well-equipped sites, and enough trails to make Deerslayer tired. High point of the park, literally, is 2,454-foot Mount Constitution, reached by road and providing a 360-degree view that is absolutely one of the world's greatest.

An observation tower, built of stone and timber by the CCC in 1936, looks out upon a panorama of water, islands, and peaks in every direction. On a clear day you can see Captain Vancouver. Also Mount Rainier, Mount Baker, the Strait of San Juan de Fuca, the Canadian Gulf Islands, Vancouver Island, Point Roberts, Bellingham, and Anacortes, where all those people who didn't set their alarm clocks are lined up at the ferry terminal waiting to get where you are.

Nearby is the only encroachment of civilization, the transmitting tower of KVOS-TV in Bellingham. Manning its controls is David Richardson, a third-generation Orcas islander. Assigned the responsibility of maintaining the fidelity of images, he has undertaken another responsibility: to help protect the reality he sees all around him.

A freelance writer on Pacific Northwest subjects since 1956, he is the author of *Pig War Islands,* an entertaining and often angry book on the San Juans and their history. Today's chapter disturbs him. He writes:

"Mainland people want to save the unspoiled character of the Islands for boating, camping, and hunting trips; while island people want their own enjoyment of their homes and surroundings saved from the growing inundation by outsiders, whose fun they resent having to support with their taxes.

"Meanwhile," he continues, "runaway development of the area continues at an accelerating pace. Everywhere in our island Eden, ribbon-flagged surveyors' stakes, popping up like fall mushrooms, proclaim more and yet more subdivisions in the making."

Overdevelopment, a shortage of water, lax regulations on sewage disposal, lot sizes and land use in general foreshadow a spreading blight, Richardson feels.

Many agree, including the board administering the state's Shoreline Protective Act which has censured the islands' local and county governments for failure to enact adequate planning and zoning controls. Richardson sees the dichotomy here too.

"I have friends, good friends, who have worked a piece of land all their lives," he told me. "Most of them never made a dime. Now they see their land becoming valuable; they look forward to selling it—cutting it up and selling it so they can travel and take life easy. Now someone has to come in and say no."

Perhaps the answer lies, as Richardson and many others view the island land use crisis, in the establishment of some sort of international seashore. Such a pattern helped save Cape Cod and Point Reyes in California from overdevelopment and at the same time made room for resident and recreationist to share their heritage.

Whatever tomorrow's nuclear family will find along the 125-mile Orcas Island coastline (all but Moran State Park in private ownership) its facilities today cater to just about every appetite. There are more than a score of resorts, ranging from an old hotel with a stuffed elk head watching the cash register to inns with heated pools, tennis courts, and lawn games. Like its sister islands of Lopez and San Juan (no man is an island, Ms. Steinem), Orcas also has a nine-hole golf course, and resorts offering year-round salmon fishing and boat rentals. For quieter pursuits, the crossroads village of Eastsound offers browsers a modest shop with an impressive stock of rare prints. Operated by Dale Pederson, the collection includes some seventy-five thousand prints for sale, including Hogarths, Houbrakens, and Cruikshanks.

Pederson's next-door neighbor is Marlowe Hartung, a talented painter in his own right whose sale gallery includes works of leading Puget Sound artists.

Leaving Orcas, the ferry passes through the tiny Wasp Islands, a name the very few San Juan liberals maintain could be applied to the rest of the archipelago (two Orcas Island teachers were once fired for requiring a reading of Woodrow Wilson), and across the channel to Friday Harbor on San Juan Island.

Friday Harbor is built on a graceful cove in which is centered a small island, Friday. Town and island are believed to have been named for a displaced Kanaka, brought to the islands by the Hudson's Bay Company to herd its sheep. From the ferry, Friday Harbor resembles a southeastern Alaska cannery town: a business district straggling up from the docks; pilings supporting storage tanks and the remains of a cannery, and air filled with the welcoming cry of gulls, sea birds, and resort owners. Just abeam of the ferry slip is a tiny plaza with a war memorial, and beyond it the business district of the San Juan Islands' leading commercial center and county seat. The town is a latecomer among communities capitalizing on the merchandizing of nostalgia. But for openers, the San Juan Hotel, built in 1884, has been restored, as have a few other structures, including a theater.

During summer months, the protected harbor is crowded with U.S. and Canadian pleasure boats, for Friday Harbor and its neighbor, Roche Harbor, are the marine gates to some of the world's most appealing cruising waters. For landlubbers, the San Juan County Fair is held here in August.

Nine miles across the island is Roche Harbor with a strip of waterfront that could have been built by Eastman for the *National Geographic*. Focal point is the gleaming-white, balconied Hotel de Haro, built in 1886 and named for the Spanish explorer, López de Haro. Theodore Roosevelt slept here, possibly crying, "Bully!" as he viewed the formal gardens and a seawall built by British soldiers in 1859 and still standing. Much of that period's furnishings and bric-à-brac has been preserved in the lobby. The stairway displays some of the original log walls left from an old trading post. Also on view is a century-old tapestry, fashioned by a thirteen-year-old convent girl in Spain and depicting Captain de Haro limned against Mount Baker and some local flora, all remarkably accurate. Across the road, a Victorian house has been remodeled into a restaurant that overlooks the harbor.

The Hotel de Haro, with its delicate lines and gardens of wisteria and myriad flowers, is a striking contrast to Rosario's severe lines. Yet both were creations of nineteenth-century industrialists who were harsh in business and tender in their private lives.

John S. McMillin, an ex-Indiana lawyer-industrialist, built Roche Harbor in 1886 as a company town to serve nearby lime deposits. McMillin's lime works became the West's biggest, with shipments moving out of Westcott Bay to markets around the world. While laborers were shooed off to a district inelegantly named Japtown, McMillin in his Victorian mansion (since destroyed by fire) and in the hotel he built for guests, brought to the island a grand paternalistic style equaled only by that of Moran.

The plant was destroyed by fire in 1923, rebuilt, and finally closed down in 1956. Only remnants are left, including a string of boxy residences built for supervisors and now remodeled into guest cottages, ideal for big families.

Not far from the hotel a wooded path leads to the McMillin mausoleum. Here amid the trees, a circle of pillars encloses a table surrounded by chairs that mark the crypts of the industrialist and his family. The mausoleum's pillars, steps, table, and chairs—all done in limestone—are a classic Masonic monument to family, church, and rugged individualism. On the back of each chair is carefully listed the McMillin clan's memberships in churches, fraternities, and other organizations. Each carries an inscription that the fiercely partisan McMillin must have regarded as the correct password in this or any other life. Republican.

Latter-day additions to McMillin's town, now a well-tended resort, include an Olympic-sized swimming pool, riding stables, a four-thousand-foot air strip and moorages for two hundred pleasure craft.

The main roads from Friday Harbor and Roche Harbor lead to the chief historic attraction of the San Juan Islands—the sites of U.S. and British Army encampments that date from a bloodless, saber-rattling incident now known as the "Pig War."

The Graustarkian episode was precipitated by some sloppy language in the description of where the U.S. and Canadian boundary line passed through the San Juan Islands. A provision of the Oregon Treaty of 1846 drew the line "to the middle of the channel which separates the continent from Vancouver's Island, and then southerly from the middle of said channel and of Fuca's straits to the Pacific Ocean." But which channel? The United States insisted it was Haro's Strait, which put San Juan Island in U.S. waters. Great Britain, alarmed over the prospect of Yankee guns dominating sea lanes leading to Victoria and Vancouver, argued that the language referred to Rosario Channel to the east, which would make San Juan Island forever England.

Tensions mounted, as correspondents are wont to say, when on June 15, 1859, an American settler killed a Hudson's Bay Post pig with an appetite for Yankee potatoes. The Bay's commandant demanded one hundred dollars for the pig. The settler spurned this demand and both sides blew the bugle. The Pig War was on. It reached its peak, logistically at least, a few months later when four hundred sixty-one Americans dug in with fourteen cannon facing the general direction of five British warships mounting one hundred sixty-seven guns and carrying more than two thousand men.

Whether or not the incident ever "brought England and the United States to the brink of war," as the marker at today's English Camp states, it was finally settled after a twelve-year bloodless stalemate. (During this period both sides established the camps now being restored.) The dispute was resolved in 1872 by Kaiser Wilhelm I, who, although not generally remembered as a great peacemaker, nevertheless knew how to draw a fine line as an arbitrator, particularly when it took some territory away from Cousin Victoria.

So the United States got San Juan Island, the island got a National Historical Park, and the San Juan County Commissioners got another headache on road maintenance.

Of the two portions of the park, English Camp and American Camp, the former has more to view: the original blockhouse overlooking narrow Garrison Bay; a gabled commissary; a small garrison building; remnants of a blacksmith shop and a small cemetery where are buried the seven Royal Marines who died of natural causes during the occupation.

English Camp also nurtures what is billed as the World's Largest Big Leaf Maple, and who is to argue? The tree is 294 years old, 24.4 feet in circumference, and measures 98 feet from the ground to crown, down six feet from its Dow Jones high of 104, set in 1966 before a trimming.

American Camp, located on a barren, windswept point overlooking disputed Haro Passage, has but a marker and the remnants of Pickett's Redoubt. Here Captain George Pickett, later to gain fame for his charge at Gettysburg, erected the Americans' first line of defense during the celebrated stalemate.

On the island's west side, San Juan County Park offers picnic grounds, camping, and ramps for boat launching.

If by now all this to-ing and fro-ing among the San Juans has kindled a desire to put ashore on your private strand, there are a number of state parks to accommodate your wish. All you need is a boat.

Boat charters, either with or without a skipper, are available at any number of marinas from Seattle to Friday Harbor. They are expensive. If you have to ask how much, as someone once observed, you can't afford them. Sailboats may be chartered at Friday Harbor and at Orcas and Deer Harbor. Rentals of smaller outboard-powered boats, from sixteen feet up, can provide another means of extending your explorations. But remember that the U. S. Coast Guard answers around five thousand distress calls each year from boaters in sound and coastal waters. In most cases they come—sometimes too late—from those who either overload their craft or ignore advice and weather reports.

Ten state-operated boaters' parks with more than seven thousand miles of shorelines are located on Matia, Doe, Clark, Sucia, Stuart, Jones, Turn and Posey islands, with more being developed. Facilities are somewhat primitive, which means no hot showers (often no water at all), no flush toilets, and no electrical hookups to enable you to watch the Game of the Week. One island, Blakely, has a popular resort shared equally by boaters and pilots who land at its beachside strip. A submerged area, Pea Pod Rocks off the east shore of Orcas, has been designated as an underwater park for scuba and skindiving. Clement's Reef off Sucia Island, which was purchased by boaters who then donated it to the state, is favored by spear fishermen seeking ling cod, snappers, black bass, and halibut. For a full list of these or other parks write Washington State Parks and Recreation Commission, P.O. Box 1128, Olympia, Wa., 98501.

From San Juan Island, ferry routes head back to Anacortes, or across San Juan and Speiden channels twenty-two miles to Sidney, B.C. En route to Sidney, the ferry passes Speiden Island, now renamed Safari Island, where sportsmen land by plane and are driven around in a jeep until they sight one of the game animals shipped there by the resort's proprietor. Then they shoot it and have it mounted as a trophy.

Just twenty minutes by small ferry from Anacortes is Guemes Island. Only eight miles square, Guemes has but one resort with a covey of cabins, some with fireplaces, located on the island's northern tip. A family-type retreat, its attractions include miles of beaches, a swimming pool, and good salmon fishing.

Guemes, not included in the San Juan chain, is well known for its own little war. It was a contemporary conflict that briefly placed it in the ranks of bumper strip causes, along with Boycott Lettuce and Stop the Bombing. It was created by a proposal to construct an aluminum plant on the island, a move that won approval from payroll-hungry Skagit County officials. The project was abandoned under Save Guemes pressure created by an alliance of environmentalists, sports and commercial fishermen, San Juan property owners (most of whom lived in Seattle), and newspaper editorialists from Olympia to Vancouver, B.C.

It was a victory for Bambi, clean waters, and island Rotarians, won by a young Seattle attorney better known for his association with another water gate, John Ehrlichman. But as David Richardson observed, it only illuminated the fact that "island and mainland people alike turned out to be less than agreed on just what it is the San Juans should be saved from." He continued:

"Island dwellers want to save their right to go on island-dwelling, without being forced to sell due to astronomical property taxes, resulting from inflated land values brought about by increasing population and industrial pressures. But they also need to save the means to earn their livelihood, which means looking to these same pressures to generate jobs."

A similar uneasiness permeates Whidbey Island, just south of Anacortes. The twenty-three-mile-long island (longest in the contiguous United States next to Long Island) is flanked for most of its distance by the shores of Pugetopolis, which stretches northward from Seattle. With two hundred miles of shoreline, eight lakes, four state parks, and a growing market for summer and retirement homes, the island has become a developer's paystreak. Whidbey real estate started taking off in 1965 when sales reached a record fifteen million dollars. They went up to thirty-six million dollars in 1969 and now are flying in a holding pattern at around thirty million a year.

As sales mount, so do land prices, and with them taxes. As a result, the island, which once supported a thriving agriculture economy, is becoming more and more oriented to the summer vacationer and the retired.

Despite its severe people pressures, Whidbey manages to retain a certain measure of the charm of its San Juan cousins, with miles of unbroken forest and beach. It can be reached by ferry from Mukilteo and Edmonds just north of Seattle, from Port Townsend (summers only) and via the Deception Pass Bridge just south of Anacortes.

The island got its name from Joseph Whidbey of Captain Vancouver's staff who in 1792 discovered that the island and its neighbor, Fidalgo, were not one, but were separated by a narrow, churning channel he named Deception Pass. Later Captain Thomas Coupe sailed a full-rigged ship through the breach and into Penn Cove on Whidbey Island. The namesake town that grew up around his 1852 claim became a very salty place indeed, with a score of retired ship's captains settling along the cove.

The bridge spanning Deception Pass, and even narrower Canoe Pass, is thirteen hundred fifty feet long and at peak tides some two billion five hundred million gallons of water rush through Deception Pass each hour at speeds up to eight knots.

Near the south end of the bridge, built by the WPA in 1935, is one of the entrances to Deception Pass State Park, which is full of picnic tables, camping sites, forest trails, beaches, and a lake that warms up enough for enjoyable swimming.

If you haven't seen a used-car lot or a franchise restaurant for a long while, Oak Harbor just ahead has more than all the rest of the San Juans combined. Up until 1940 the population of Oak Harbor hovered around four hundred and most of its land was occupied by Dutch farmers working some of the state's richest soil. The farms, some fifty-five in all, were removed to make way for the Whidbey Island Naval Air Station. Today, more than ten thousand call Oak Harbor home, making it the area's largest community.

A half hour's meander down the highway is a fine old bath-down-the-hall inn, the Captain Whidbey, overlooking Penn Cove. Built in 1907 of madrona logs, it has a dining room with meals of great gusto, a bar, and lots of nooks awash in seas of books and magazines. Accommodations include comfortable rooms with partitions so thin they provide an entertaining night with Ted and Alice and George and Louise and Bruce and Kay and Walter Cronkite and Howard K. Smith. It also offers a scattering of cabins, some with fireplaces and all with less propinquity.

A few miles south is Coupeville, where Captain Coupe and his fellow skippers settled down with a sigh on Penn Cove. Penn Cove remains relatively undisturbed and the old false-front buildings of the town's main street have renewed their lease on life by becoming places in which to dine, drink, and shop. But recently gone is the doctor, who, with a talent not found even in McCann-Erickson or J. Walter Thompson, composed this copy for the sign over his office: SPECIALIZING IN THE DISEASES OF MEN, WOMEN AND CHILDREN.

Coupeville also has a score of Victorian houses for viewing and a tidy city park (picnicking only) overlooking Penn Cove and, beyond it, the Cascade Range. A Whidbey Island visitor in 1911 told of counting more than three hundred harbor seals in the cove, part of a fleet of engaging submersibles that once numbered in the tens of thousands. Today you may look in vain, for there are but an estimated eighteen hundred in all of Puget Sound, Grays Harbor, and Willapa Bay. More than ten thousand were destroyed between 1943 and 1960 when the State Department of Fish and Game offered a bounty on the mistaken assumption the seals posed a threat to salmon runs. The bounty was eliminated when the Department ran out of funds. Today it recants by stating in a recent bulletin, "With wise management and protection of key colonies, the seals can prosper without unduly threatening sport and commercial interests."

Across the narrow island, overlooking Admiralty Inlet, is a freeze-frame picture out of an old newsreel, Fort Casey, established in 1890 to repel any invaders heading down Puget Sound. The Fort's main batteries were ten-inch guns so mounted that they sank down behind their parapets after each firing. The guns all went off to scrap during World War II, but a couple of duplicate models, plus two three-inch rapid-firing guns, were salvaged from Fort Wint in the Philippines and have been installed in the old emplacements. Here kids sight down the barrels and fire at oncoming ships, usually Japanese freighters. The state-operated fort includes a picnic ground and an interpretive center in an old lighthouse.

South of Coupeville a side road leads to Ebey's Landing, a strand of beach where Colonel Isaac Ebey settled in 1850, and seven years later was murdered and beheaded by a raiding Indian party. Ebey had a bit part in the Pig War when, as a U. S. Collector of Customs, he got into a hassle with the British over some sheep they had landed on San Juan Island (he maintained the British were trying to pull the wool over our isles). He was killed by a marauding tribe of

Northern Indians seeking the scalp of a white *tyee* (chief) in revenge
for the death of twenty-seven Stikine Indians the year previous near
today's Port Gamble. The British, who blamed the incident on Kake
Indians from Russian America, later retrieved Ebey's head and sent
it home for burial.

Heading south, we pass a winery and vineyards of loganberries—
the world's largest, the sign says. Near the island's southern tip, South
Whidbey State Park has picnicking and swimming facilities. A few
miles south, the road branches to the coastal town of Langley, site
each August of an old-time county fair, replete with competing jars
of mincemeat, bread-and-butter pickles and wild blackberry jam,
hangings of afghans, crocheted pillowcases and tied quilts, Rebekahs
selling pie and cake, and a guitarist singing soulfully and reproach-
fully about a girl with a che-heating heart.

Beyond that is Clinton and the ferry to Mukilteo. We're back on
the mainland.

"Islands have always been fascinating places," wrote John Stein-
beck in *Sea of Cortez*. "The old storytellers, wishing to recount a
prodigy, almost invariably fixed the scene on an island—Faery and
Avalon, Atlantis and Cepango, all golden islands just over the horizon
where anything at all might happen."

What's the future for Puget Sound's islands, not just the San Juans
but all those that punctuate the Sound from Lummi to Hartstene at
its southern reach?

Well, anything at all might happen. But each new resident, each
new visitor—like you and me—will accelerate change. To date, man's
fear of being separated from his automobile, even for a ferry ride,
has protected the islands and left most of them relatively unpopu-
lated. Anderson Island lies within sight of the industries and lights
of Tacoma, but in a hundred years it has attracted but a hundred
residents. Hartstene to the south, less than that.

But today they attract the disenchanted, who, seeing and savoring
this bucolia, desire it for therapy. So they buy the wooded island lot,
ignoring the rows of stakes soon to be filled with houses and neighbors; soon to be followed by wider roads, a traffic signal, and then
the service station, the supermarket, laundromat, and all the rest of
whatever it was they were running away from.

There are answers, of course, and a few of them even are being
heeded. Washington has enacted a Seacoast Protective Act, which,
while weak, will hold back the very worst of the developments. Parts
of the California coast and Wisconsin's rivers have been saved by
conservation easements. In Ottawa, the province has purchased one
hundred thousand acres for a protective barrier. Richardson up on

his perch on Orcas Island looks—to date in vain—for an International Seashore, similar to the national effort that spared Cape Cod. (A U.S.-Canadian commission in 1973 recommended creation of an international park embracing the San Juan Islands and the Gulf Islands in British Columbia, but there has been little response to date from Ottawa or Washington. Reaction of islanders has been generally negative.) All call for large public expenditures. But paying for wars, past and future, has placed such appropriations low on our priority list, heading us back to the days when House Speaker Joe Cannon could say—and be heeded—"not one cent for scenery." Lacking protective legislation, and the funds to back it up, only economics will determine land use.

Today, developers' flags flutter across the islands from Orcas and San Juan to Harstene and Anderson. And on Anderson Island, Hazel Heckman, one of this region's talented writers and a long-time island resident, writes in *Island Year:*

"Anderson Island is no Grand Canyon, no Everglades, no redwood forest to arouse public indignation. It is only one of the 'little wild places,' one endangered island in Puget Sound. But great losses are made up of small losses. We cannot shrug this off as progress." Sic transit.

THE LEWIS AND CLARK
TRAIL

Before the Protozoic era, Washington got along just dandy without the Cascade Range. This promoted cross-state travel. Dinosauria summered in the San Juans. Fish swam languidly around the Blue Mountains down in the state's southeast corner. There followed a rather exciting period during which there were great disturbances in the land mass. When it was all over and the last flow of lava and ice was stilled, Washington was divided by the Cascade Range.

Travel hasn't been the same since.

Part of a system of ranges that extends from Baja California to the St. Elias Range in Alaska, the Cascades in Washington include more than a hundred peaks higher than eight thousand feet.* Covered in deep snow during all but summer months, the Cascades are breached by three railroad tunnels, five highway passes (two of which are closed in winter), and a river-level route along the Columbia.

From Vancouver, let's follow the Columbia upstream into eastern Washington on the trail of Lewis and Clark. The river is an inland sea here. It extends smooth and broad a hundred miles west to the

---

* The highest: Mount Rainier, 14,410; Mount Adams, 12,307; Little Tahoma, sometimes mistaken for a part of Rainier, 11,117; Mount Baker, 10,778; Glacier Peak, 10,528; Mount St. Helens, 9,677; Mount Bonanza, in the Glacier Peak Wilderness Area, 9,511; and Mount Stuart, in the Cascade's eastern fringe, 9,470.

Pacific and another forty miles east to Bonneville, its flow contained there by the first of the Columbia's big dams.

Viewing it from Highway 14 eastward out of Vancouver, the Columbia's thrust to the sea appears deceptively unhurried. It's only when a bulky river tug comes into view, straining with its tow against the current, that the river's powerful sweep becomes apparent. It's a picture that could be captioned with William Cullen Bryant's lines from *Thanatopsis:*

". . . the continuous woods where rolls the Oregon, and hears no sound, save his own dashings."

Camas, fifteen miles upriver from Vancouver, is named for a lovely blue—sometimes white—flower with a bulb once sought here by the Indians for its starch. (It also proved to be a valuable nutrient to the Lewis and Clark party, who found it made up into an "excellent beer.") It is the site of a big Crown Zellerbach pulp mill—in fact, the mill is where you'd expect the town square to be. It's one of the world's biggest, the kind with a dozen belching stacks, like something from a Russian postage stamp. To compensate for its intrusion, Camas had made the rest of its downtown as attractive as possible, with a main street mall lavish in tree and floral paintings. Camas had been the "City of Paper" ever since 1884 when its first mill was built at nearby Lake Lackamas. Tours at 10 A.M., 1 P.M., and 3 P.M. (no 3 P.M. tour wintertime) may be arranged by telephoning the Crown Zellerbach communications department at Portland, (503) 227-6481.

For the next twenty miles, the highway flirts with views of the Oregon shore, a colorful collage of forested hills, rocky palisades, and misty waterfalls. From Washougal, a pleasant woolen milling community two miles east of Camas, State 14 climbs above the river for a better look. The view is largely obscured by growths of maple and alder, but nineteen miles from Washougal, you can, wind willing, discover one that is truly unobscured—almost a thousand feet above sea level. This is Beacon Rock, named by Lewis and Clark after the Corps of Explorers found it marked the beginning of the tidewater Columbia. Beacon Rock is more than nine hundred feet high and is said to be the second highest single block of stone in the world by those who believe all the world's rocks have been measured.

In 1901 the monolith was climbed for the first time. On reaching the top, its conqueror unfurled a strange device—a banner advertising a river steamboat company. They don't make them like that any more along ad row. Today, climbers use Beacon Rock for practice. For the less venturesome, a walkway of planks and iron railings switches its way to summit views of the Columbia Gorge and Cascade peaks.

Across the highway, a road leads into Beacon Rock State Park, one of the state's largest, equipped with picnic grounds, tent sites, hot showers, electric stoves, a playground, and trails leading to two waterfalls. Along the shore, not far from where Lewis and Clark camped in 1805 and again on their return the following year, is a boat ramp and harbor with limited facilities for picnics and camping.

For more than a century the monolith was known as Castle Rock, stemming from a name given by a Scotch fur trader, Inshoach Castle. It was not until 1916 that the Board of Geographic Names restored it to Beacon Rock, which indeed it was.

To Lewis and Clark, Beacon Rock was a milepost celebrating the fact they had at last triumphed in a mission virtually unequaled in the history of land explorations. The worst of the long haul from Missouri was over. True, ahead lay months of wet and hungry misery at the Columbia's mouth and the disappointment of finding no ship there awaiting their splashdown as promised by President Jefferson. Ahead, too, was the long return to civilization with everything save sickness in short supply. But behind them were the hazardous portages and the terrors of mountain passes made even more fearful by the imminent prospect of failure or death. Much of the Columbia beyond Beacon Rock was still a mystery. But it was broad and smooth and the explorers eagerly noted its tidal qualities and rejoiced in the emerging greenery. Of the terrain, Lewis simply noted that it was "more handsome."

(It wasn't that Lewis was programmed, like today's astronauts, for unpoetic simplicities. Indeed, he agonized over the literary quality of his observations. For example, after penning a description in the Journal of the Great Falls of the Missouri, he wrote in chagrin:

("After writing this imperfect description I again viewed the falls and was so much disgusted with this imperfect idea which it conveyed of the scene that I determined to draw my pen across it and begin again.")

Most of the names Lewis and Clark so carefully bestowed on their discoveries of mountains, streams, flora, and fauna were ignored later by geographers, zoologists, botanists, and their bureaucracies. In an age when beacons have become the cheap inventions of speechwriters, the name they gave this massive rock rings true.

Three miles east of Beacon Rock is another monolith which has served as a sort of beacon for today's river tamers: Bonneville Dam. Here at the penstocks of the towering dam ends (save for a fifty-seven-mile stretch between Priest Rapids Dam and Richland) the last free-flowing stretch of the Columbia within Washington's borders. For the next eight hundred miles, the Great River becomes the Great Powerhouse, its flow harnessed by eleven dams. Bonneville and

Grand Coulee Dam were the first of these publicly financed river corrals. As Stewart Holbrook observed in *The Columbia,* "They changed much of the Pacific Northwest as nothing else since the coming of the covered wagon trains." And not always for the better, as we shall see.

Bonneville, with its surrounding rim of forested hills, is an ideal rest stop, well equipped on both sides of the river with parks, a rose garden, a visitor's center with guided tours, fish ladders, and huge locks. Here tugs and barges carrying everything from Alaska urea to wheat from Washington and Oregon are raised or dropped up to fifty feet on their journeys. Behind the dam, extending for forty miles to The Dalles Dam, is a lake covering a series of falls.

The dam, completed in 1937 and named for Lieutenant Colonel Benjamin Louis Eulalie de Bonneville (who as poet commandant provided seed money—with interest—to General Grant when he was planting potatoes back at Vancouver Barracks), is an engineering triumph, providing electrical energy, flood control, and navigation, the trinity of the Army Corps of Engineers. Built in a period when technology had an answer to every problem, including those it created, it is equipped with a series of pools aptly described as fish ladders that lead the migrating salmon to the upper dam level. There they head upriver. It's a fascinating sight, these great fish, fertile and impatient, thrashing upward to consummate a drive that has brought them thousands of miles in their return to the gravel bed in which they were born.

Trouble is, less and less salmon survive to close this cycle. An appalling number die each year from the effects of supersaturation: excessive amounts of nitrogen created when air is trapped in the waters rushing over the dam spillways.

Fisheries experts disagree on the fatality count. Federal fish biologists have put the death toll as high as ninety percent of the runs. Those in state service say the number is substantially less, and contend that not all deaths are attributable to supersaturation. They maintain further that the toll is decreasing, pointing out that the 1972 chinook salmon run was the best since 1938. That of 1973, they say, was average.

But all agree that over the years the river's salmon runs have become seriously depleted. Today, the runs are measured not in pounds or cases, but in individual fish. Around eighty thousand salmon ran the gauntlet in 1972.

It took a bit of doing to add the Columbia River salmon to our list of endangered species. For seventy-five years, they have survived the most ingenious attempts by modern man to destroy them. Over the years, the salmon were caught by seiners, trollers, gillnetters, and even horse-drawn seines. But the most efficient were fish traps. These were simply screens thrown across migratory routes. Equally effective and ingenious were the giant fish wheels that once churned these shores with seventy-two installations from the Cascades as far up as The Dalles.

Adapted from those used by Alaska and river Indians, the wheels, up to forty-four feet in diameter and eight feet in width, scooped the salmon from the river. With their motive power being that of the river current, they were great money-makers, costing around ten thousand dollars to install and capable of amortizing that investment in less than a season. One Columbia River fish wheel in the Cascades area hoisted out ten thousand salmon in a single twenty-four-hour period; thirty tons of sturgeon being lifted during a similar period. Another, during its thirty-one years of operation, caught 4,625,776 pounds of salmon.

Rudyard Kipling on viewing the Columbia River fish wheels termed them "infernal arrangements." A companion, who apparently had a better writer, was quoted as saying, "Think of the black and bloody murder of it!"

Actually, the wheels caught less than ten percent of the river's annual catch, and along with drag seines and traps, have long since been outlawed. But the Columbia's dams are here to stay, to be followed within this century by up to a score of nuclear generating plants. We have, for better or worse, wedded what most accept as the good life of the Pacific Northwest to the kilowatt, trading salmon runs for low cost, clean energy. The scientists are now back at the drawing board. Some are confident that dams and salmon can someday occupy the same stream bed. Others not so optimistic foresee the eventual demise of the Columbia's salmon runs.

From Bonneville Dam, a side road to the north leads to Bonneville Hot Springs, where for a buck you can swim all day in naturally warmed waters. A few miles east, the Bridge of the Gods crosses into Oregon. It's a toll bridge unless you're a card-carrying god. The bridge got its name from a tedious legend blamed on Indians about a natural span that arched over the river until the gods got angry and withdrew their support. If you're interested in closer views of those waterfalls you've been seeing across the river, this is a good place to cross over. The Oregon side of the Columbia is strewn with almost a score of fine parks between Troutdale, opposite Camas, and The Dalles. One, Rooster Rock State Park, is dandy for a picnic on a grassy lawn or a swim from a mile-long sandy beach.

Just beyond Stevenson on State 14, a side road (State 141) heads north along the Wind River, through the town of Carson and into the depth of the Gifford Pinchot National Forest. Just west of Trout Lake at road's end is one of the region's many ice caves, created twenty thousand years ago by volcanic action. The Forest Service has made access easy by a ladderlike staircase, which enables you to drop into this four-hundred-foot cavern and play like you're the Thing from the Earth's Core. The cave (and two-mile-long Ape Cave, just south of Mount St. Helens) is a favorite with spelunkers. More than six hundred of them met here a few years ago for the convention of the National Speleological Society, which isn't as stuffy as it sounds, judging by the song they sent echoing down the cave:

"It ain't catshit and it ain't ratshit, so it must be batshit."

This southern flank of the Gifford Pinchot National Forest is a fitting namesake for the Pennsylvania gentleman who coined the word "conservation" while horseback riding through a Washington, D.C., park. It lies between Mount Adams and Mount St. Helens, embracing 660 miles of streams, 310 small lakes, 1,300 miles of trails, and enough roads to make Justice William Douglas sick. The mountain's roads, complains the distinguished jurist, who has tramped Adam's slopes since boyhood, are "claiming even the remote refuges and converting them into public squares."

One nearby refuge accessible by trail is Indian Race Track on Adam's southeast slope. Tribes met here in the dim past to pick berries and play games, including the racing of ponies across this meadow. Over the years the races cut a furrow, still visible, that at points is ten feet wide and a couple of feet deep. If they did that to-day, I'll bet they'd hear from Justice Douglas.

The roads and trails along this forest stretch are heavy with ranks of blackberry vines and huckleberry bushes, making it a popular locale for pickers and bears. You'll find them—the berries, that is—on sale in early fall at Carson and nearby White Salmon, which hosts a Huckleberry Festival each September. State 141, as it winds along the Wind River, also serves three Forest Service campgrounds, one of them a handy gateway to the ice caves.

Five miles east of the Stevenson junction, State 14 crosses the crest of the Cascades, a milestone not readily apparent along this low-level route, save for the gradual replacement of Douglas fir forests with those of the Ponderosa pine of the eastern slopes.

Just ahead are Bingen and White Salmon. The towns feuded for years over who should get the rail depot, which was settled by naming it White Salmon-Bingen, the only stop so blessed, at least according to Ripley. Bingen, named by early German settlers for Bingen-on-the-Rhine, is the site of a riverside park with picnic and boat-launching facilities. There is steelhead fishing on the Little White Salmon, and five miles north of White Salmon anglers seek rainbows in Northwestern Lake. The lake, formed by a mossy old-timer of a dam operated by Pacific Power and Light Company, has a public park with picnic grounds amid the firs, but no swimming.

At Bingen, a toll bridge crosses the Columbia into Hood River, famed for its apples and pears and one of the gateways to Oregon's Mount Hood recreation area.

East on State 14, between the old highway and the new is Rowland Lake Park with swimming, picnic tables, and a boat-launching ramp for fishermen. A nearby highway rest stop and picnic ground looks down on what is left of flooded Memaloose Island, once an Indian burial ground. The obelisk you see is the last resting place of Victor Trevitt, pioneer saloonkeeper from The Dalles, who selected this watery grave while in his cups.

Fifteen miles east of Bingen, just beyond the town of Lyle, a side road leads down to the river bank and into Horsethief Lake State Park. Located on a grassy peninsula, it's equipped with electric stoves, sun shelters, and facilities for picnics, swimming, and camping. Origin of the name is hazy, but it was along this stretch that William Clark wrote of guarding their stores against Indian theft, "which we were more fearful of than their arrows." (The Indians were probably Wishrams, the *mafiosa* of the upper Columbia, but they were outclassed by a party of downstream Chinooks, who, when invited to a parley to discuss their thievery, stole Clark's peace pipe.)

The Dalles Dam, visible from here, has its own grassy picnic grounds as well as a visitor center, views of fish ladders, and a walkway across the crest of the spillway to its locks. At the visitor center they will tell you the dam is 8,700 feet long, has a 120-foot spillway that will generate 1,119,000 kilowatts, and creates Lake Celilo, extending twenty-four miles to the base of John Day Dam. But there is no tape recording of what lies below the surface.

Back in October 1956, as a newspaper reporter I visited this stretch of the Columbia. I was covering the last Indian fishing season at Celilo Falls, which for centuries has been fishing grounds for the Nez Perce, Umatilla, Yakima, and other horse Indian tribes. It was a sight to remember, the black rocks overlooking the cataracts festooned with crude wooden platforms from which Indians with dip nets and spears harvested their last catch of migrating salmon.

I talked to a graying Indian, Harrison Lott, a member of the Nez Perce Tribal Council who had come from Idaho to Celilo Falls each year for twenty years to fish. He patiently recited the provisions of the treaty signed with Governor Isaac Stevens at Walla Walla in 1855, in which was promised "exclusive and perpetual" fishing rights for the tribes at this stretch of soon to be drowned rapids.

"Now we are told we have no rights," Lott told me. He paused to watch two young Indians who stood poised with their spears like figures on a Grecian frieze. Then he continued with little apparent conviction, "We will bring to Washington the words spoken by Governor Stevens to Chief Looking Glass." He trailed off, knowing full well he was shouting into the wind. Then he resumed his watching.

Just beyond Wishram, a star trek away from any apparent reason for its being, is Maryhill Castle. High above one of the most unattractive reaches of the Columbia on a sagebrush plateau, Maryhill was the folly and pride of Sam Hill, a multimillionaire North Carolinian who married the boss's daughter. Hill was the son-in-law of Empire Builder James J. Hill. He also was a Quaker, apostle of good roads and European royalty, and a hatchetman in Hill's railroad wars, none of which explain the location or purpose of Maryhill Castle.

Construction started in 1913. For thirteen years intermittent droves of workers toiled, building a three-story mansion of concrete and stone, fashioning it in formal Flemish style and surrounding it with appropriate formal gardens and driveways lined with poplars. All of which did little to brighten the surrounding seven thousand acres of drylands. During the construction, Hill gave several versions of just what in the Sam Hill he was up to. On one occasion he told an interviewer that his project was to be "an international museum of fine arts, and a library."

"It will be a school of all the people," he elaborated, suddenly providing a populace where none existed. "The farmer folk could come out here to find solutions to their problems." The latter remark would have puzzled his father-in-law, who had busied himself creating railroad rate structures that created farmer problems often solved only by bankruptcy.

Then in 1926, Maryhill Castle was completed. Down the driveway came Queen Marie of Romania, accompanied by a proud Sam Hill and an entourage that included the aging Loie Fuller, undoubtedly the only ex-star of the Folies Bergères to play a matinée on the Columbia. A lover of pomp and publicity, Hill and his royal party had already been feted in Portland, one hundred and fourteen miles away, and were now ready for the formal dedication of the sagebrush château.

Queen Marie, inheritor of a large dose of grandmother Victoria's sagacity, went along with the act with the same aplomb and eye on the cash register that had marked her successful foreign aid tour of the United States. Her words, now inscribed on the portal of the castle, are a masterpiece of genteel obfuscation:

"Sam Hill is building not only for today, but tomorrow. There is much more in this building made of concrete than we see. There is a dream built into this place. Some may smile and scoff, for they do not understand. But I came in understanding of his dream. For those dreamers I would say good things are not only for this life but for beyond."

Today, more than sixty thousand visitors each year troop through Sam Hill's castle on the Columbia, which, if it hasn't become a school of all the people or served much of a role as an ombudsman headquarters, has excelled in its role as "an international museum of fine arts."

Run by a private board without public funds, its twenty-two galleries are officially described as housing "Paintings, Sculpture, Ceramics, Glass, Mementos of European Royalty, Gallery of Chessmen, Old Dolls, French Mannequins, Old Guns, Northwest Indians Collections."

My wife, a delightful commoner, more aptly describes it as "royalty's attic." And with some exceptions, notably its fine Indian collection, it is.

Here, in well-lighted, immaculate galleries is an eclectic inventory not to be seen this side of Topkapi. A few examples:

Greek vases from 900 B.C., gift of Elizabeth, Queen of Greece; a throne chair from Queen Marie's Bucharest palace; her gold lamé coronation robes; gold chalices and altar vessels; two pieces of wood and an iron keel plate from the *Mayflower;* Cézanne and Delacroix etchings; a Rembrandt, a Corot sketch and one of Tahitian women by Gauguin, all keeping company with seven Alaska oils by Sydney Laurence and Rodin sculptures; Samurai swords, stone axes, muskets, pistols, bows and arrows, chessmen, decanters, and milk glass; models of early Columbia River steamers and autographed pictures of European royalty, all looking appropriately decadent. And much, much more. And on the top floor is Sam's room, hung with mementos of that which he held dearest in life: recognition.

Here, sharing space with a plaque proclaiming Hill's life membership in the Oregon State Motorists Association, is his French Legion of Honor certificate. A parchment appointing him honorary Consul General of Belgium holds equal rank with a cup inscribed: "A reminder of pleasant relations. From your gas man, 1904." Another cup, from the Harvard Club of Minnesota reads: "He filled the bumper fair." It's a good exit line.

Hoist one to Sam Hill. Another to the three Princes of Serendip.

Together they have built a showcase shared by Impressionist painters and aboriginal basket makers, Romanoffs and Babbitts; depositors of mildew and glitter in this outrageous castle with a river for its moat. The very improbability of it all teases us with Marie's benediction: "There is much more in this building made of concrete than we see."

Whatever Hill's dream, his legacy is worth every mile of the journey to its place of fulfillment, the Maryhill Museum of Fine Arts, open daily, holidays and Sundays included, March 15 to November 15, between 9 A.M. and 5:30 P.M. Admission 75 cents; students twelve to eighteen, 40 cents, and those under twelve, free when accompanied by an adult.

Just beyond Maryhill, a road just east of the Sam Hill Memorial Bridge at Biggs leads to Maryhill Park, operated by the Corps of Engineers, providing a grassy picnic ground, swimming beach, boat ramp, and an old steam locomotive. East of where State 14 intersects with U.S. Highway 97 is another durable monument to Hill's eccentricity, a scale model of Stonehenge, built by him as a monument to World War I dead, now a park operated by Klickitat County. From its appearance, today's Druids have forsaken painting themselves and instead deface their altars with spray paint graffiti.

Along the Columbia between Maryhill and Pasco two Army Corps of Engineers dams, John Day and McNary, provide the usual opportunity to inspect their inner and outer workings. Both have transformed the Columbia into placid lakes, stocked with salmon, whitefish, trout, and other fish. You can swim, picnic, launch your boat, or fly your kite from a number of parks along their shores. Or you can just sit and watch the tugs lock their way through with cargoes of grain, logs, piling, chemicals, and other products. Around five million tons a year move through these locks, most of it heading for Portland. (The Port of Portland continually infuriates its bigger rival, Seattle, by counting the river grain shipments twice; once when they arrive at elevators from upriver, and again when the grain is loaded for overseas destinations. Portland adds up the totals and then writes promotional ads that say, "Nyaaa, we handle more cargo than Seattle!")

ON THE TRAIL
OF EXPLORERS

Dr. Samuel Johnson's top banana, James Boswell, once set him up for another one-liner by asking if the Giant's Causeway was worth seeing. To which Dr. Johnson replied, "Worth seeing? Yes; but not worth going to see."

At Maryhill, where U.S. 97 heads north over Satus Pass and into the inviting Yakima Valley, we can make the same magisterial distinction. As long as we're in the neighborhood, let's continue on our State 14 for a few miles into Pasco, Richland, and Kennewick. They're worth seeing.

The three communities comprise an area known inelegantly as the Tri-Cities. On two occasions during the past hundred and fifty years they have served as crossroads in man's explorations of what he has presumed to be his domains.

We find the first of these historic junctures on a point of land that elbows into the Columbia at Pasco. Here on October 16, 1805, the Lewis and Clark party came down the Snake at last to meet the Columbia, which they found "remarkably clear and crowded with salmon." Near where the explorers pitched camp is Sacajawea State Park, a pleasant, grassy plot that provides the usual picnic amenities and a small, well-tended museum displaying a collection of arrowheads and Indian tools. But nothing to illuminate the historic role of

Sacajawea, who has been sentimentalized into something between the "Shoshone Deirdre" of Bernard De Voto and the dusky Debbie Reynolds of the late-late show.

One may detect a whiff of history's male chauvinism in this relegating of Sacajawea to the role of a simple-minded camp follower. But we have done little better to make flesh and blood of Lewis, Clark and company, who have been dispatched to the Eagle Scout wing of our pantheon of heroes.

Across the Columbia from Pasco, another museum, larger and more costly than that at Sacajawea State Park, attempts to tell the story of the ultimate milestone in exploration—the splitting of the atom. It too transforms an epic into a bore. Located on the ground floor of Richland's ten-million-dollar Federal Building, the pretentiously named Hanford Science Center is a maze of aisles lined with typical trade show exhibits: models, photomurals, pegboard graphs, and tinny, taped messages, all unrelated in graphics, theme, or continuity. They attempt to tell the story of the frontiers man has crossed since the day when plutonium brewed here at Hanford set off man's first nuclear explosion in the New Mexico badlands.

Nowhere, save perhaps Hiroshima or Nagasaki (which are timorously ignored in the displays), could there be a more fitting theater for this chapter in history. Here in this desert community, hatched overnight in World War II during the race to split the atom into a weapon, is assembled one of the world's largest collection of scientific thinkers and their tools. All are geared to bending nuclear science into plowshares. But as told in the Hanford Science Center, the story has all the bravura of a "Know Your Military Police" training film. You'll find more illumination and excitement in one of Ma Bell's county fair exhibits.

There is something disturbing about the inability of Sacajawea's museum at Pasco to recapture the past and that of the Richland museum to celebrate the future. Why not create one imaginative facility that could combine the drama of two of man's great explorations? Why not fashion a tapestry from the homespun of Lewis and Clark and the alchemist's gossamer of the atom? Where else could these two disparate events play under the same tent?

Here on the banks of the Columbia, not far from where Clark dispensed eyewash to the Indians and made points with a chief by rubbing his cranky wife with camphor, Hanford laboratories are fashioning nuclear batteries that are implanted in the body as pacemakers.

Where Thomas Jefferson instructed his secretary, Captain Meriwether Lewis, to study "the soil and face of the country, its growth

and vegetable productions; especially those not of the U.S.," Hanford
scientists study rocks brought back from the moon.

Within sight of where Lewis and Clark reached the Columbia after
groping their way across much of the continent, not sure if they
wouldn't meet llamas or, as Jefferson hoped, a lost tribe of thirteenth-
century Welshmen, men create equipment for skylabs. On nearby
Rattlesnake Mountain scouts with radio telescopes scan the routes
of tomorrow's Corps of Explorers.

President Jefferson believed, as he dispatched his scouts westward,
that America contained land for our descendants "to the thousandth
and thousandth generation." At Hanford, biologists seek programs to
curb our population.

It would take a Corita Kent to graphically illuminate an era when
a president instructed his far-ranging aid to bring back word of "the
dates of which particular plants put forth and lose their flowers," and
another where the men of Hanford seek means to dispose of wastes,
including those of the atom that could make the world leafless and
lifeless.

But these and a hundred more parallels and differences between
the centuries are elements needed to stir a museum into something
with meaning and life. They are subjects for some future Hall of
Science here in the Tri-City area, entertaining and instructing us with
the story of a party of explorers with distance in their eyes, and those
who have embarked all of us on a journey that may forever remain
uncharted.

To date, more than a billion dollars in public funds has been invested in Hanford. Perhaps the next time another Atomic Energy
Commission budget is being marked up, funds might be included for
development of a museum here that might illuminate the dark of
yesterday and the brightness of tomorrow. (NOTE: Since writing this,
the appointment of Dixy Lee Rae as head of the AEC makes such a
project, if not more likely, as least more plausible. Dr. Rae formerly
directed the Seattle Science Center and is highly regarded for her
ability to translate science into meaningful and entertaining exhibits.)

Perhaps when this Hall of Explorers is being designed, room can
be found for space to focus attention on one passage from Thomas
Jefferson's instructions to Meriwether Lewis. It too speaks of a
science, perhaps stillborn, that of man's relation to man:

"In all your intercourse with the natives treat them in the most
friendly & conciliatory manner which their own conduct will admit;
allay all jealousies as to the object of your journey, satisfy them of
it's innocence, make them acquainted with the position, extent, character, peacable & commercial dispositions of the U.S., of our wish to

be neighborly, friendly & useful to them, & of our dispositions to a friendly commercial intercourse with them; confer with them on the points most convenient as mutual emporiums, & the articles of most desireable interchange for them & us, if a few of their influential chiefs, within practicable distance, wish to visit us, arrange such a visit with them, and furnish them with authority to call on our officers, on their entering the U.S., to have them conveyed to this place at public expense. If any of them should wish to have some of their young people brought up with us, & taught such arts as may be useful to them, we will receive, instruct & take care of them."

There is little in the appearance of Pasco, Richland, or Kennewick to indicate they are the legatees of a billion-dollar inheritance. Those facilities, the research labs, the plutonium grist mills, the world's most powerful nuclear generator, and others, are located out on the desert a score of miles away.

There, amid the sagebrush, are located the think tanks where daily some sixty-five hundred men and women assist in probing into physics, marine sciences, metallurgy, chemistry technology, and a host of environmental sciences. Fueling these are annual budgets of more than $160 million, dispensed under contract with the Atomic Energy Commission, by corporations that read like the Big Board of 2001:

Computer Sciences; Nuclear Co.; Hanford Environmental Corp.; Douglas Nuclear Inc.; Atlantic-Richfield Hanford; Martin-Marietta; Battelle Northwest and Holosonics, Inc., the latter busy at developing acoustical holography, a sort of X-ray with pictures created by sound, more acute than X-ray and without its harmful side effects. Other researchers from the University of Washington, Washington State University, and the University of Oregon are at work at a sixty-five-acre graduate center.

While virtually all of these facilities are privately operated, much of the Hanford Works project, some five hundred square miles in all, remains an empty, off-limits wasteland, owned by the Atomic Energy Commission. Sections are being released gradually for cultivation as part of the Columbia Basin irrigation empire that stretches northward from the Tri-Cities. Almost a billion dollars a year in farm crops are harvested from the Basin's half million acres, and the Tri-Cities ports flourish as funnels for this wealth. Pasco also thrives as a rail center and Kennewick augments its income with that of grape processing plants.

Of the three, only Richland has avoided the plastic look of communities suckled by the automobile. It accomplished this by undertaking a face-lifting following its transition from a federal city to one of private ownership. Along the river, a landscaped esplanade with

boat ramps, picnic grounds, and a playground provides this largest
of the Tri-Cities with one of the few waterfronts in the entire state
that doesn't resemble a city dump. Two resort hotels overlook the
Columbia at this point. Here you can thoughtfully sup and drink
while watching the incongruity of tumbleweeds floating past in the
Columbia. Downstream four miles is 417-acre Columbia Park, operated by Benton County, a pleasant greensward of picnic and camping
grounds, a swimming beach, golf course, tennis courts, and boat
rentals. The riverfront is the site each July of the Atomic Cup hydroplane races and the Tri-City Water Follies.

Ten miles up the Snake River via U.S. 12 and State 124 are Ice
Harbor Dam and Lake Sacajawea, extending thirty-two miles to the
foot of Lower Monumental Dam. Both offer self-guided tours, and
the lake has a boat-launching ramp for fishermen. Overlooking the
dam is a memorial, including a well-preserved petroglyph, honoring
local Indians, or at least their former fishing grounds.

Just north of Pasco, White Bluffs Road, a dead-end gravel byway,
provides a rare chance to savor the flavor of the innocent Columbia
before it was damned. Between here and Priest Rapids Dam, fifty-
seven miles in all, is the last free-flowing stretch of the Great River
(or as free-flowing as a dam-regulated stream will permit), wending
past Indian campgrounds, deserted as the abandoned reactors nearby.
Woodlands and coves are homes for ducks, geese, golden eagles, blue
herons, kingfishers, wintering white pelicans, and other bird life. The
river-level road parallels about ten miles of this strand, a favorite
for rock hounds seeking agates deposited in gravel beds at the foot
of the white bluffs that give the road its name. The Army Corps of
Engineers, which looks on any remaining stretch of unharnessed river
with great and persuasive sadness, has plans for a dam to rectify this
oversight. But the proposal is being determinedly fought by a group
united under a newly formed Columbia River Conservation League,
which envisions the stretch as a National Recreation Area. The abandoned reactors, appropriately enough in this age of Sudden Shock,
would become museums. Perhaps displaying a stuffed engineer or
two.

From Pasco, the Lewis and Clark Trail (over U.S. 12) crosses the
Snake near Sacajawea State Park, then follows the big bend of the
Columbia as it flows through the McNary Wildlife Refuge. The river-
bank thickets and grasses are popular hunting grounds for ducks and
Canada geese. During fall months you can hear flocks of buckshot-
tattered wildfowl angrily flapping by, crying, "Some refuge!" For bird-
watchers, there are chances for viewings of the long-billed curlew,
valley quail, avocet, and the burrowing owl.

At the southern boundary of the eight-thousand-acre refuge, U.S. 12 brushes by the doorstep of Wallula, another Columbia River community of drowned memories. Wallula, once the site of two frontier forts and later a riverboat port for wheat carriers, was, back in the seventies, the terminus for a railroad that could have been the pattern for the Toonerville Trolley. Huffing along under the full-blown name of the Walla Walla and Columbia River Line, it connected Walla Walla with Wallula over thirty-two miles of wooden rails covered with strap iron and held in place by rawhide strips. Nearing its destinations, the narrow-gauge locomotive was preceded by a barking collie, the Indians having stolen the cowcatcher. But the line succeeded in driving down the wagoner's price of hauling wheat from six dollars a ton to $1.50. It made so much money for its founder, a dropout doctor, that he even could manage a smile over the name the locals had hung on his one passenger car—the Hearse.

Today the contained Columbia has inundated all signs of Wallula's past. The relocated hamlet consists of two short tree-shaded streets and a combination bus depot, post office, and tavern look down on a pulp mill. Back from the highway is one of the state's biggest cattle-fattening centers, a feed lot accommodating on an average day thirty-five thousand steers and heifers. They are fed for a hundred and forty days and gain about three pounds a day. Cowboys ride around the lot crooning, "Get it on, little dogies."

Beyond Wallula, past the view of the rocky cleft where the Walla Walla River meets the Columbia, you can begin coloring the land green. Abruptly, almost like the crossing of one of those magical borders in Oz, the gritty flavor of the drylands is rinsed away. The old-horse-blanket look of the tumbleweed country gives way to the pastels of grasslands and irrigated fields against a backdrop of the Blue Mountains, which really are. Over this range, harsh and challenging in winters, the Lewis and Clark party clawed its way home.

Before the settlers' plow broke its sod, this valley was knee-deep in native grass and supported a small village of Cayuse Indians, who ranged their horses here. In 1847, in two days of terror, this became Washington's bloodiest ground.

A well-marked side road leads to the site where in 1836 Dr. Marcus Whitman and his wife, Narcissa, built their Presbyterian mission. In November 1847 they died with eleven others under the tomahawks, knives, and guns of the Cayuse. Some fifty survivors were captured by the Cayuse, then ransomed a month later by Peter Skene Ogden of the Hudson's Bay Company.

This dark story is told, museum fashion, at the Whitman Mission Historic Site. It is Ford's Theater reduced to a vacant lot. An interpretive center houses artifacts of the period and a doll's-house staging of the tragedy. Outside, a self-guided tour wends through the grounds, the story of the mission and its untimely end related by pushbutton narrators.

But the old ruts in the Oregon Trail flanking the mission plot are real. Over them had creaked the emigrant wagons and their followers who turned down this road to find the solace, medical treatment, and advice the Whitman Mission provided. The Cayuse probably kept no accurate record of this traffic. But even without counters, they must have uneasily watched the growth: two dozen wagons in 1841, one hundred fourteen the following year, and more and more until by 1847, the year of bloody decision, more than three thousand settlers eased to a halt here amid the fields of rye. And that year along with the wagons arrived smallpox, ravaging the Cayuse and sowing fear and distrust among its leaders, who became convinced they were being poisoned by the white shaman and his wife.

The visitor trail winds up a knoll, passing a monument and graves of the dead. At its crest it provides a sweeping view of cultivated fields and a meandering stream, and beyond, the curve of the Blue Mountains over which Narcissa Whitman walked with her husband down into the valley. Impatient with her Indian charges, whom she described as "proud, haughty, and insolent," she saw their redemption only in terms of their adaptation to farming, and what she discerned as their acceptance of the Word.

"We have been teaching them the Ten Commandments," she wrote near the end, "with which they are very much pleased."

After 1847 the smoke from the burning mission billowed into a settlers' war against the Cayuse. This was followed still later by the flames of Indian wars that flickered across Oregon Territory until 1877, when Chief Joseph etched an epitaph to resistance with his famed valedictory. As in most wars, the territory's major battle with the Indians began with a peace treaty, this one signed a few miles away in what today is Walla Walla.

There's an unhurried air to Walla Walla that makes you thirsty—for a milk shake. Some liken this quality to evidences here of the transplanted Midwest, or even upstate New York. But to me, a milk shake in a cool Walla Walla emporium with the Naugahyde booths commanding a view of Main Street is as flavorful as beer in Milwaukee or sidewalk coffee in New Orleans. The atmosphere belongs to a period when most main streets were like this, anchored at their corners by J. C. Penney, Sears, Montgomery Ward, and Marshall Wells. Between them are two- and three-story brick buildings with upper windows that are arched eyebrows, housing lodge halls and advertising dentists, and a Liberty Theater with a faded invitation, "Let's go to the Movies."

Bustle is still the word for Walla Walla's sidewalks. Vehicular traffic is shepherded by signals set for eighteen miles an hour. Fringing the business district, roomy old residences sprawl with a kind of ungirdled relaxation in the shade of leafy locust trees. I've never had the pleasure of exploring one of these beckoning Victorians, but Nancy Wilson Ross, who did, draws back the lace curtains in her *Farthest Reach:*

"Inside the houses one finds heirlooms and 'antiques': camphorwood chests, melodeons, and glass that came round the Horn, carefully preserved little fanciful landscapes of moss, shells, and fungus, made by territorial ladies when they began to acquire their first leisure, or samples of weaving left from older and less leisurely days when women had to grow their own flax and make their own cloth in the gentle Oregon valleys in which the first emigrants settled."

Walla Walla was anything but a gentle valley when its first populace arrived in the sixties, itching and scratching from the Idaho gold fields. In succeeding years, the frontier town provided enough gunsmoke to fuel a whole series of television westerns with cattlemen feuding with sheepherders, rustlers riding the range, and vigilantes hanging the evildoers right downtown. But it was all over in a decade. Farmers replaced the prospectors, the Territory's first bank, department store, and newspaper bespoke a disappearance of villainy, and soon the area's first wheat crop was making its way to market over Dr. Baker's rawhide railroad to Wallula.

Today, Walla Walla thrives on a bib-overall economy nurtured by wheat and cannery crops as well as sugar beets, cucumbers, grapes, lawn seed, and a delectable sweet onion that you can eat like an apple. Cattle raising and horse breeding augment these crops and provide such social outlets as the annual horse shows sponsored by breeders of Appaloosa, Tennessee walkers, Arabians, and other breeds represented by the four thousand horses in the county.

The many streams entering the valley give Walla Walla its Indian name, meaning "place of many waters." Townsfolk have patiently endured all the jokes it has generated and not long ago topped them all by hiring as manager for the Walla Walla baseball team a chap named Joe Ditto.

Visitors, particularly hunters, use Walla Walla as a stepping-off point for elk and deer safaris in the Blue Mountains; or pheasants, waterfowl, and chukars in the Grande Ronde Valley, and rainbow and brown trout in the Tucannon Lakes, Mill Creek, and the Touchet River.

Walla Walla's two largest institutions are Whitman College and the Washington State Prison. Both provide steady payrolls and innumerable Rotary Club discussions over the policies of their administrators and future of their charges.

Whitman College, founded in 1859 by the Reverend Cushing Eells, a co-worker and friend of Dr. Whitman, should cause little concern among those who watch closely for signs of blight in the groves of academe. A recent survey of its prelaw students, for example, showed eighty percent ranking above the national average. In the past decade, eighty-two percent applying for admission to medical school were admitted, compared to a national average of fifty percent. Always ranked high among the nation's smaller colleges, it modestly acknowledges the graduation of a Nobel Prize winner in physics, Walter H. Brattain, as well as a U. S. Supreme Court Justice, William O. Douglas.

Physically, Whitman, like downtown Walla Walla, evokes sighs for the good old days; bricked walks and turreted buildings shaded by elm, locust and birch trees, an honest-to-Tom-Brown greensward with a duck pond, formed by Mill Creek, all nicely mixed with unobtrusive examples of more contemporary architecture.

Also on campus is a seventeen-ton rock. On it, writ in bronze are words commemorating the role of a Nez Percé chief, Lawyer, who played a key role in the Treaty of 1855 by lobbying for its acceptance in the face of strong opposition from his co-chiefs, Old Joseph and Looking Glass. He was rewarded by a federal land grant and a $1,500-a-year annuity.

The treaty parley was attended by Territorial Governor Isaac Stevens, General Joel Palmer, Oregon Territory's Indian Affairs superintendent, and the chiefs of the Nez Percé, Walla Walla, Yakima, and Cayuse Indians. Held on a May day on a grassy plain near today's downtown Walla Walla, the ceremony drew more than two thousand mounted tribesmen, and Governor Stevens' party of about a hundred, including fifty soldiers. From the description of one of Governor Stevens' aides, Lieutenant Lawrence Kip, the peace parley must have been as colorful as that of Versailles, and in the interest of a lasting peace, about as productive.

Wrote Lieutenant Kip of the scene:

About 2500 of the Nez Percé tribe have arrived. It was our first specimen of this Prairie cavalry, and it certainly realized all our conceptions of these wild warriors of the plains. Their coming was announced about ten o'clock, and going out on the plain to where the flag staff had been erected, we saw them approaching on horseback in one long line. They were almost entirely naked, gaudily painted and decorated with their wild trappings. Their plumes fluttered above them, while below, skins and trinkets and all kinds of fantastic embellishments flaunted in the sunshine.

Trained from early childhood almost to live upon horseback, they sat upon their fine animals as if they were centaurs. Their horses, too, were arrayed in the most glaring finery. They were painted with such colors as formed the greatest contrast; the white being smeared with crimson in fantastic figures, and the dark colored streaked with white clay. Beads and fringes of gaudy colors were hanging from the bridles, while the plumes of eagle feathers interwoven with the mane and tail fluttered as the breeze swept over them, and completed their wild and fantastic appearance.

When about a mile distant, they halted and half a dozen chiefs rode forward and were presented to Governor Stevens and General Palmer in the order of their rank. On came the rest of the wild horsemen in single file, clashing their shields, singing and beating their drums as they marched past us. They formed a circle and dashed around us while our little group stood there, the center of their wild evolutions. They would gallop up as if about to make a charge, then wheel round and round, sounding their loud whoops until they had apparently worked themselves up into an intense excitement. Then some score or two dismounted, and forming a ring, danced for about twenty minutes while those surrounding them beat time on their drums.

After these performances, more than twenty of the chiefs went over to the tent of Governor Stevens, where they sat for some time smoking the "pipe of peace" in token of good fellowship, and then returned to their camping ground.

Not far from town on Garrison Creek is Fort Walla Walla Park which still houses remnants of the military post built during the wars that followed enactment of the uneasy treaty.

(A clue to its failure might be found in a letter written by Governor Stevens' wife, Margaret: "Mr. Stevens has them [the Indians] right under his thumb. They are afraid as death of him and do just as he tells them.")

The Fort park offers campsites in the fields and woods and a museum operated by the Walla Walla Valley Pioneer and Historical Society. It displays a pioneer schoolhouse, cabins, a blockhouse, country store, railway depot, grain-thrashing equipment, and other shards from the midden heaps of the nineties. Open 1 A.M. to 5 P.M., June to September.

Children will enjoy a visit to the Walla Walla Game Farm at 498 North Thirteenth Street where game birds are raised. Hatching season is April through June, and the farm is open daily from 8 A.M. to 8 P.M.

Like most Washington cities, Walla Walla bills itself as a gateway to the sportsman's outdoors. It's a fair claim, and points out one of the ironies of the Lewis and Clark saga.

For in following the course of the Snake River the Corps of Explorers were taken on a route barren of game, "empty gut country" in which dogs were considered a table treat. (Clark alone seemed to have rebelled against this entrée, observing wryly, if not doggedly, "All the Party have greatly the advantage of me, in as much as they all relish the flesh of the dogs.")

Had the party held to a more southern route they would have eaten better. Today one of the state's most productive hunting grounds is the Blue Mountains, and particularly the W. T. Wooten Wildlife Recreation Area. You can reach it by driving north on State 12 to Dayton, a pioneer town on the Lewis and Clark Trail, and heading south a dozen miles. There in the wild Tucannon Valley, the 11,344-acre sweep of mountains, timbered hills, and grass-covered ranges abounds in elk, deer, bighorn sheep, bear, rabbit, grouse, quail, partridge, pheasant, turkey, dove, as well as cougar and bobcat. Eight lakes and the Tucannon River provide excellent fishing.

It's approximately two hundred fifty miles from Vancouver to Walla Walla over the route we've just completed. The distance is noteworthy for the history it spans, the beguiling changes in terrain, and the fact this river-level route is about as far as you can travel on the level in the entire state.

Ahead, the Lewis and Clark Trail moseys its way toward the Idaho border through some of the state's most productive wheatlands (68.49 bushels per acre is Columbia County's boast), passing through buckboard towns like Waitsburg and century-old Dayton, where seventy-five of the town's residences are vintage pieces from the nineteenth century. Now the Columbia County seat, Dayton's setting on the grassy flats of the Touchet River made it a favorite campgrounds for Indian tribes. Here, too, Lewis and Clark rested as they headed home in May 1806.

Just beyond Dayton turn off onto State 261, which will take you about thirty miles to a crossing of the Snake River and on to Palouse Falls, a cataract that tumbles two hundred feet over a lava cliff into a rimrock basin. A nearby state park offers picnic grounds and limited camping facilities. (NOTE: The falls are best viewed in spring and fall; during July and August the cataract often becomes a trickle.) Nearby is Marmes Rock Shelter, where North America's oldest man was unearthed by Washington State University archeologists.

The Washington portion of the Lewis and Clark Trail ends about sixty miles northeast of Dayton at the Snake River towns of Clarkston and Lewiston, just across the river in Idaho. From here, State 195 climbs north over a dizzying serpentine route that could have been designed for a late-movie chase sequence, then stops with a sigh at the sleepy college town of Pullman and the dramatic campus of Washington State University.

At Lewiston, riverboats carrying from twenty to forty passengers make a two-day run down America's deepest gorge, the precipitous and scenic canyon of the Snake River.

However you view this route of Lewis and Clark, by highway or air, it is a trail that as former Interior Secretary Stewart Udall once said, "fired a national spirit of adventure which still persists."

SPOKANE'S
WORLD AFFAIR

America's most widely read sports columnist, Jim Murray, writes about cities with the same degree of courtesy that Westbrook Pegler once accorded the Roosevelts. Cities are to Murray what night club audiences are to Don Rickles.

Louisville he described as "America's Bar Rag, the kind of town that should have a tattoo on its bicep—two hearts and the word, Wanda." Cincinnati "looks like it's in the midst of condemnation proceedings." Murray mellowed a bit while visiting Spokane:

"There's nothing to do there after ten o'clock. In the morning. But it's a nice place to go for breakfast."

That's not a very nice thing to say about Washington's second city, a community whose residents were, up until 1974, content to live in the "capital of the Inland Empire," and the place where in 1903 Father's Day was born. (It was invented in 1910 by Mrs. John Bruce Dodd of Spokane, who, some say snidely, wanted her father to give her a pony.)

It is obvious that Jim Murray's insensitive appraisal was penned before Spokane, with a population of but 175,000, became host to Expo '74, a World's Fair celebrating ecology. Spokane thus became the smallest city ever to sponsor a World's Fair; the first city to hold one in honor of ecology, and the only community, large or small, to host a World's Fair celebrating ecology and to locate the fairgrounds on the banks of a polluted river.

Thanks to the fair, Spokane has been shaken out of its high-button shoes. New shops, hotels, and office buildings and the planting of five hundred trees brighten a once drab downtown. Just bringing to the city the Russians, Japanese, Iranians, Koreans, Nationalist Chinese, and other foreign exhibitors diminished Spokane's insularity. And the Expo '74 site along the Spokane River has transformed a grubby commercial riverfront into a series of pleasant esplanades, opening for the first time in a century an unobstructed view of spectacular Spokane Falls, only a short walk from the city center.

Whether or not Expo '74 has demonstrated how man can live in harmony with his environment, as billed, or whether, as Spokane's maverick attorney Carl Maxey charges, it made no contribution to ecology other than to increase Spokane's air pollution, is academic. All such exposition themes should be believed no more than political platforms or a fight manager's predictions.

Ever since Philadelphia burghers held a fair in 1876 to celebrate the centennial of the Declaration of Independence, all U.S. expositions have had but one purpose, to generate trade and travel and put their community on the map. This being a rather materialistic *raison d'être*, expositions are cloaked in a theme. So, following the example of Philadelphia, Chicago fashioned a magic city in cardboard Gothic, and in 1893 (missing by a year) celebrated the four-hundredth anniversary of the landing of Columbus. St. Louis developed a thousand-acre display in 1903 to observe the Louisiana Purchase Centennial. Chicago in 1933 celebrated, with a straight face, a Century of Progress. Even the Seattle World's Fair had to cobble together a centennial theme to give Congressmen a reason for appropriating $12,500,000 for its keystone Federal Science Pavilion.

"Why nineteen sixty-one?" That was the question arising at Congressional hearings through which Senator Warren Magnuson was steering the Seattle fair appropriations bill. Lights burned late at the Library of Congress as the search for an appropriate centennial date went on. It became painfully apparent that the main events of 1861 were the start of the Civil War and the first federal taxes on income. Neither called for much of a taxpayer-sponsored centennial gala. Then someone in desperation recalled that the last marker along the border between the United States and Canada was erected at Point Roberts, north of Seattle, in 1861.

So it was in 1959 that President Dwight D. Eisenhower sent Congress a message urging support of the World Science Pan-Pacific Exposition at Seattle in 1961 to celebrate the wonders of science and to "commemorate the centennial of the final physical fixing of the world's longest unfortified frontier."

The appropriation finally passed (it somehow ended up as an amendment to the Mutual Security Act, passed an hour before adjournment) and the Seattle World's Fair opened, a year late, as Century 21. By this time everyone had forgotten whatever it was they were supposed to be commemorating.

So much for the ecology theme of Expo '74. That fair is providing entertainment and perhaps a bit of education on environmental problems. It converted an area of riverfront blight into one of public enjoyment. More important, enough Spokanites were stung by the "eco-phony" charges to launch long-range plans for cleaning up its dirty river basin. And along with the upgrading, the city hasn't had so much fun since the time in 1890 when Judge Turner gave Mayor Clough a shiner and the intervening bailiff had to be carried out of the courtroom with a busted leg.

Despite this growing up, no one is going to write a song about a night in Spokane. A diner may, as we did, still encounter a waiter-person who takes down your order of steak tartare with a solicitous whisper, "You know, of course, that's raw meat?" But thanks to Expo '74, Spokane has become something more than a nice place to go for breakfast. Symbolizing the change has been the conversion of the old American Legion Hall with its Art Deco decor (no, Myrt, he wasn't the post commander) into an haute cuisine restaurant, A La Parisienne, a creation of a young French restaurateur, John Paul Kissel. Its menu of escargots à la Bourguignonne, Quilcene oysters, quiche Lorraine, omelettes, and other offerings should return to downtown Spokane the kind of dining all but forgotten since the Hotel Davenport offered one of the coast's finest kitchens.

Beyond the city limits, not much has changed. Which is just as well, for no other Washington community is surrounded by such a beguiling collection of lakes, rivers, forest and desert hideaways. They demonstrate, for the time being, one way man *can* live in harmony with his environment.

Spokane's success at escaping the ills of megalopolis can be attributed to the city's far corner location as well as to its youth. This is a sudden city. Approaching by plane, your jet gushes in for a landing over the heads of grazing cattle. Next to the highway, forest and field march right up to the city's doorstep. Spokane is a young city. By 1870, Seattle had elected its first mayor and, with a population nearing two thousand, was challenging Olympia and Walla Walla for the lead in population. Talk of railroads coming stirred every hamlet. Yakima was planting its first orchards. And while all this was going on, Spokane was a sleeping valley, deep in bunchgrass, peopled only by an Indian tribe whose name, the Spokanes, meant "children of the sun."

Two years later a pair of Montana stockmen, possibly horse thieves, took up claims along the falls. The eclipse of the children of the sun had begun. Settlers followed. Mills grew up along the falls. By the time the first train puffed across the river in 1881, Spokane Falls was a town of a thousand lumberjacks, prospectors, construction workers, and adventurers. Among the latter was a man of many talents, D. C. Corbin, who first connected Spokane Falls by rail with the mineral riches of Idaho, thereby making it into a city. The line was the Coeur d'Alene Railway and Navigation Company, which John Fahey in his *Inland Empire* describes as "one of the more fanciful rail systems devised by man." Fanciful or not, during its first year it hauled out ten thousand tons of concentrates from the Bunker Hill and Sullivan mines, providing, as Idaho's governor said, "the entering wedge which opened the marvellous treasure of the Coeur d'Alene to the world." Passengers were less impressed, being required to sit on benches in the caboose when they weren't obliged to walk.

Fahey tells of one rider who recalled:

"A light fall of snow would block the trains . . . It was a common occurrence for the passengers for the Canyon Creek towns and mines to abandon the train and walk to their destinations or back to their homes. On the least indication that the train would not be able to get through, the conductor would hurry through the cars and collect the fares before the passengers realized that they would have to walk."

With the coming of the railroads, great effort was made to attract settlers through circulars dripping with hyperbole. My favorite: "The beauty of Ladore, the poesy of Minnehaha, and the majesty of Niagara are mingled in the falls of the Spokane . . . It is no exaggeration to say that Eastern Washington presents the combined landscapes of Switzerland and Italy, the highlands of Scotland and the English lake region, the whole forming a panorama capable of expressing every type and emotion of scenic beauty . . ."

By the early nineties, having shed the falls from its name, Spokane had become a Far West Omaha, the biggest rail center and largest inland city between Minneapolis and the Pacific. The city by the falls was on its way to becoming the prosperous wheeler and dealer of the grains, ores, timber, and other resources that finally gave Spokane the title "Capital of the Inland Empire." No longer a frontier town, it had grown up into a city with streetcars, electric lights, an array of handsome buildings and a sprawl of rail yards and viaducts that were to cut off the downtown from its riverfront vistas until 1974 when a World's Fair restored that heritage.

Some of that early-day affluence remains encased today along Riverside Avenue, a leafy concourse above the Spokane River near where the city began. Facing the drive as it nears the city center are the elegant and impregnable redoubts of the city's long-entrenched Establishment. Here in comfortable propinquity are the city's leading church, the Lady of Lourdes Cathedral, its Masonic Temple, the Elks Club, the Chamber of Commerce, and the crusty Spokane Club, which some call City Hall. At the end of this hardening artery is the ten-story old brick tower of the *Spokesman-Review,* the empirical voice of the Inland Empire. Megaphone of the Cowles family, which also owns the only other Spokane daily as well as its NBC television outlet, the *Spokesman-Review* has until recent years held to a course slightly to the right of Charles de Gaulle. One widely quoted story has a campaigning Harry Truman halting his motorcade in front of the *Spokesman's* constricted tower, which looks like a Bavarian castle viewed through a distorting mirror, and shouting:

"There is the worst newspaper in the United States!"

The story is not true. What Truman did say, at the nearby depot, was that the *Spokesman-Review* was the nation's *second* worst paper, placing it a runner-up to the Chicago *Tribune* in the HST ranking.

Truman's outburst, even had it been widely publicized in Spokane, would have gained him but few votes. The waning but sinewy conservatism of the *Spokesman-Review* is but a reflection of the city, strongly rooted in the doctrines of Calvin Coolidge. Most Spokane GOP voters view Washington's popular Republican governor, Dan Evans, as a West Side radical. The handful of Democratic legislators elected from Spokane bring to Olympia viewpoints that would be warmly accepted in Texas. Unabashedly patriotic, Spokane on any given day flies more U.S. flags downtown than Seattle does on the Fourth of July. A bit of disappearing Americana worthy of Norman Rockwell's brush is one of Spokane's street sweepers at work, his cart flying the flag as proudly as a cavalryman's guidon.

A few blocks upriver from where the *Spokesman-Review* building glowers down at the U. S. Court House is the site of Expo '74, strung along the river's shores and on two islands, Havermale and Cannon.

Beyond Spokane's compact borders, there is little debate over the quality of the environment. At its doorstep is a chain of lakes—seventy-six of them within a fifty-mile radius. Roads lead to a desert waterfall, mountain forests, or wheatlands that are either as tawny as a Jersey's flank or so green you can discern their color in the dark.

For a sampler before heading out of town, pick up a map showing the route of Spokane's thirty-three-mile Drive. It wends through fat-cat residential districts and a series of parks, pausing at museum, forest trails, and floral gardens. Riverside State Park, just three miles outside the city limits on this route is fifty-five hundred acres of woods and volcanic formations. Together with Downriver Park, they embrace a public golf course, camping and recreational sites along the river, and miles of forest trails. Nearby, where the Spokane and Little Spokane rivers meet, is the Spokane House Interpretive Center, housing dioramas and artifacts telling the story of the fur trading post built here in 1810 by David Thompson and the North West Company, the territory's first permanent white settlement. Open summertime, 10 to 7, Wednesday through Sunday.

A brilliant-hued contrast to the grayness of the low-budget Spokane House museum is the new million-dollar Pacific Northwest Indian Center located on an old Indian campground above the Spokane River on the Gonzaga University campus. If Indian lore excites you at all, it is probably the top attraction of its kind anywhere, and certainly the outstanding stop on this drive.

The museum was first conceived a decade ago by three scholars of Indian life, Jerome Peltier, author and rare-book dealer; Father Wilfred Schoenberg, Gonzaga University archivist, and Richard Lewis, photographer and collector. The five-story structure houses more than thirteen hundred manuscripts and eight hundred published volumes on Indian language; five thousand volumes on Northwest history and the Lewis collection of thirty-two hundred photographs taken on Indian reservations. For less scholarly viewing there are hundreds of artifacts including masks, wood carvings, beadwork, clothing, tools, weapons, saddles, and tepees, among which is a rarity of painted buffalo hide.

In addition to its function as an attraction for researchers and visitors, the Indian Center, operated as a private nonprofit corporation, will offer leadership education programs and technical assistance to Indians.

If your young tribe is interested in artifacts of a more contemporary scene, hustle them off to the Crosby Library on the Gonzaga campus. The library is the gift of the singer, who is a Gonzaga alumnus and a regent. In addition to its serious works, it has a room housing Bing's original hit records, his Oscar and other memorabilia dear to the hearts of the Geritol set. Open October through May, Monday through Friday, 8 A.M. to 11:30 P.M.; Saturday, 8 A.M. to 5 P.M.; Sunday, 1 P.M. to 11:30 P.M. June through September it is open

Monday through Friday, 8 A.M. to 5 P.M., and Saturday, 8 A.M. to noon.

Other worthwhile way stops on the thirty-three-mile drive include: the Finch Arboretum, with more than a thousand varieties of trees and shrubs along a meandering creek, and a picnic grounds; Manitou Park on Grand Boulevard, featuring a splashy fountain and Japanese gardens; and Fort Wright College of the Holy Names, a former frontier fort that includes a museum of pioneer and military history of the region. Open Sunday, 1 to 5.

For one of Washington's most comprehensive and entertaining pictures of early Northwest history as well as its geology, bird life, and Indian arts and artifacts, visit the Cheney Cowles Memorial Museum, operated by the Eastern Washington Historical Society at West 2316 First Street. Open Tuesday through Saturday, 10 A.M. to 5 P.M.; Sunday, 2 P.M. to 5 P.M. Adjoining is Campbell House, a late-nineteenth-century mansion with nineteen rooms and ten fireplaces, now restored. The Museum has a large art gallery with local works as well as traveling shows. Open Tuesday through Saturday, 10 A.M. to 5 P.M.; Sunday, 2 P.M. to 5 P.M.

If you're into a later scene, try *schlepping* around 2nd City at 605 First Avenue in downtown Spokane, a warren of shops, galleries, and boutiques. Along its second-floor corridors are offerings of regional painters and sculptors, pottery makers, weavers, and crafters of leatherwear, jewelry and toys. For other appetites, there's a health juice bar, a coffee house, and a specialty restaurant.

Although Spokane is at the doorstep of Washington's desert and adjoins the nation's most productive wheat-growing belt, it's also a land of forests and lakes. There are scores of lakes in Spokane County alone, some offering the state's best trout fishing. Add such Idaho lakes as Priest, Coeur d'Alene, and Pend Oreille, plus those of adjoining Stevens County, and the lake census tops a hundred.

Most of Spokane County consists of rolling prairies supporting crops and livestock. But along its fringes prairies give way to low mountains. The city's own peak, Mount Spokane, is but thirty-five minutes from town, a state park with a view-packed road leading to its 5,878-foot summit. Ample facilities for picnics. A year-round chair lift serves the indolent. A new ski resort, Snowblaze, has twenty-two major runs for novices and experts, including a mile of downhill slope illuminated for night skiing during the December to mid-April season. The all-season condominium has an ice-skating rink and a heated pool overlooking a valley that appears deserted as far as the eye can see.

An hour's drive south of Spokane just off U.S. 195 is towering Steptoe Butte. The landmark and memorial park at its base was named for an Army commander who while en route to the Colville area with his troops in 1858 was forced to retreat after a clash with a united force of Spokane and Coeur d'Alene Indians. The battle was little more than a skirmish. But to save face a retaliatory campaign was launched, resulting in the slaughter of nine hundred Indian horses and large quantities of food, ending the Indian resistance. The park includes a picnic ground and a road leading to the summit.

About twenty miles southwest of Spokane near Sprague, just off Interstate 5 is the seventeen-thousand-acre Turnbull National Wildlife Refuge. Pick up a pamphlet at the entrance and take a self-guided tour through the ponderosa pine and along its lakes. You may see a spring of teals, a charm of goldfinches, or even a murder of crows. (I didn't see any of these, but I've waited years to use those designations.)

But those are side trips. My favorite routing to savor the variety of the areas surrounding Spokane heads north and crosses the Selkirk Mountains to Colville and Kettle Falls, loafs back along the shores of Lake Roosevelt, pausing at old Fort Spokane, then cleaves through rolling wheatland before returning to the city. It's a trip that can be made in a day. But it's more rewarding if extended to a weekend or longer, particularly if you have a carful of wriggly gum-chewers who can conjure up more stops than Baedeker.

Head out of Spokane over the ugly gut that is U.S. 2, which fortunately soon gives way to open country, becoming increasingly forested with pine as the Selkirks begin. About forty-five minutes out of Spokane is venerable Pend Oreille State Park, with a pleasant picnic and campground in a virgin forest. A few miles beyond, U.S. 2 bends east for Newport on the Pend Oreille River, gateway to Lake Pend Oreille, Priest Lake, and other Idaho gems. Leave U.S. 2 and continue ahead on State 311 and 31.

At Tiger, with its scatter of old Snuffy Smith barns and one general store, turn left onto State 20 (which, having just been renumbered, may still appear as State 294 on your road map). Within a few miles a series of sharp switchbacks elevates you into the cool fastness of the Selkirks. At the crest, Lake Gillette, one of a chain of mountain lakes, has a well-developed Forest Service recreation area, including a sandy swimming beach. Other Forest Service camps are at Lake Leo and Lake Thomas. Gillette, Heritage, and Thomas lakes also have resort facilities.

(While this recommended routing involves heading west at the crossroads of Tiger, an alternate would be to continue north from

Tiger through Metaline Falls, and on into Canada for a looping exploration of the unspoiled Kootenay Lake country. En route to the border is Crawford Cave State Park (open June 1 to September 15), ten miles northwest of Metaline Falls. As yet undeveloped, the facility provides a rude entryway to an 820-foot limestone cavern that's real neat if you're into stalactites, flowstone, rimstone pools, and speleothems. Farther to the north off State 31 a vista house overlooks Boundary Dam, a Seattle City Light facility with its powerhouse encased in a man-made limestone cave 477 feet long, 76 feet wide, and 170 feet deep, with no stalactites. Tours available.)

As State 20 starts down into the Colville Valley, it briefly parallels the Little Pend Oreille River. A side road leads to a vista lookout atop 5,774-foot Old Dominion Mountain.

Colville sits neatly in a flat green valley surrounded by rolling hills, pungent with the smell of freshly sawn timber from a half dozen mills. From its strip of business houses, residential streets mount the hillsides, cool and dim in the shade of spreading trees. Three old grist mill wheels at its civic center and a downtown museum are reminders of the past.

For the unhurried, Colville is a good rest stop on this circle route out of Spokane. Motels, while limited in number, are the best you'll find in this area. Restaurants offer good steaks, rare in Washington, where most steaks in the cattle belt taste like one. For campers and brownbaggers, Colville provides visitors with a cool city park with covered stoves and a playground, and at nearby Kettle Falls, a spacious, well-equipped National Park Service campground and recreation area on the Columbia.

The Kettle Falls cataracts, which like those at Celilo Falls made this an Indian crossroads and fishing grounds, have long since disappeared under the waters of the dammed Columbia. They cover some notable footprints. Down this valley, following the Indian trails, came trappers, traders, and goldseekers. The wide-ranging David Thompson passed through here and watched the Indians bartering and netting salmon. Liking what he saw, Thompson moved Fort Spokane to this new site on the transcontinental trading trail he had blazed. It was a good move for the North West Company, and in 1822, after building four canoes at Kettle Falls, Thompson inaugurated the first major shipment of furs for London, via the Columbia.

"On the 22nd [of April 1812]," he wrote, "two of the canoes were loaded with 25 packs, two with 20 packs and two with 16 packs, in all 122 packs, each weighing 90 pounds. In addition each canoe carried 300 pounds of dried meat and five men." It was another first for Thompson, added to an impressive list that included being first to travel the entire Columbia from source to mouth; founding the first Columbia River trading post, and first to map the Pend Oreille and countless other rivers. Later the Colville post became a link in the Hudson's Bay Company's route, dispatching bateau loads of furs to Vancouver, and taking on the name of one of the Company's directors, Lord Colville. You can follow this trading route by heading north on State 25 as it keeps company with the Columbia on its way to Canada.

For that matter, the visitor can find inducements in any compass heading out of Colville. To the south, in addition to our route along Lake Roosevelt, another highway, State 395, angles off through pleasant vales to Chewelah, a gateway to the Colville and Kaniksu National Forest and the new ski resort on Chewelah Mountain, called 49° North.

To the west, Highway 30 knifes through the pines of 5,575-foot Sherman Pass, the state's loftiest, to Republic. Now a center for tourists and sportsmen, Republic once boasted an opera house and twenty-eight saloons for those drawn by an 1896 gold strike. One mine, the Knob Hill, continues to operate, but at age seventy-five, its veins are all but atrophied.

The most rewarding variety of terrain on the roads leading out of Colville, however, is via State 25 southbound. From this lush valley with its backdrop of pine, it's but ninety miles down Roosevelt Lake to Davenport, as dry and brown as its surrounding wheatfields.

Just outside nearby Kettle Falls, where this southbound leg back to Spokane begins, is the restored St. Paul's Mission, built by Jesuit fathers in 1845. Limited camping facilities are located in the pines. A pioneer cemetery overlooks the drowned rocks where Thompson watched the Indians fish.

Heading south, State 25 bends with the shores as the tamed Columbia becomes Roosevelt Lake, as broad, blue, and tricky as Puget Sound. Between tiny villages tucked in mountain folds, Herefords graze. Pastures, interspersed by orchards and alfalfa fields, are guarded by high deer fences. Small campgrounds, a half dozen on this stretch, nestle in coves.

At Gifford, a ferry with capacity for nine cars crosses the lake every hour to Inchelium ($1 for cars and campers, running time, fifteen minutes). Ten miles from Inchelium, a Colville Indian Reservation village, are Twin Lakes, rated among the Pacific Northwest's most rewarding waters for trout fishing. The Log Cabin Resort on South Twin Lakes has accommodations, trailer hookups, boat rentals, and a store. An hour's drive from the forested lakes country will take you to Nespelem, a town as bleak as the nearby graveyard where is buried Chief Joseph, the Northwest's greatest Indian warrior.

If you elected not to make this detour into history, State 25 hurries along Lake Roosevelt toward Davenport, where U.S. 2 heads eastward into Spokane along the fringe of the Big Bend wheat country. South of the town of Gifford, the highway drops to the shores of the lake where the National Park Service has created a shaded recreational area with attractive facilities for picnics, camping, and swimming. Above the river is Old Fort Spokane, built in 1881 to keep Joseph and his resettled tribe on the reservation. The fort, now being restored, includes a museum and self-guided tours.

Beyond Fort Spokane, the land changes its colors. Within a few miles, the precipitous hills of evergreens reflected in Roosevelt Lake become the rolling slopes of wheatlands. Trees survive only along creek banks or in windbreak plantings. But save for disastrous drought years—such as 1972–73, when both winter and spring wheat plantings were wiped out—these lands are among the world's most productive breadbaskets.

Davenport, where State 25 intersects with U.S. 2 on our route back to Spokane, is a typical community that leans on this fickle staff of life. Next to Moses Lake and Ephrata, it is the largest town on the Columbia plateau, and its tree-shaded streets lined with yellow and red brick buildings have changed little since the days when townfolks dug breastworks around the courthouse to prevent the rival town of Sprague from stealing the county seat. Just off its main street, a museum traces the painful growth of this region from homesteader's fields to a world granary. Faded pictures capture some of the excitement that swept Davenport and other wheat communities following demonstration of the wheat combine, a ponderous machine that combined cutting and threshing, and was to revolutionize wheat growing. Farmers came from fifty miles around when the first combine, powered by a massive groundwheel and pulled by thirty-two horses, moved out into the waiting grain of the California Ranch at nearby Harrington in 1890.

The combines cut the average threshing crew from twenty to six, and created a new folk hero, the driver, who perched high on a ladderlike platform, directed thirty-two horses (or mules) on a single hitch over the rolling hills. The driver controlled only the two lead animals. These swung the rest of the team, which in a thirty-two-horse hitch would be lined up in five rows of six each. Then in the twenties, horses and mules gave way to tractors. Today, harvest crews that once numbered more than thirty consist of but three or four hands, including the combine driver.

Those elevators housing the bulk grain you see clustered along the highway between Davenport and Spokane could be the tombstones of these old crews, for the first to go were those displaced by the elimination of sacks, the sack sewers and jiggers. They were followed into oblivion by the header punchers, the straw bucks, the hoe-down men, and the teamsters who with muscles, tempers, and lungs kept horses and mules in line.

Their disappearance left a gap in the wheat belt communities that doze along the tracks. Thirty years ago, Giles French, editor of the *Sherman County* (Ore.) *Journal* wrote their obituary in an editorial entitled "One Hundred Acres a Day":

"They plow a hundred acres a day now, that is, day and night; great, brightly-painted, dust-covered behemoths, like army tanks, go charging over the landscape dragging along strings of plows . . .

"Time was, and not too far distant, when they plowed with six horse teams . . . and five acres was considered enough for any man or any team.

"And Saturday night or Sunday the whole crew went to town.

"Now the men who turn over 50 acres a shift are lonesome men . . . They grab their lunch at noon or midnight between gear shifts and have communication with neither man or beast in their work . . . There is more efficiency, but no one is happier and there is no life around the town. Farming that was once a way of life . . . is now a business, geared to the machine as surely as any factory; and the raillery of the crews has been stilled by the rattle of valves."

Sic transit.

BUCKLE ON
YOUR SUN BELT

When nature had finished rearranging this far corner, she left in the lee of the Cascade Range a convulsed area with a climate and terrain that has produced the state's most vivid contrasts.

Scattered along a hundred-mile swath between the Canadian border and the Yakima Valley are ranks of snowy mountain spires so remote they remain unnamed and often unclimbed. In their shadows are desert wrinkles as deep and brown as the Grand Canyon. It's a thinly settled region that has raised a bumper crop of superlatives: the nation's most productive fruit bowl (the Yakima Valley), its deepest chasm (Lake Chelan), and the biggest man-made masonry structure since the Great Wall of China (Grand Coulee Dam).

Yakima, Ellensburg, or Wenatchee are good entreports to this sun belt. With completion of the North Cascades Highway it may be explored on a weekend loop trip from Puget Sound, or a visit can add spice to a cross-state journey. The region becomes particularly rewarding when Puget's curse moves in on the west side, dimming sun and spirits. On those days the Cascades become a dam, holding back Pacific-brewed fog and clouds, producing within a few miles some of the country's greatest differences in climate. At the crest of Snoqualmie Pass, rainfall reaches a hundred inches annually. Eighty miles below in the Kittitas Valley the fall is but ten inches and a few miles to the east it trickles down to five.

This is not to imply the region is Palm Springs. Winters are among the state's coldest. In one northern Cascade region they arrive so closely on the heels of fall that the area appears on maps simply as Early Winters. But from May through September the sun works overtime. Which is one reason that a community like Yakima, with a population of less than fifty thousand, has a score of public swimming pools and almost a thousand hotel and motel rooms.

A delightful approach to this sun belt from the West Side is to wend down Stevens or Snoqualmie passes, or circle down White or Chinook passes from Mount Rainier.

Let's try a lesser-used route that touches most of the region's attractions. Drive north on U.S. 97 from the Columbia River highway, starting at Sam Hill's Maryhill. It's a route that will take you from the gaunt Columbia gorge up through the timbered Horse Heaven Hills, a wild rangeland over which an estimated five hundred untamed horses still graze. The terrain changes as the highway approaches Yakima, becoming reminiscent of northern Mexico, particularly at sunset when mountains loom purple against a reddened sky.

About fourteen miles south of Yakima, at Toppenish, headquarters for the Yakima Indian Reservation, a side road will take you to Fort Simcoe, built during the Indian wars of the 1850s. The fort, now a state park, dozed through the wars like a British outpost in India, occasionally sending out a force to show the colors, but engaging in little action. It has been lovingly restored, including the original commandant's house. The grassy parade grounds, barracks, and blockhouse are just right for a raid by any restless bad guys you might have in the back seat. A museum displays Indian artifacts, foodstuffs, plants, and pioneer furnishings. Picnic tables are scattered through the shady grounds. Open Wednesday through Sunday, 9 to 6, May 1 to October 1; October 15 to May 1, open daily, 8 to 5.

Yakima is pleasantly spread along wide tree-shaded streets, planted back at the time when settlers believed their town was destined to become a territorial capital. After a venomous campaign launched by Ellensburg and Olympia, during which Yakima was described as being "alone and desolate on an alkali desert," it lost the bid. The hamlet then looked to the desert, which turned out to be so rich that today's crops are valued at $175 million annually, all raised on irrigated land.

Some of Yakima's past is displayed at a historical museum in Franklin Park, including exhibits of a blacksmith shop, pioneer post office, and Indian artifacts. Open Wednesday, Thursday, and Friday, 10 to 4; Sunday, 2 to 5. Another nearby attraction is Yakima Sportsman's Park with a fishing pond for kids under fourteen, a campground in the forest, and a playground.

North out of Yakima, U.S. 97 heads for Ellensburg, squeezing through the narrow Yakima River Canyon. Hillsides are bright in springtime with wild flowers. This is a favorite area for hunting agatized rock and wood created by prehistoric lava flows.

Ellensburg is another cow town with a randy past that has been purified by progress. Once known as Robber's Roost, it became a cattleman's Saturday night corral. Today it's a prosperous ranching and college community. The lone surviving harness shop is surrounded by places featuring pizzas and organic food to slake appetites of hands who ride into town on ten-speed bikes from nearby Central Washington State College.

The leathery past is not forgotten, however. Each Labor Day weekend the cry of "Let 'er buck!" opens a rodeo and Indian pageant that for caliber of riders and events is matched only in the Pacific Northwest by the Pendleton (Oregon) Roundup.

To the east, the highway leads to a unique park set amid the remnants of a forest that flourished here during the age of dinosaurs. At Gingko Petrified State Park on the Columbia near Vantage, an interpretive center displays portions of logs from scores of trees, including redwood, magnolia, palm, teakwood, and the ginkgo, which provided the climax forest of fifteen million years ago. All were wiped out, then preserved by a series of massive lava flows. From the center, a short side path leads to a gulping view of the Columbia far below. A few Indian petroglyphs are mounted here, including one looking remarkably like yesterday's peace symbol. Picnic tables are scattered among a welcome grove of latter-day trees.

Wenatchee, the only other large community in this sun belt, is the self-styled Apple Capital of the World, shipping out almost twenty thousand carloads of Delicious, Winesap, Jonathan, and other varieties each year. Seasoning this economy is income from pears, cherries, aluminum, and the harvesting of visitors, particularly during the annual Apple Blossom Festival in the spring. One of Wenatchee's most popular visitor attractions is Ohme Gardens, painstakingly planted high on a bluff above U.S. 97. The nine-acre plot is a cool retreat of alpine plants, evergreens, flowers, brooks, and shady glens, most of them covered by busy golden mantle squirrels. Open daily from April 15 to October 15. Admission: $1.25; students, 75 cents; children under twelve, free.

The North Central Washington Museum at Chelan Avenue and Douglas Street features Indian picture rocks, relics, and pioneer items, and for rockhounds, a changing exhibit of cut and polished stones from the area.

Like Yakima, Wenatchee's eminence as one of America's most bountiful orchards is due to its lava-enriched soil, a heavy dose of sun, and water that since completion of the Highline Canal in 1903 has defeated the desert. Located at almost the exact center of the state and close to millions of acres of national forests, this city on the Columbia also has become a hub for outdoor recreationists.

A dozen miles west, a combination of winter sun and powder snow attracts almost a hundred thousand visitors annually to the Mission Ridge ski area. Between Thanksgiving and May a chair lift will hoist you to Shangri-La views of Mount Rainier, the Cascades, and the orchard valleys below.

Nearby, tucked in the foothills of Wenatchee National Forest, is Leavenworth on the U.S. 97 route to Seattle through Stevens Pass. A few years ago a tired logging community, Leavenworth called in some University of Washington planners and rebuilt itself into a Bavarian mountain village. It's a sham as commercially packaged as Disneyland. But somehow Leavenworth manages to carry it off, becoming both colorful and enjoyable down to its annual Autumn Leaf Festival each fall (late September and early October).

Wintertimes, the hills turn white with powder snow, drawing some of the nation's top skiers to the Leavenworth International Ski Jumping Contest, one of the nation's oldest ski meets, held the first Sunday in February.

Approximately midpoint between Wenatchee and Leavenworth is the spic-and-span apple town of Cashmere, site of the Pioneer Village and Willis Carey Historical Museum. Open daily during summer months, they include well-crafted restorations of cabins, a jailhouse, a saddle and shoe shop, offices of pioneer doctors and dentists, a mission blacksmith shop, assay office, and other original buildings. These preservation efforts of the Chelan County Historical Society have been accorded national recognition, including the top award of the American Association for State and Local History.

Another spoke in the Wenatchee hub points north. Here, since completion of the North Cascades Highway, has been added a route that embraces some of the state's most intriguing desert, valley, and mountain terrain. Included are Lake Chelan, Grand Coulee Dam, the Dry Falls of the Columbia, the Methow and Okanogan valleys, and the North Cascades National Park. Let's head north.

Seven miles north of Wenatchee as U.S. 97 aims for Lake Chelan is Rocky Reach Dam, a $275 million giant completed in 1962 by the

Grand County Public Utility District, providing muscle for Wenatchee's aluminum plant. Behind it, fifty-five-mile-long Lake Entiat is popular with fishermen seeking salmon, steelhead, trout, and bass.

Rocky Reach Dam's visitor center, in contrast to its sterile counterparts along the Columbia, has been lavished with acres of lawn, thousands of flowers, including a sixty-by-forty-foot flag of red, white, and blue petunias, picnic grounds, playground, sundeck dining area, underwater viewing of migrating salmon and a museum.

If the museum at Richland mirrors a lack of imagination, that at Rocky Reach Dam is so detailed and all-inclusive as to be formidable. Included in corridors that seem to stretch for a mile are well-crafted exhibits that display everything from early Indian life to a complex history of electricity.

To the north of the dam are two riverside parks, Silocosaka and Will Risk, with facilities for picnicking, camping, swimming, and boat-launching. A ferry crosses the lake to Daroga Park, privately run with tree-shaded camping sites, an excellent swimming beach, boat ramps, and a lake stocked with rainbow.

Nature hasn't quite tired of rearranging this region, created by the greatest upheavals and lava outpourings this planet has ever witnessed. Just beyond Entiat is a reminder. Here an overlook, Earthquake Point, gazes down on the still visible results of a heavy temblor that rocked this region in 1872, temporarily blocking the Columbia and causing devastation at Lake Chelan.

Lake Chelan to the Indians was "Tsill-ane," meaning deep and rushing waters. It's an appropriate title, for at points it's fifteen hundred feet deep, making it America's deepest chasm. The reference to rushing waters, we may assume, came from upheavals such as the 1872 quake that massaged Chelan's bottom, which at points is four hundred feet below sea level.

The Indian name was Anglicized by General George B. McClellan when he passed through the region, ostensibly on a railroad survey. Actually what he was up to was to engage in a series of sneaky feints on behalf of his commanding officer, Secretary of War Jefferson Davis, who let it be known he didn't want any railroad linking up those no-account, antislavery northern states.

So the good general obliged and spent most of his time avoiding Indian tribes which for decades had been moving back and forth across the mountains through a dozen passes. General McClellan kept sending out plaintive communiques such as, "There is nothing to be seen but mountain piled upon mountain, rugged and impassable." Dutiful to a higher calling, he never did advance through the Cascades.

So the railroads bypassed Lake Chelan, but not before a lot of stock was sold. Included were some nicely engraved offerings of an enterprise W. C. Fields could have touted, the Lake Chelan, Stehekin Valley and Horseshoe Basin Railway. Yass.

Prospects of a railroad led to the sale of a thousand lots around the lake, causing momentary embarrassment when it was discovered they were all on Indian land. The ownership status was appealed to Congress, which after some musing decided the issue in favor of guess who. Today the selling of lots and the care of visitors vie with apples as Chelan's most productive crops.

Fortunately, less than half of Lake Chelan's fifty-five-mile length is accessible by car, a factor that may spare it the fate of Lake Tahoe and other overused alpine recreation areas. But along the twenty-five miles of road rimming the southern shores, familiar signs of blight are everywhere. The town of Chelan, which bills itself as "the capital of America's Switzerland," is a plain-Jane village bereft of any attempts to make it more pleasant—other than to hang canned music speakers from lampposts. The lakeshore itself at this point is covered with a sprawl of developments. Spacious homes with lawns running down to the beach share the lakefront with huddles of mobile homes, warehouses, and an array of resorts ranging from tacky old-time Kozy Kabins to modern "villas," with balconies overlooking a pool and the lake.

Apart from this regrettable inattention to appearances, Lake Chelan's public and private developers have assembled a playground of wide-ranging tastes, including swimming, tennis, golf, and fishing. Lake Chelan State Park is a busy hive of one hundred seventy-eight tent sites and hookups for twenty-five trailers, boat moorage and picnic and swimming facilities. Boats may be launched or rented at a half dozen stops between Chelan and road's end at 25-Mile Creek.

As a colorful end-of-the-season romp, the Pacific International Yachting Association is host to a regatta on Lake Chelan during the last weekend in September. Given a sunny day with a good wind, the blue lake, dotted with varicolored spinnakers, creates a picture as gay and frivolous as a Miró painting. It's one of the few views at this crowded end of Lake Chelan that lives up to its billing of "Switzerland of America." But you'll find peaceful alpine vistas in profusion by heading up the lake.

Every morning at 8:30 between May 15 and September 30 (limited service, other months), a no-frills passenger boat, the Lady of the Lake, heads out on its four-hour run to the lake's farthest reach at Stehekin, then returns. Fare is $7.50 round trip from Chelan. Children, six through eleven, half fare; under six, free. If you're in a hurry, you can fly one way on a float plane in a half hour for $14. Same rates for children as above.

Leaving Chelan, the Lady of the Lake churns its way up a blue channel often less than a mile wide, passing orchard-covered lowlands and high crags from which descend glaciers and waterfalls. Except during hunting season, forests are the undisturbed home of deer, bear, and cougar. At higher reaches, the peaks accommodate a few mountain goats.

At one time, Chelan's goat herds numbered in the thousands, drawing hunters from throughout the United States, until finally they were virtually wiped out. As one early traveler wrote in 1891:

"One could row all day without losing sight of large bands. It was no uncommon occurrence to count 100 of these goats in a single band and large numbers of them were shot from rowboats, often falling over the cliffs into the water." Sic transit, you departed Capricorns.

Chelan's upper reaches include a half dozen small resorts, all but two of them near the Stehekin entrance to the Lake Chelan National Recreation Area and the southern fringe of the North Cascades National Park. Most popular is the North Cascades Lodge at the Stehekin boat landing; thirty-three rooms, some in an alpine lodge, others scattered in cabins among the pines. A good place to rusticate, or go fishing, take a rubber raft trip down the Stehekin River, or hike. Numerous camping sites are provided by the National Park Service all along the old twenty-three-mile road that leads from Stehekin into a valley terminating at the foot of the Cascade peaks.

Other favored treks for backpackers include hiking into the Glacier Peak Wilderness Area from the old mining camp of Holden, now a Lutheran retreat. Holden can be reached by taxi (ah, wilderness!), a twelve-mile trip from the boat stop at Lucerne, but the rates are as steep as Holden's slopes. An easier hike from Lucerne takes you about three miles to Domke Lake, where the U. S. Forest Service maintains two small campgrounds, among the eleven it operates at various boat stops along the lake.

Beyond the lake area, the Columbia, Methow, and Entiat rivers are favored among steelhead fishermen, and nearby Wapato, Jameson, and Alta lakes are among the state's most rewarding for those dipping a line for big rainbows.

It's but an hour's drive from Chelan's icy blue depths to a viewpoint overlooking a multihued chasm where thundered one of the great waterfalls of all times. This is the Dry Falls of the Columbia, once bigger than a hundred Niagaras, now part of the Sun Lakes State Park recreational area.

Below here during the glacial age flowed the yellow, silt-heavy Columbia, diverted from its course by an ice dam where Grand Coulee Dam now rises. The flood, laden with boulder-encrusted icebergs from the glacial plain, gained speed here, dividing to plunge eight hundred feet downward in two giant horseshoe falls, each two miles wide. Behind the receding flood that lasted for six thousand years emerged a lava plateau rent with sculptured coulees. To the south was a mosaic of pothole lakes, mesas, and soils of incredible richness.

The story of this prehistoric cataclysm that shaped the terrain and economy of today's Washington is told in an interpretive center at this Dry Falls viewpoint. Open Wednesday through Sunday, 9 to 6, May 1 to September 30.

(Some spoil-sport scientists doubt this theory of the mighty cataract. A pioneer of the region, Charlie Younger, shared their skepticism.

("Hell!" said Younger. "I've been around here more'n sixty years, and all I ever seen going over them Dry Falls was just a trickle.")

Just below the interpretive center, near the base of those vanished falls is Sun Lakes State Park, a collection of busy play pens scattered along the shores of Park Lake, Dry Falls, Perch and Rainbow lakes. A good base for serious explorations of the coulee country or for swimming, boating, golfing, fishing, and camping.

Beyond Sun Lakes, two smaller state parks are under development: Lake Lenore, so named for its prehistoric cave shelters, and Summer Falls, where in irrigating season, a 165-foot waterfall drops into Billy Clapp Lake. At the southern tip of this belt created by the pre-historic Grand Coulee ice dam is Soap Lake, supporting a strip of modest resorts and parks catering to those drawn by its mineral waters.

From the Sun Lakes area it's about an hour's drive up State 155 to where Grand Coulee Dam shackles the Columbia. Here, where the river was once blocked by a monstrous wall of ice, a mass of concrete rises 550 feet above bedrock and extends for almost a mile. The monolith, 550 feet thick at its base, raises the Columbia's waters 354 feet, creating Roosevelt Lake, which extends northward to pene-trate 150 miles into Canada.

As a man-made structure, Grand Coulee Dam has few rivals. Compared to its natural predecessor, it's something patted together at the seashore for the ice dam that once existed here towered above the river for eighteen hundred feet and stretched off to be lost in the shadows of the Okanogan Mountains to the north.

Grand Coulee Dam carries a clout as big as its superlatives. Back a few years it lost its crown as the world's most powerful dam to the Bratsk Dam in Siberia. But by 1975, installation of six generators in the new powerhouse will restore those laurels. I suggest that at the dedication ceremonies, Washington's senior senator, Warren Magnuson, who more than any man fought and won Grand Coulee's appropriation battles, might recall the words the president of the American Society of Civil Engineers used in opposition to its construction:

"A grandiose project of no more usefulness than the pyramids of Egypt."

It was quite a putdown for the dam that since has irrigated 516,000 acres of desert and sold $845 million worth of power, and for better or worse has made possible the Hanford project and the resultant birth of the atomic bomb and the concept of nuclear power that has followed.

There is such an inhuman scale to Grand Coulee Dam that it is hard for the viewer to be more than momentarily awed. Once real living guides would accompany your tour with a spiel that gave the giant some measurable dimensions. So in those days we gawkers learned that the spillway is twice the height of Niagara, that its main irrigation canal carries as much water as the Colorado, and that each of the two generator buildings is twice the size of a football field. Those are the kinds of statistics that send you away singing "Yankee Doodle."

Grand Coulee's third powerhouse, to continue in the fashion of yesterday's guides, is longer than three football fields and is half as high as the Washington Monument. When completed, it will generate as much power as all fifty-one powerplants built by the Bureau of Reclamation in the past seventy years!

On the drawing board for Grand Coulee Dam are all kinds of plans for expanded visitor facilities. These included funiculars, an Indian exhibition center, an outdoor cafe, open-air concert hall, and other glories. But right now, while the Bureau of the Budget is doing its contemplation exercises, the best way to view this monumental achievement is to take a look from one of the vantage points that can bring it into focus.

Turn off State 155 directly above the dam's pumping plant for a view that includes the dam and a close look at the massive pipes that reach up from the reservoir below. If there were a human guide around he could tell you that the big pumps can lift in one minute enough water to supply the daily needs of a city bigger than Seattle. From here the pumped waters flow through a concrete-lined channel into Banks Lake, the distribution point for a two-thousand-mile network of smaller canals that irrigate the half-million-acre Columbia Basin Project.

Visitors leaving Grand Coulee Dam find themselves covered with statistics. A good place to rid yourself of them is in any one of the parks surrounding the dam. One of the best is Douglas Park in the town of Coulee Dam, with shaded picnic sites overlooking the river. A public swimming pool is nearby. Coulee City Community Park includes boat ramps, a sandy beach and picnic grounds. Electric City provides a campground and boat ramp. Grand Coulee, a playground and picnic tables. Some of the most spectacular scenery can be viewed from Steamboat Rock State Park between Electric City and Coulee City on State 155. The largest camping area this side of Sun Lakes State Park is Spring Canyon, operated by the National Park Service on Lake Roosevelt just off State 174 with almost two hundred tent and trailer sites, a beach and a marina. Beyond Spring Canyon, Lake Roosevelt's six hundred sixty miles of shoreline are the site for thirty-one parks and a dozen swimming beaches. Elsewhere throughout the Columbia Basin, the backwaters of the dammed Columbia have created a network of potholes and reservoirs that have become popular fishing and waterfowl hunting grounds. One of the largest, thirty-two-mile-long Banks Lake, is stocked with trout, bass, perch, crappie, and bluegill. Four public access areas on Banks Lake are provided by the state as well as a park popular with boaters, Steamboat Rock on State 155, just south of the town of Grand Coulee.

While finishing your coffee at one of these rest stops, consider a couple of routes from Grand Coulee Dam to round out this visit to Washington's sun country.

The first, State 165, passes through the Colville Indian Reservation headquarters town of Nespelem, where is buried the Northwest's greatest Indian warrior, Chief Joseph. From Nespelem the highway penetrates into the historic Okanogan Valley and heads north into Canada. At nearby Okanogan, Highway 20 heads for the North Cascades pass to the West Side.

The alternate route from Grand Coulee would be State 174, which visits Chief Joseph Dam and old Fort Okanogan on its way to the Okanogan Valley.

If your brood is hollering "not by a dam site," hurry on to Nespelem and the grave of Him-mah-too-yah-kelt (Thunder-which-comes-over-the-water), better known as Chief Joseph.

The town, the cemetery, and the few tribesmen who live on the 1,300,000-acre Colville Reservation are poor, for our generosity toward the defeated has never been extended to Indians.

Like Chief Seattle's grave at Suquamish, that of Chief Joseph is a simple marker. But Seattle looks out on the land and water he and his people called home. Joseph gazes on alien soil, hundreds of miles from the Wallowa mountains and fertile valleys from which he, his family and tribesmen were driven. Joseph, son of a pacifist and himself a reluctant warrior, fought back in a classic thousand-mile retreat toward sanctuary in Canada. He led an exodus of seven hundred, including men, women, and children, over steep and rocky trails, meeting and defeating superior forces of U.S. troops in three major pitched battles. Near Eagle Creek, Montana, he was surprised by a large force. After the second day of fighting, he capitulated.

"I am tired of fighting," he said in his famed farewell. "Our chiefs are killed. Looking Glass is dead. Tu-hul-sote is dead. The old men are all dead. It is cold and we have no blankets. The little children are freezing to death . . . Hear me, my chiefs, my heart is sick and sad. From where the sun now stands I will fight no more against the white man."

Joseph and his people probably would have lost no more had they continued to fight. For after the surrender, the U. S. Government broke its pledge of a reservation in Idaho. Joseph never reached his promised land. Instead he and his tribe were shipped to Oklahoma Indian Territory, part of the journey jammed in boxcars. After eight years, during which one third of the tribe died of disease, Joseph and the remaining Nez Percé were permitted to return to the Northwest—to today's Colville hills. There at Nespelem rests, possibly, Joseph, chief of the Nez Percé, who once said:

"All men were made by the same Great Spirit Chief. They are all brothers. The earth is the mother of all people, and all people should have equal rights upon it."

Beyond Nespelem, State 155 swings east to join up with U.S. 97 which heads for Canada along the banks of the Okanogan River. During autumn when banks and hillsides glow with the state's brightest colors, the river is roiled by thousands of salmon heading for their last fertility rites.

This is one of Washington's oldest highways, first used by Indian tribesmen, then fur traders who by canoe and horseback packed their furs from New Caledonia to Astoria and returned through Fort Okanogan with trading goods.

Following in the traders' aching footsteps came the prospectors who during the Cariboo Gold Rush trod these same banks, racing toward rainbow's end in British Columbia. The gold rush towns survived long enough to send big cattle drives streaming into Canada over this Okanogan trail.

Despite the fact herds are being reduced due to recreational land demands, cattle raising is still big business in the Okanogan Valley. The Thursday cattle auction at Okanogan will move as much as two million dollars' worth of beef on the hoof. True, there are more pickup trucks than horses in the auction parking lot and the wrangler's roping is more of a spectator sport than a way of life. But each year the men are still separated from the boys at the rodeo, the Omak Stampede, held in August and climaxed by a hellbent horse race down a steep bank into the Okanogan River. (The past also is recreated in a quieter setting at the Fort Okanogan State Park interpretive center just east of Brewster, near where John Jacob Astor established his ill-starred trading post in 1811. Open Wednesday through Sunday.)

About one third of Okanogan County's annual income comes from livestock, outranked by harvests of fruits. Of its three and a half million acres, which make it the state's largest county, forty-two percent is in woodland, most in national forests. The town of Okanogan is headquarters for this National Forest Service realm that includes more than fifty campgrounds and a network of roads and trails that tap many of its thousand lakes and countless streams.

Scoffers around the corner poolhalls claim the fishing in lowland streams and lakes is productive only for about an hour after the state fish and game tank truck has dumped one of its loads of rainbows. But there are enough mountain lakes—more than two hundred of them above the four-thousand-foot level—to challenge the more dedicated. Overall, the piscatorial mortality rate is satisfyingly high. Those who make up fish stories for county records claim around 1,750,000 fish, mostly rainbows, are taken each year from Okanogan County waters. They also estimate some thirty thousand hunters in a year will bag around ten thousand deer, as well as innumerable game birds, a few goats, and an uncounted number of cattle. For those who are into rock and gem hunting, the area is lumpy with garnets, tungsten, quartz, soapstone, and other rock-hound finds. (A line to Fran and Ollie's Rock and Gem Shop, 123 First Avenue in Okanogan, will help you learn where they are.)

At Omak, State 20 heads for Twisp and Winthrop. Here the old road begins its new role as the North Cascades Highway. Until this cross-state link was opened in 1972, the highway dead-ended at Winthrop, creating a backwater country as remote, insular, and cloistered as the Cumberlands. A picture of that past is glimpsed in this account from a guide book of the forties:

"The Methow Valley has no large towns. The people live on their farms, or engage in bounty hunting, trapping, herding, prospecting and logging. They regard towns as places in which to trade, vote and spend holidays—the traditional attitude of the Old West. On weekdays and special occasions those trading centers take on the appearance of pioneer towns, with hitching rails, haphazard sidewalks and crude plumbing; riders on horseback, buckboards and buggies; the men with tanned faces and alert eyes in chaps and spurs, or blue jeans and Stetsons."

Near Winthrop is a drive-in, the Virginian. The name sets the tone of today's Winthrop which has rummaged around the attic and donned cowboy regalia to head the visitors off at the pass. The drive-in's name comes from the fact that back in the 1880s Owen Wister came out to the Methow to visit an old Harvard roommate, Guy Waring. A onetime architect, Waring was living contentedly in the valley as a cattleman, shopkeeper, cook, carpenter, justice of the peace, author, and dropout from the wicked East Coast. From the area and its men (or from Waring's book *My Pioneer Past*) Wister possibly drew some inspiration for his subsequent novel, *The Virginian,* best known for its steely eyed one-liner, "When you call me that, smile!"

It's doubtful if either Wister or Waring would smile at today's Winthrop, all corseted up in false fronts purporting to give it that Old West look. The sham is entertaining but not convincing. None of the frontier-styled business houses, including Three Fingered Jack's, the Winthrop Palace, the General Store, and others along the two blocks of planked sidewalks ever existed in the past. The result is imitation Scottsdale, including such coy bits as cloaking the service station in barn planks and hanging out a faded sign reading FUEL YARD. Counterfeit fakes, harmless to all, save perhaps the throngs of visiting moppets who discover the General Store is but another Rexall and are reminded again that nothing is quite what it's billed to be.

Like Leavenworth with its "Bavarian village," Winthrop's masquerade was adopted to encourage tourism and ease the unemployment that makes this region one of the state's most economically depressed areas. To date, it has made the town a tourist mecca. With a few additions it could be a genuine pleasure to visit.

Instead of the modern-day Potemkin Village to gull the tourist, why not add a bit of the true West to the false-front village? Build a gristmill along the Methow or Chewak rivers, both of which course unnoticed through town. Subsidize a blacksmith shop. Demonstrate gold-panning. Or candle dipping. Build a water-powered sawmill like the one that operated seventy years ago at nearby Chesaw, a wonderful Rube Goldberg contraption in which falling water filled up a series of cups mounted on a thirty-five-foot wheel, thus turning the saw. Then augment these working demonstrations by building a museum for a collection of saddles, harnesses, wagons, and old mining machinery. To finance these operations, sell bread from the gristmill, souvenir horseshoes from the blacksmith shop, coffee tables made of pine fresh from the sawmill, or snacks served from an old cookout wagon.

Winthrop could become both entertaining and instructive, a Mystic, Connecticut, in chaps. It could leave visitors with something more than the feeling someone has been pasting bogus snapshots in the family album.

If you want to get a more nourishing taste of the Old West, free from additives, walk up the hill from the movie-lot village to Guy Waring's old cabin. The rambling cabin has become a museum, jammed to the beams with the lifelong collection of a Winthrop merchant, S. W. Shafer. Situated in a shaded yard cluttered with an old Rickenbacker car, a buggy, a farm wagon, and an old train bell, the cabin is sagging into a comfortable relaxation that would have warmed Waring's architect heart. Among the Methow Valley memorabilia is the sign that once swung over Winthrop's only saloon, the Duck Brand. Unlike the ornate, heavy-serif lettering found in restored Winthrop, that of the original sign is slender and graceful. The sign's illustration, taken from the owner's cattle brand, is as gentle as Picasso's dove.

Another display includes a reproduction of an old Remington painting of a group of mounted Indians looking across the Okanogan River at the first fences of the settlers, and with it, one of Wister's less distinguished verses:

> Of old, when Okanogan ran
> Good medicine for horse and man,
> The winged shaft was wont to fly
> In peace or war, beneath the sky.
> Gone is the arrow, and instead
> The message of the white man's drink—
> These lessons by the river-brink
> Are learned, where Okanogan ran
> Good medicine for horse and man.

You'll find Remington hanging around just about every pioneer museum this side of Dodge City, which must give his shade a chuckle, for his sympathies didn't exactly lie with the men who opened the West. Once when asked to speak before a pioneer group's national convention, Remington laid it on the line, telling the assembled crowd of Westerners:

"In my book a pioneer is a man who comes to virgin country, traps off all the fur, kills off all the wild meat, cuts down the trees, grazes off all the grass, plows the roots up, and strings ten million miles of bob wire. A pioneer destroys things and calls it civilization. I wish to God that this country was just like it was when I first saw it and that none of you folks were here at all."

Someday a museum curator with a good deal of financial independence is going to hang that statement next to the Remington collection.

A few miles southwest of town is Sun Mountain Lodge, which
along with Rosario on Orcas Island and the Lake Quinault Lodge
ranks among the state's best resorts. It's atop Sun Mountain, a foothill reached by a five-mile-long road that winds past two lakes on its
climb from the Methow Valley floor. Along the way is Moccasin Lake
Ranch, its ranges dotted with the fast-growing Charolais cattle, blond
French imports that are slowly replacing Herefords and Black Angus
in many of today's computerized cattle ranches. Visitors are welcome.

Sun Mountain's 360-degree outlook into the valley and surrounding
misty mountains is as rewarding as the natural wood and stone decor
of the lodge, cantilevered over a brow of the peak. The entire complex, including its swimming pool, tennis courts, and stables, is com-
plemented by lawns, plantings, and natural growth. Trails lead to
forest glens. For seventy-five dollars a wrangler will pack you into
high lake country and set up camp for you for a week's stay.

Like the few accommodations found along this strip of the sunshine
belt, the lodge draws heavily on West Side escapees from Puget's
clouds. Sunny weather usually begins in May and continues through
September and October. July and August are hot, cooled occasionally
by thunderstorms. The storms are reminiscent of Hawaii, with sun-
bright mountains and valleys darkened by moving cloud shadows.
Sheets of rain bring with them sweet smells of dampened earth. At
time of writing, rooms were not air-conditioned, although this is
planned for early installation. The inn is closed between November
and April.

If you're continuing west over the North Cascades Highway, Winthrop is just about the last chance for gas, refreshments, and restrooms
for about eighty miles. There is a small gas station near the cutoff
road to Harts Pass, thirteen miles from Winthrop on that highway.
But the station has been operating all these years with a hand-cranked
gasoline pump, which must be one of the few remaining anywhere.
By now the owner may have sold it to a collector and retired.

Because of its name, many are under the impression the North
Cascades Highway passes through the North Cascades National Park.
While some of the park's peaks are visible from the highway, the
highway (State 20) is bounded for its entire length by national
forests, save on its western slope where the Ross Lake National Recreation Area takes over. At some future date, a tramway may be
built up the slopes of Ross Lake into the park, but until then, to get
into the park, you hike. A score of trails leads into its glaciated can-
yons, forests, lakes, and streams. (For a detailed list write for *Dar-*

vill's Guide to the North Cascades at P.O. Box 636, Mount Vernon, Washington.)

Aside from a few view turnouts, the North Cascades Highway is virtually nonstop, with but four campgrounds and no commercial food facilities at all. Of two-lane construction and with but one passing lane each way, it can be a slow and congested route, particularly on weekends. But the scenery is unmatched, a combination of the Cascades' hoariest peaks, combined with ranks of upthrust rocky pinnacles more likely to be seen in Colorado or the Yosemite Valley.

About thirty miles west of Winthrop, a side road leads a half mile to the Washington Pass overlook, the highway's high point, clinging to a rocky slab high above the valley. Within view are the massive peaks of 7,750-foot Liberty Bell Mountain and Early Winters Spires, as close to a Swiss postcard as you'll find this side of the Canadian Rockies, all nicely framed by forests of fir and tamarack.

The North Cascades National Park is as tailored for today as Rainier was for yesterday. Rainier National Park shares this same Cascade range. But it was born of a day when national parks were pleasure resorts to be enjoyed from a sightseeing bus or the verandah of a lodge. They grew up in the definition applied by Congress when it established our first national park at Yellowstone: "Dedicated and set apart as a public park or pleasuring ground for the benefit and enjoyment of the people." And so to meet this amiable concept, Rainier was graced with a chain of mountain lodges, hundreds of rental cabins, stables, and a golf course at Paradise Valley. At one time a funicular up its side was considered!

North Cascades National Park is the antithesis of this concept of a "pleasuring ground." Its adherents wouldn't be found dead in an *après ski* cocktail lounge? They're off heeding the words of John Muir "to climb the mountains and get their good tidings."

Muir would like the North Cascades Park for its size and terrain. It embraces 1,053 square miles that house more than three hundred glaciers, hundreds of spires, scores of alpine lakes, icefalls, and ice caps and coverings that range from rain forests to the dry shrublands of the eastern slope. You'll see none of these from a car, a camper vehicle, a cabin, or a mountain lodge.

The North Cascades National Park, a bench mark in conservation, represents something of what Aldo Leopold was talking about when he said:

"We abuse land because we regard it as a commodity belonging to us. When we see land as a community to which we belong, we may begin to use it with love and respect."

And the North Cascades Highway? Perhaps it too represents the

future, the forerunner of a day in which having reached our turn on
the computerized waiting list we pack our family off to the Outdoor
Recreation Reception Area. There we'll be sealed in a battery-
powered, glass-domed car and sent nonstop over a mountain road,
pausing but once for ten minutes at a viewpoint. We might expect an
artificial village at each end, one Western, the other Bavarian. Or one
of the campgrounds of the future being planned today by an outfit
called Hi-Rise Campsites, Inc. Projected for construction at New Orleans, it will be twenty stories high. You will drive in and park your
camper at any one of two hundred forty campsites. All are built on
artificial turf, surrounded by artificial trees. On the rooftop is a swimming pool filled with purified water.

The park rangers, we may anticipate, will be suited up by Bill Blass
and known as Natty Bumppos.

Sic transit.

VISITOR INFORMATION

Dept. of Commerce & Econ. Development, Tourist Promotion Div., Olympia, Wa. 98501

State Dept. of Game, 600 N. Capitol Way, Olympia, Wa. 98501

State Dept. of Fisheries, 115 Gen. Adm. Bldg., Olympia, Wa. 98501

Coulee Dam Nat'l Recreation Area, Box 37, Coulee Dam, 99116

Nat'l Park Service, N.W. Regional Office, 4th & Pike Bldg., Seattle, Wa. 98101

U.S. Forest Service, Federal Bldg., 1st and Marion, Seattle, Wa. 98100

Washington State Ferries, Pier 52, Seattle, Wa. 98100

Seattle–King County Visitor and Convention Bureau, Tower Building, 1815–7th Avenue, Seattle, Wa. 98101

Automobile Club of Washington, 330 Sixth Ave. N., Seattle, Wa. 98109

TELEPHONE NUMBERS
OF WASHINGTON CHAMBERS
OF COMMERCE

Anacortes	293-3832	Ocean Park	665-5165
Bellingham	734-1330	Ocean Shores	289-2451
Blaine	332-6737	Okanogan	422-3730
Bremerton	373-9595	Olympia	357-3362
Brewster	689-2541	Olympic North Beach	276-5518
Camas	834-2472	Omak	826-1880
Cathlamet	795-3231	Orcas Island	376-3411
Centralia	736-3161	Pasco	547-9755
Chehalis	748-8885	Pateros	923-2461
Chelan	682-2022	Pomeroy	843-1841
Clarkston	758-7712	Port Angeles	452-2363
Cle Elum	674-2460	Port Townsend	385-2722
Colville	684-2528	Poulsbo	779-4740
Coulee City	632-5231	Pullman	564-1217
Coulee Dam	633-0470	Puyallup Valley	845-6755
Davenport	725-1261	Raymond	942-3503
Dayton	382-2511	Republic	775-3322
Ellensburg	925-3137	Ritzville	659-1568
Ephrata	754-4656	*Seattle	622-5022
Everett	252-5106	Sedro-Woolley	855-6241
Ferndale	384-1161	Sequim	683-4131
Forks	374-6292	Shelton	426-2021
Garfield	635-3176	South Bend	875-5829
Goldendale	773-4791	Spokane	624-1393
Grand Coulee	633-1350	Tacoma	627-2175
Grays Harbor	532-1924	Tonasket	486-2150
Ilwaco	642-2439	Toppenish	865-2491
Issaquah	392-7552	Tri-Cities	586-4015
Kalama	673-4561	Twisp	997-3122
Kelso	423-5922	Vancouver	694-2588
LaConner	466-3141	Waitsburg	337-6781
Lake Chelan	682-2022	Walla Walla	525-0850
Leavenworth	548-5821	Wapato	879-9411
Longview	423-8400	Wenatchee	662-2116
Lynden	354-4474	Westport—Twin Harbors	268-3250
McCleary	495-3401	Central Whidbey Island	678-4221
Metaline	446-4131	North Whidbey Island	675-3535
Montesano	249-4331	South Whidbey Island	382-4808
Morton	496-5124	Wilbur	647-2202
Moses Lake	765-7888	Winthrop	996-2311
Mount Vernon	336-2522	Woodland	225-4061
North Bend	888-2439	Yakima	457-5123

* Seattle–King County
Visitor Bureau 622-5022

READING LIST

The Dam Book	George Sanisbury and Nanci Hertzog
Exploring the Olympic Peninsula	Ruth Kirk
The Hidden Northwest	Robert Cantwell
Inland Empire	John Fahey
The Last Wilderness	Murray Morgan
The Northwest Coast	James G. Swan
Pig War Islands	David Richardson
Salt Water Fishing in Washington	Raymond Buckley
Seattle	Nard Jones
Skid Road	Murray Morgan
Washington State Fishing Guide	Stan Jones

F